THE IMAGINATION OF CLASS

THE IMAGINATION OF CLASS

Masculinity and the Victorian Urban Poor

Dan Bivona and Roger B. Henkle

The Ohio State University Press
Columbus

Copyright © 2006 by The Ohio State University.
All rights reserved.

Library of Congress Cataloging-in-Publication Data

Bivona, Daniel.
  The imagination of class : masculinity and the Victorian urban poor / Dan Bivona, Roger B. Henkle.
    p. cm.
  Includes bibliographical references and index.
  ISBN 0-8142-1019-8 (cloth : alk. paper) — ISBN 0-8142-9096-5 (cd-rom) 1. English prose literature—19th century—History and criticism. 2. Urban poor—Great Britain—History—19th century. 3. Social classes in literature. 4. Masculinity in literature. 5. Sex role in literature. 6. Poverty in literature. 7. Poor in literature. I. Henkle, Roger B. II. Title.
  PR878.P66B58 2006
  828'.80809352624—dc22
                             2005030683

Cover design by Dan O'Dair.
Text design and typesetting by Jennifer Shoffey Forsythe.

The paper used in this publication meets the minimum requirements of the American National Standard for Information Sciences—Permanence of Paper for Printed Library Materials. ANSI Z39.48–1992.

In Memory of
Roger B. Henkle
1937–1991

- CONTENTS -

Preface		ix
Foreword by Patrick Brantlinger		xiii
INTRODUCTION		1
CHAPTER 1	Sensational Journalism, Male Detachment, and the Feminized Victim	25
CHAPTER 2	Culturalism, the Feminized Poor, and the Land of Deadened Affect	67
CHAPTER 3	Morrison, Gissing, and the Stark Reality	104
CHAPTER 4	Hell Hath Its *Flâneurs:* The Discourse of the Abyss	137
CONCLUSION	Representing the Poor and Forestalling Abjection	179
Notes		183
Works Cited		191
Index		201

- PREFACE -

*W*hen he died suddenly of a heart attack at the age of fifty-four in October of 1991, Roger B. Henkle left behind many grieving family members, colleagues, and students, past and present, from Brown University, where he taught for many years. I was one of the latter. Roger directed my dissertation, which I completed in 1987. As with all the others, I appreciated Roger's wit, his enthusiasm, his intelligence, his energy, and his *bonhomie*; and, like the others, I felt his loss keenly.

Roger also left behind a very interesting but unfortunately rather incomplete manuscript which he had been working on up to the time of his death. It was entitled *The Imagination of Class: A Study of the Middle Class Victorian Representation of the Urban Poor*. At the request of a number of Roger's colleagues and friends at Brown, including Robert Scholes, Michael Silverman, and L. P. Curtis, I agreed in 1992 to take on the task of writing, rewriting, and reconstructing the manuscript. Roger's wife and literary executor, Carol, generously agreed to make me coauthor and gave me permission to make whatever changes were necessary to bring the manuscript up to final form.

I was somewhat reluctant at first to take on this task. I had just finished my first book and had begun research for my second, and I was wholly unable at the time to forecast when I might be able to begin the labor of reshaping Roger's manuscript. The project itself I also found somewhat daunting in conception: however much freedom I had been given to remake the manuscript, it was not my manuscript. I worried about the expectation that I would produce "Roger's" book and whether or not I could reconcile my vision of the material with his. The manuscript itself needed more than simple editing: there were unwritten chapters and written ones in need of some rather dramatic changes; the amount of work involved would require that I dedicate more time to mastering the material than Roger had. Moreover, to be asked to take on someone else's manuscript is rather a strange affair when you think about it. I felt myself anything but a clone of Roger Henkle and not at all well equipped psychologically for the task of bringing someone else's dream to realization through my own efforts. I was not even sure that I agreed with his thesis. Would I want to write a book that contested his main claims?

In any event, the demands of my own career required me to put off serious work on the manuscript until four years ago when I began researching the subject in earnest. During the process of researching I discovered my own interest in the issue of poverty and its representation in discourse. I began to see my own way through the material. When I began rewriting the manuscript in earnest after having done the research, I felt a renewed appreciation for what Roger had already accomplished, but I also felt tensions emerging between my view of the material and his. At times, it seemed as if I was carrying on an argument with the dead. I had always been more of a post-structuralist than Roger, and differences between the way I would word something and the way he had worded it threatened, at least in my own mind, to promise irreconcilable conflicts of perspective that might find their way into inconsistencies in the book. What struck me initially as a serious, and potentially project-ending, problem became, as I worked my way through the material, an opportunity to refashion the material in a way that took cognizance of these differences. My argument with the dead, finally, I think, helped me to sharpen the argument. At least I hope it did. The jury is still out. In any event, I do feel obliged to acknowledge that the "we" of this text is a more factitious "we" than is usually the case in coauthored books. My "collaboration" with Roger on this book was, unfortunately, never face-to-face.

I benefited greatly from the advice of a number of people in putting together this book. These include Patrick Brantlinger, who read and commented on the original manuscript, and Roger's colleagues at Brown, Robert Scholes, Michael Silverman, and L. P. Curtis. I am indebted to Carol Henkle for agreeing to allow me coauthor status, and for not losing faith that I would ultimately bring this project to completion. I wish to thank the English Department at Arizona State University for supporting this project by assigning me some research assistants who assisted me greatly. They include Laura Nutten, Heather Hoyt, and Amy D'Antonio. The latter two gave especially useful advice on the manuscript. I appreciate the advice I received from colleagues at a number of conferences at which I presented this material in recent years including the Interdisciplinary Nineteenth-Century Studies conference, the Midwest Victorian Studies Association conference, and the Pacific Coast British Studies conference. I also want to thank the students in my seminar "Imagining Class in the Nineteenth Century" in spring of 2002 who contributed, sometimes despite themselves, to helping me think through the issues discussed here. I also wish to thank Kara Wittman for many discussions that helped to sharpen my thoughts.

None of these people should be blamed for any inconsistencies, omissions, or incomplete thoughts in the final product, not even Roger Henkle, my coauthor. For those, I take full responsibility myself.

Lastly, I want to thank my family: my wife, Jeanne, and my children, Laura, Michael, and Kate. They consistently had greater faith that this would be finished than I did.

Dan Bivona
Arizona State University
May 2005

- FOREWORD -

by Patrick Brantlinger

On the contributors' page for the Spring 1992 issue of NOVEL, the editors list Roger Henkle, whose article on George Gissing, Arthur Morrison, and urban poverty in late-nineteenth-century British fiction it contains. Following Roger's name, they indicate that he "was at work on a book-length study of the fiction of urban poverty in late-Victorian England before his untimely death on October 5, 1991." Thanks to Professor Daniel Bivona of Arizona State University, *The Imagination of Class* is at last the completed version of that book-length study. I am certain that Roger, our mutual friend and Dan's former mentor and dissertation advisor, would be more than pleased with and proud of the result.

In the same contributors' notice, the editors of NOVEL announce that I had "agreed to edit the almost completed manuscript." Friends of Roger's at Brown University, including L. P. Curtis and Mark Spilka, had indeed asked me to take a look at and hopefully edit the manuscript of what is now *The Imagination of Class*. I gladly did so and recognized that it was, like his earlier book *Comedy and Culture* (1980), original, ambitious, and on its way to becoming a major contribution to Victorian studies. However, the manuscript was less complete than we hoped. Though much of it was finished, major portions remained to be written, and I did not feel that I was the right person to become Roger's coauthor. That person turned out to be Dan Bivona, who deserves much praise not just for finishing the portions that Roger was unable to complete but also for bringing the entire project up-to-date in a well-informed, sophisticated manner. He says in his preface to this volume that he often felt he was "arguing with the dead," but in my view the collaboration was much more about agreement than about argument.

The Imagination of Class deserves to take a prominent place among recent—and I stress recent, especially in the sense of up-to-date—studies of nineteenth-century British literature focused upon urban poverty and social class. Bivona has brought this book into dialogue with such recent works as Seth Koven's *Slumming* and Simon Joyce's *Capital Offenses,* both published in 2004. Whenever the issue of Victorian representations of slums and the poor arises, one thinks immediately of Dickens, from *Oliver Twist* to *Our Mutual Friend*. But numerous Victorian novelists, economists, journalists, and social critics dealt with aspects of class and urban poverty. These include Henry Mayhew, Hector Gavin, James Greenwood, Walter Besant, Richard Jefferies, H. G. Wells, Margaret Harkness, Beatrice Webb, Charles Masterman, and many others. Henkle and Bivona make the case that the British, bourgeois "imaginary" was significantly shaped and empowered by its interest in, writing about, and various "reformist" and "social work" attempts to cope with the urban underclass or "residuum." Class formation or identification takes place through a process of othering, of differentiation; and it also takes place hegemonically—that is, through getting the "public" of a given society to consent to or acquiesce in always unequal power relations, including class hierarchies based in large measure on wealth and poverty, the possession of private property and dispossession.

As Henkle and Bivona point out, the subject of urban poverty was central not just to middle class identity formation, but more specifically to several types of masculinity, from the *flâneur,* or explorer of the slums and "lower depths" of London, to the social reformers, journalists, and increasingly professional sociologists such as Mayhew, Greenwood, and Charles Booth. They argue that "the interests of a predominately male professional class, which was in the process of formation throughout the nineteenth century, strongly influenced, indeed determined, the ways in which the Victorians represented poverty in the city of London." Depictions of "the abyss" were also a staple of fictional realism, from Dickens to Gissing, Morrison, Jack London, and beyond. As well as any previous study, *The Imagination of Class* demonstrates the crucial nature of the cultural or ideological work that focusing on "the lower depths" performed in late-Victorian Britain. The authors stress that the "representations of urban poverty" they analyze are not necessarily inaccurate, ideological distortions of social reality. And yet these "representations may tell us more about what it meant to be male and middle class in the nineteenth century than they tell us about what it meant to be poor."

Henkle and Bivona's analyses of works by such writers as Mayhew, Greenwood, Gissing, and Morrison are careful, cogent, and persuasive. If there needed to be a further compelling reason to read this study, it might well be the reason that it also should send readers back, repeatedly, to Roger's *Comedy and Culture*. More humorously and persuasively than most, that book makes the case for both comedy and culture as central to the study of nineteenth-century British history. Humor, and indeed laughter, may not seem to accord well with the abject, often tragic subject of poverty. But Dickens set a tone and a model, combining laughter with deep concern for social justice, that Roger Henkle exemplified throughout his career as a teacher and scholar.

In her tribute to Roger in the memorial issue of *NOVEL*, Diane Elam, also one of his former students, writes: "I remember the open vibrancy of his laughter as he made some remark, and I remember laughing out loud. It's his laughter that I'll always hear and the risks that I'll always remember to take that were Roger's real gifts to me" (327). Elam also says: "Simple dogma was never good enough for him, because he always believed in the possibility of a social justice which could not be the product of quiet acceptance" (326). In the rest of the commentaries in that memorial issue, other colleagues and students stress Roger's generosity, his sense of humor, his irreverence for the solemnities of academia, and—most memorably—his laughter. "What I remember is the effect of Roger's laughter," writes another former student, Christina Crosby; while serving as editor of *NOVEL*, "he humanized the whole business of scholarly production" (322) and made it fun.

I, too, remember Roger Henkle's laughter and "his rich appreciation for the sublime and the ridiculous in all parts of the profession," as Caroline McCracken-Flesher, still another former student of his, writes (321). During several of my visits to New England, I experienced Roger's hospitality—and his laughter. Perhaps, then, it is fitting to end this foreword to a book on middle-class Victorian representations of urban poverty by recalling how on one of those occasions Roger drove me around Providence in a car from an outfit called "Rent-a-Wreck." His wife, Carol, needed their own car to commute to work. I think the "wreck" was held together, barely, by rubber bands. I remember the window on the passenger's side was stuck open, and I'm pretty sure the door on the driver's side was permanently locked. But Roger was just as proud of it as if it had been a Rolls Royce, in part because, in his

Dickensian way, he could make it the subject of endless jokes and laughter, mostly about himself and his own bad taste in rented jalopies.

In the editorial that leads off the memorial issue of NOVEL, Mark Spilka declared: "It seems fitting that Roger should be widely known for his protégés and disciples. His devotion to them was legendary, as was and is their return devotion" (232). Of those many successful "protégés and disciples," none has returned Roger's "devotion" more fully and appropriately than Dan Bivona by becoming the coauthor of this book. Thanks to him, *The Imagination of Class* is not just at long last completed, but is also a major new contribution to studies of Victorian literature, its interest in social justice, and its reciprocal influence on social class formation. It's a *Festschrift* and then some to the memory of a great friend and teacher.

- INTRODUCTION -

The poor were always with the English. Poverty had been of broad social concern since the Elizabethan period at least: the topic of ongoing debate, periodic legislation, sporadic philanthropy. But the London poor of the nineteenth century—particularly from the 1840s on—seemed to present a different phenomenon. The spectacle of poverty and associated degradation in Central and East London, and later in South London, gave rise to a new set of imaginative and cultural representations. It developed from and in turn created new relationships between an ascending urban middle class and the worst victims of the metropolis. Poverty became, as Gertrude Himmelfarb notes, "a cultural rather than an economic condition" (*Idea of Poverty* 366). The character of the London poor broke into the public consciousness as if it were a *discovery*, which was "at once painful and alarming" in the words of one observer, and the "sense of novelty did not seem to disappear till the 1890's" (*Victorian City* 1: 18). New terms, such as "slum," entered the vocabulary, and from the Victorian period on, almost as one conceived of the big city, one conceived at the same time of a festering, teeming, sullen nether world within it. The state of London's poor came to exercise a strong imagistic influence, shaping the discourses of journalism, social work, government activity, and high culture.

At the heart of this development is the consciousness of class itself. The change in the relationship of the middle class toward those around it, such as the urban poor, ensues from the awareness, most strongly felt in the growing urban bourgeoisie, of itself as a class, in opposition to other classes and in need of defining and asserting its own imperatives. Such an awareness had been forming for some time, but it began to solidify into what we have since come to associate with middle class culture only in the mid-nineteenth century. The city was crucial to this development, for its growth corresponded in large part to the rise of the middle class, and it was also the field in which the middle class carved out new ideals and new personal relationships that would replace the old ones of a society dominated by the rural-based upper classes. Moreover, the city's dynamism was destabilizing older class relationships. The new middle class order was supplanting the old relations of paternalism and special influence, and this new order felt pressed to define the ways in which it would represent itself, how it would exercise power, what means of control it would be able to impose.

One of the early survey/studies of the East End slums illustrates how closely the construction of this imagined community was tied to middle class ethical imperatives. Hector Gavin's *Sanitary Ramblings: Being Sketches and Illustrations of Bethnal Green* appeared in 1848, on the heels of the first systematic analyses of the deplorable sanitary conditions of East London, and in the wake of a cholera epidemic. Gavin was a practitioner of forensic medicine, and his study, a street-by-street description of the filth, stench, overcrowding, incidence of disease, conditions of buildings, and sanitary facilities, is one of the most praised and thoroughgoing instances of reportage. Yet he indicates in the opening paragraph of his report that more is at stake:

> To believe that the middle and upper classes were fully cognizant that multitudes of their fellow-beings have their health injured, their lives sacrificed, their property squandered, their morals depraved, and the efforts to christianize them set at nought by the existence of certain well-defined agents, and yet to find them either making no effort to alleviate, or to remove these misfortunes, or with a stern heart denying their existence, would be to charge these classes with the most atrocious depravity, and the most cruel heartlessness and selfish abandonment. It is impossible to suppose that love and charity are so utterly unknown to this great Metropolis . . . and I believe that the hearts of many will be warmed and their spirits aroused to assist those who have undertaken the great work of sanitary improvement and social amelioration. (Gavin 3)

The ethical and pragmatic challenges are neatly joined here. Social responsibility is directly linked to class self-definition. Furthermore—

and this is crucial—the discarded poor of Bethnal Green, the people often characterized during the century as the "residuum" and "outcast London," are now brought directly into the broader body politic; they are made part of our human condition as residents of "this great Metropolis." Gavin is, as well, no dry statistician; his mode of assessing the conditions shares with many of the journalistic explorers of the slums whom we shall read a personal, lively eye for vivid writing. Of Diby-St, Globe-Road, he writes, "In this *most dirty street*, exists one of the most atrocious nuisances which it is possible to create. A person named Baker, lately dead, here formed a receptacle for every kind of manure. . . . The decomposing organic particles which are always being set free from this putrescent mass, are wafted by each wind that blows, over a population to whom they bring disease and death, as surely as, though more insidiously than, the deadly simoon" (Gavin 9–10). Even so, at another spot, Whisker's Gardens, amidst this putrescence, a "few gentlemen" have cultivated flower gardens. Of one Gavin says, "When seen in his damp and dirty home, he is generally accused of personal uncleanliness, and a disregard of the commonest appearances of decency and regularity; yet, in his garden, he displays evidences of a refined taste and a natural love of beauty and of order. The two are irreconcilable, and as the one sentiment is natural and spontaneous, we are irresistibly led to regard the personal uncleanness of the poor, and the impurities which surround their houses, as the results of agencies foreign to the individual" (Gavin 12). This disclosure of a slum-dweller's "evidences of . . . a natural love of beauty and of order" places him on a cultural continuum with his betters. He and his kind are for a moment absorbed into the values—beauty and order—of the middle class, even as they display an absence of the other essential virtues of cleanliness and regularity. And the forces which distance the slum-dweller from "decency" and "regularity" are explicitly identified here with agents beyond the individual's control that infect him from without.

It is not our intention here to suggest that the work of slum clearance, sanitary reform, and private charity in the Victorian age served only to soothe the consciences of the middle classes and had no benefits to the victims of poverty. Nor are we arguing that the middle class professional stance of detachment—the aspiration for objectivity inherent in sanitary reports, for example, the ethical imperative to understand social conditions accurately, independently of the writer's own biases—is invariably meaningless ideological illusion, a "pseudo-detachment" disguising class bias and darker desires lurking beneath.

The Victorian age was one of the great ages of reform and the achievements of many of its reformers were genuine and helpful to actual people. Moreover, what we call the "professional middle class ethos," to which figures like Gavin subscribe, can be seen as part of a larger commitment within Victorian culture to the ideal of "detachment." As Amanda Anderson has recently reminded us, "detachment" had a range of meanings, most of them quite positive, to the Victorians themselves:

> The cultivation of detachment involves an attempt to transcend partiality, interests, and context: it is an aspiration toward universality and objectivity. The norms through which that aspiration finds expression may be situated, the aspiration may always be articulated through historically available forms, but as an aspiration it cannot be reduced to a simple form of illusion, or a mere psychological mechanism. (*Powers of Distance* 33)

However, our contention here is that no discourse attains total transparency to its object, no matter how fervently the writer may aspire to achieve it. Discourse is a complex symbolic phenomenon in which the triangulated relationship among writer, reader, and object of representation must be taken into account. And when these elements are taken into account, the writings we discuss here reveal a complex picture in which postures of detachment were deployed as much to stage the virtue and comprehensive vision of the urban explorer as to bring the reality of urban poverty to the urgent attention of the British reading public. The writerly persona and its inscribed reader are fictive constructs but powerfully compelling fictive constructs. We analyze these constructs not to dismiss the real service reform brought to the victims of urban poverty, but to point out how the discourse on urban poverty also infused middle class writing about that social problem with an urgency and symbolic imagery that, in retrospect, can now be seen as contributing to middle class self-definition.

While the Victorians wrote about the slums for a variety of reasons and motives, our central contention here is that many of the images that they constructed served the purpose of self-definition of an emerging—and largely male—professional class. We have chosen the title we did to emphasize that our focus is on an imaginary construct. Since the publication of Benedict Anderson's influential *Imagined Communities*, the term "imaginary" used as a noun has come to refer to the complex way in which people experience their relationship to others on a variety of psychological levels, some of which are governed by assumptions that are not subject to question, assumptions, in many cases, never rising to conscious articulation. Commonly held beliefs about the shape of time and space—new ideas about simultaneity, for example—help to construct a shared, but ultimately authorless, lived "imagination" of the "nation," in Anderson's view. These assumptions or beliefs are lived but seldom more than sporadically interrogated. To cite another example, the philosopher Charles Taylor justifies his choice of the term "imaginary," in the title of a recent book, because he is interested less in what social theorists have consciously articulated about how one is to judge human behavior according to certain norms than he is in how ordinary people "imagine" their relationships to others in a way that is often best expressed in shared "images, stories, and legends" (Taylor 23). We cite Anderson and Taylor not to suggest that none of the representations of urban poverty that we discuss here are accurate. Far from it. Rather, what we assert is that the representations may tell us at least as much about what it meant to be male and middle class in the nineteenth century as they tell us about what it meant to be poor. Anchored in commonly held middle class assumptions about "character," "space," "temporality," and so on, the middle class imaginary of the urban poor is very revealing—although only partly revealing about the lives of those who would seem to be the main objects of its representations. In that sense we are examining a discourse that is notably situated.

The male middle class imaginary of urban poverty presents a complex picture, one in which anxieties about competition, violence, class-based resentment, individuality, and the need to differentiate oneself from the scions of inherited wealth influence the ways in which the urban poor are represented. As James Eli Adams notes in *Dandies and Desert Saints*, the growth of the professional middle class in the Victorian age was accelerated by the decay of fixed distinctions of rank, as the new industrial class system gradually supplanted the traditional patriarchy dominated by the landed aristocracy and gentry. New definitions of "the gentleman," associating him with, for instance, a new internalized ethic of self-control, are put forth to differentiate the new middle class "gentlemanly" class from the older, rank-based status category. Along with this comes a significant set of new anxieties, as the "manliness" of the mainly intellectual labor performed by this Victorian professional class "gentleman" is called into question (Adams 1–9). The new rising class, in Adams' view, is an anxious class, concerned with its social and political legitimacy, its ability to command the fealty of the lower classes it would hope to command, its identity riven by the tensions that unrestricted competition breed.[1]

As we will see in this book, one response to this anxiety was to hollow out a new sphere of manly adventure. The descent into the "slum" (and later, the "nether world" or "the abyss") became a means of asserting that intellectual labor—indeed, the act of writing itself—could entail manly exploration, requiring the exercise of extraordinary self-control if not personal courage. Social exploration in the urban slums became an act of adventurous roaming unfit for the more genteel readers whom Pierce Egan mocked in 1823 in *Life in London* as *"fireside heroes and sprightly maidens, who may wish to 'see life' without receiving a scratch"* (Egan 19). Egan is, of course, mocking his own readers, whose experience of the slums is beholden to his representations of them as a realm apart from middle class experience. Despite his taunts, the book nonetheless invites his readers to visit this realm cautiously but vicariously—with Egan as docent. Many of the writers we examine here, from Dickens and Mayhew through Greenwood, London, Masterman, and others, cast themselves in the role of reporters on a realm of experience that is either not immediately available to their own readers or too threatening for the more genteel among them to risk visiting in person. The "immediacy" of life in the slums becomes a carefully constructed experience to be widely shared in an age of growing literacy and the proliferation of newspapers and journals: its smells, its criminality, its outrages to the sense of decency presented by a writer who often parades his own mediating role between classes as his prime credential. Such a discursive strategy often shifts the focus somewhat from the poor, the object of these representations, to the affect of the reader and the risk-taking of the reporter, as if the main point of the writing were to demonstrate the manly courage of the reporter and the possibility for sympathy—or moral outrage—latent in the reader. In *The Imagination of Class*, we explore, above all, the ways in which the discourses on the urban poor create distance and the illusion of vicarious immediacy: how they "spectacularize" the urban poor for a growing Victorian readership.[2]

Males and the Urban Poor

The male experiential relationship with the urban poor thus takes on a special significance in this context. In the early Victorian period, the writings of Dickens and Mayhew spread out before the male reader a lively otherworld or sphere of masculine experience. As Richard C. Maxwell observes, "street life comes to embody dreams and desires that London brings out generally; dramas of freedom, reconciling an environment that 'assassinates you with reality' and an individual sensibility that wants alertness and mobility" (Maxwell 102). It lures the reader with its imagery of undiminished personal vitality. The vision of the underworld of the 1850s and early 1860s follows the brief efflorescence in the 1820s and 1830s of the so-called Newgate novel, in which the protagonist was often larger than life, modeled after the criminal MacHeath of John Gay's *The Beggar's Opera*, Henry Fielding's Jonathon Wilde, or Dick Turpin and other fabled blackguards chronicled in the *Newgate Calendar*, a popular record of infamous careers of crime. Their bravado, their charisma embodied, as much popular literature does, a set of desires, fantasies, and anxieties of the time—albeit ambiguously indulged by the middle class male reader.[3] These scoundrels, like Edward Bulwer Lytton's Paul Clifford, were often committed to sentimentalized and obscurely political schemes of social reform. They actually wanted to do something about the state of neglect and inequity, rather than recline in the immobility of guilt. They represented as well a kind of flamboyantly asserted subjectivity, much as the Byronic myth did on a more romanticized (and socially elevated) scale during the same period. The Newgate novel came on the scene at a moment when the possibility of assertive, individual agency was threatened by the growing constraints of modern society, with its divisions of labor, its enhanced domesticity, its diffusion of authority and affect. It seemed to arrest, for a moment, the descent into a nation of clerks and bureaucrats. Among men, the spectre of the loss of the capacity to act independently, even aggressively, acquired almost a mythic status, and the spurious image of a freer, bolder realm in the recent past found voice in the bravura renditions of such literature.

Another chronicler of the London slums, J. Ewing Ritchie, muses, in *The Night Side of London* (1861), "I should not like a son of mine to be born and bred in Ratcliffe-highway. That there would be a charming independence in his character, a spurning of that dreary conventionalism which makes cowards of us all, and under the deadly weight of which the heart of this great old England seems becoming daily more sick and sad, a cosmopolitanism rich and racy in the extreme—all this I admit I should have every reason to expect, but, at the same time, I believe the disadvantages would preponderate vastly" (Ritchie 98). So compelling is this myth of the bold and free male of worldly experience that James Greenwood, probably the most influential journalist writing on the slums after Mayhew, finds himself compelled to fight off the residual influences of the earlier versions of romantic roguery:

> The literature of the country is from time to time enriched by bragging autobiographies of villains confessed, as well as by the penitent revelation of rogues reclaimed, but, according to my observation, it does not appear that perseverance in the humbler walks of crime leads invariably to the highway of infamous prosperity . . . It is almost impossible to exaggerate the amount of mischief that is likely to result from such false and inflammatory pictures of . . . evil. . . . It tends to magnify the thief's importance . . . with precisely the same kind of gallows-glory as is preached by the authors of 'Tyburn Dick.' . . . (*Seven Curses* 71)

Gallows-glory is certainly not being sought in any bourgeois reverie, but the allure of a vital realm of adventure, mobility, and action cannot be discounted. It splices onto the mentality of the 1850s that nostalgized image of what was always a mythic masculinity. It seems to provide a spectacularized male subjectivity, as a cover for, or evasion of, the contradictions that beset the ideology's construction of established capitalism's bourgeois subject. Tellingly, it also introduces an element of social resistance—overtones of outlawry, nomadry, even misogyny—into middle class masculine discourse. The urban slums (and the literature of imperialism) provide the ingredients for such a rebellious fantasy, although it would not be fully developed until the latter part of the nineteenth century.[4]

To be sure, these literary constructs owe some of their appeal to changes in the bourgeois household that took hold especially between the 1830s and 1860s, changes which increasingly separated, for bourgeois males, the spheres of home and work, and which attempted to confine their emotional lives increasingly within the bosom of the middle class nuclear family. That era is identified by John Tosh as the "heyday" of masculine domesticity: "Never before or since has domesticity been held to be so central to masculinity. For most of the nineteenth century home was widely held to be a man's place, not only in the sense of being his possession or fiefdom, but also as the place where his deepest needs were met" (Tosh 1). While this would change somewhat after the 1870s as increasingly men were bidden to embrace, at least imaginatively, "the view that domesticity was unglamorous, unfulfilling, and—ultimately—unmasculine," that change itself testifies to unsettling emotional accommodations that surely lay just under the calm surface of the period of masculine domesticity of the previous three decades (Tosh 7).⁵

If the outlaw nature of these discourses suggests that they served as emotional or psychological compensation for the increasingly domesticated nature of male middle class life, we cannot, nonetheless, look at the relation of the bourgeois male with the East End as simply an encounter with the Other, an encounter which, by contrast, provides the observer with a definition of what he is not. It should be seen as a discourse: a set of negotiated, ambiguously phrased, imaginary relationships. Like any such discourse, this one favors certain figural and spatial patterns that sustain, in a displaced form, the desires and anxieties that inform it.

One of these patterns is that of the labyrinth: the East End coiled and twisted in narrow, dark streets in alleys and courtyards, in dead-ends, and then, deeper, into cellars, sewers, rat-ways.⁶ The journalist James Greenwood loved to chart those hidden passages. He describes in *Low-Life Deeps* a "condemned" alley in which it was discovered that underneath the street and many of the houses was a walled pit in which a brewery had once stored beer, and which was known to be haunted by the ghosts of at least two suicides. All these mazes glimmer with the luminosity of submerged life. "It must have startled innocent folk to learn that, but a year or so ago, no less than a hundred and seventy of the notorious St. Giles's cellars were still in use as human habitations, and that, after the manner of rats and other burrowing animals, as many families, consisting of mother, father and a more or less numerous swarm of big and little children passed their lives in these dismal holes under the houses . . . all in the damp and dirt and dark" (*Low-Life Deeps* 168).

What connects the middle classes to such a spectral existence? Again, and again, they tell the tale of the immersion, of the plunge into the maze, of the attraction of being "lost" for a spell in the cellar of the City. Greenwood styled himself as the "Amateur Casual," a master in disguise, who was so adept at passing as a slum dweller with petty criminals that he could move unnoticed among them, and participate in their awful mysteries. His most famous sketch is that of "A Night in the Workhouse," in which he treats his readers to the processes of transformation, to that strangely exquisite moment when one passes out of respectability and security—out of "bourgeoisdom"—and into the vulnerability and *frisson* of another state:

At about nine o'clock on the evening of Monday, the 8th inst. (Jan. 1866), a neat but unpretentious carriage might have been seen turning cautiously from the Kennington Road into Princes Road, Lambeth. The curtains were closely drawn, and the coachman wore an unusually responsible air. Approaching a public-house which retreated a little from the street, he pulled up, but not so close that the light should fall upon the carriage door.... From [the carriage] door emerged a sly and ruffianly figure, marked with every sign of squalor. He was dressed in what had once been a snuff-brown coat, but which had faded to the hue of bricks imperfectly baked.... Between the neckerchief and the lowering brim of the hat appeared part of a face, unshaven, and not scrupulously clean. The man's hands were plunged into his pockets, and he shuffled hastily along in boots which were the boots of a tramp indifferent to miry ways. In a moment he was out of sight; and the brougham, after waiting a little while, turned about, and comfortably departed. This mysterious figure was that of the present writer. He was bound for Lambeth workhouse, there to learn by actual experience how casual paupers are lodged and fed, and what the 'casual' is like.[7]

Of course Greenwood is only impersonating poverty. He can return to his middle class life; the brougham will fetch him back at the end. But many a reader must dwell upon the excitement of this experience, torn from the moorings of one's customary context and behavior, into the realm of danger, adventure, irresponsibility itself.

Whether escorted by Greenwood, or Mayhew, or Ritchie, or Dickens' Inspector Bucket, the English reader could venture across the line of class life and find a stimulation and connection. The trajectory is a symbolic one; it signifies interaction, penetration, imaginative participation. The discourse remains open in a special way, allowing a mode of psychic extension, for the middle class male, at least, which makes the excursion more than an adventure, more than a vicarious thrill. The motif of impersonation signifies an imaginative dissolution into the situation of the Other, a displacement of aspects of one's own desires. Although the later discourse from the 1870s on retains traces of this transference, it does not accommodate the full play of the masculine myth. From then on excursions into the urban slums are inflected by the language of the sociologies, the social service worker, the education inspector, and the cultural arbiter, even when, as in the case of Jack London (as we shall see in chapter 4) the reporter is a well-practiced novelist attempting to duplicate Greenwood's feats of impersonation.

Mayhew, Dickens, and Male Competitiveness

Henry Mayhew is perhaps the most important writer on the slums during the early-to-mid-Victorian period. While he is interested in the domestic lives of the poor, he is particularly interested in what they do for a living: how labor shapes them as people. He catches a phase when all manner of economic mobility appears possible—and when it seems that mobility and exchange are themselves the tokens of individualism. Eileen Yeo, writing of "Mayhew as Social Investigator" in *The Unknown Mayhew*, argues that he came upon the scene during a crucial transition between two phases of capitalism, when a more regulated and humane economy was giving way to a stage of intense competition, and that he had the rare insight to capture this change in terms of the social relationships of production (Yeo and Thompson 95). In the studies of the silk-weavers, needlewomen, tailors, and boot and shoe makers of Spitalsfield who make up the contents of *The Unknown Mayhew*, he chronicles the demise of independent craftsmanship in the face of cheap labor piecework and market instability. In *London Labour and the London Poor,* he records a different facet of this transitional period: the sudden, almost aberrational explosion of individualistic commercial activity. He ponders over it himself:

> It would be itself a curious inquiry to trace the origin of the manifold occupations in which men are found to be engaged in the present day, and to note how promptly every circumstance and occurrence was laid hold of, as it happened to arise, which appeared to have any tendency to open up a new occupation, and to mark the gradual process, till it became a regularly established employment, followed by a separate class of people, fenced round by rules and customs of their own, and who at length grew to be both in habits and peculiarities plainly distinct from the other classes among whom they chanced to be located. (Mayhew II: 147)

London Labour and the London Poor links together laborers, criminals, destitute victims, and street-sellers, but it is the latter, the costermongers and the various small entrepreneurs, hawking along the margins of the new economy, that dominate his account. As Stallybrass and White note, there is a carnivalesque quality to the study. That quality links the old cultures of country peddlers and small tradesmen to something new, to the emerging subculture of the sellers of trinkets, souvenirs, leftovers, and cheap imitation goods. As Richard Maxwell remarks, the subeconomy that Mayhew describes engages in the metamorphosis of the jetsam of a culture that is speeding up its mass production of goods, that is beginning to waste things. The street folk survive on findings, on rags and discarded clothing and cigar butts and human and animal excrement. "The street-people, like London itself, could be defined through their relationship to junk. The class was itself a form of waste, individuals thrown out by the economic machine of the city as superfluous human beings. This economic irrelevance became a source of identity, pointing such people towards the universe of excrement or cast-off things—a universe they were specially equipped to transform, since only they could feel towards it that combination of empathy and miserly delight which *London Labour* describes" (Maxwell 96).

Marginalized as these people are, they parade a kind of cocky *joie de vivre* in their resourcefulness. Consider this antic example from Mayhew:

> Fly-paper came, generally, into street-traffic, I am informed, in the summer of 1848. The fly-papers are sold wholesale at many of the oil shops, but the principal shop for the supply of the street-traders is in Whitechapel . . . A young man, to whom I was referred, and whom I found selling, or rather bartering, crockery, gave me the following account of his experience of the fly-paper trade. He was a rosy-cheeked, strong-built young fellow, and said he thought that he was "getting on" in his present trade. He spoke merrily of his troubles, as I have found common among his class, when they are over.
>
> "I went into the fly-paper trade,— it's nearly two years ago, I think— because a boy I slept with did tidy in it. We bought the papers at the first shop as was open and then got leave of the deputing of the lodging-house to catch all the flies we could, and we stuck them thick on the paper, and fastened the paper to our hats. I used to think, when I was in service, how a smart livery hat, with a cockade in it would look, but instead of that I turned out, the first time in my life that ever I sold anything, with my hat stuck round with flies. I felt so ashamed I could have cried. . . . I could hardly cry 'Catch 'em alive, only a half-penny!' But I found I could sell my papers to public-houses and shop-keepers, such as grocers and confectioners, and that gave me pluck. The boys caught flies, and then came up to me, and threw them against my hat, and if they stuck the lads set up a shout." (Mayhew I: 435–36)

The fly-paper lad is only one of many Mayhew characters who lift our spirits with their intrepid ingenuity in the face of insecurity and humiliation. They speak the spirit of commerce, even of capitalism itself, in their own small-bore way. They sing the song of individualism. And yet they will be the first victims of capitalism. Most of these one- and two-man operations will be squeezed out, or if commercially viable (like fly-papers) they will be taken over by "legitimate" businesses that will mass produce and mass market. Those who make a living by sweeping the street, or disposing and trading in refuse, will disappear as these functions are assumed by municipalities or large contractors. Some labor-intensive marginal "occupations" such as match-box making will persist for several decades, and the English slums and lower working class areas will support its own subeconomy of services and trades, but essentially the commercial fair of Mayhew is doomed. After all, Maxwell is right: these people are themselves a form of waste. They are the tailings of the commodified economy.

As Mayhew himself often passionately argued, the underclasses of London illustrate the effects of the modern competitive society: the toll on the body of the worker, the displacements brought on by the caprices of the market and the introduction of more efficient mechanical production, the psychological deprivations of piece-work and of the marginality of the costermonger existence. Gagnier and Thompson and Yeo have described Mayhew's complex and shifting attitude toward the English economic order, as he intensifies his attack on the unregulated and exploitative market and yet revels in the vitality he witnesses in its most chaotic realms. The *London Labour* vision of the underworld is governed by an ambivalent response that Dickens and other contemporary writers share toward the competitive ethos itself. Anyone working with the novel of mid-century England must remark to himself how strange it is that the great "plot," the central narrative paradigm of male bourgeois life, is so rarely told in mid-Victorian England: the story of the man rising in the business world, whetting himself on competition, defining his subjectivity by the competitive process itself. The story is being told in actual lives all over England; it is the grist for books such as Samuel Smiles' popular *Self-Help* (1859). But it is rarely the epistemic text of cultural expressions; the middle class man on the make almost never becomes the protagonist. This is the denied element in the representation of the middle class male. This is the contradiction in the bourgeois capitalist ideology of mid-Victorian England.

While competition, and the acquisitive urge that Max Weber contends is imbricated in capitalism, are not foregrounded in the great novels and much of the cultural discourse of the period, they are nonetheless present there as sites of highly contradictory energy. If one were to take the pulse of the Dickensian text, were to analyze those modulations that tell of the loci of libidinal investment, one could find the muffled, irregular rhythms of the contradictory attitude by the author—and of his ideology—toward competition. There were few men as competitive as Dickens, few who could squeeze or summarily cashier a publisher as he did, few who reveled more in the give and take. Whenever the text acquires a darkly dramatic intensity in Dickens, we are likely to be in the city of individual competition and the driven man. Dickens can never fully mediate the immense psychic attraction the competitive struggle has for him. That is the reason why the "dark" scenes of his novels register so much more energy than the domestic ones, and why he so rarely ventures (after *Pickwick Papers*) into the "merry England" countryside. That is the reason why, as well, the endings of his novels prove so dissatisfying, why they never seem to produce an abatement of the energies he has unleashed in them. He has not worked through the contradictions of his attitude toward competition and economic struggle.

Nor has the ideology of the English middle class worked through the contradictions in which it sheathes competition. Capitalism and competitive business activity are socially constructed in terms of the deferral of pleasure that is innate to the middle class ethos. Embarrassed by the distasteful, "unChristian," and ungenteel aspects of the marketplace and finance, the official culture sought to shift value away from the process of competition, often crude and selfish, and onto its goals. John Stuart Mill and others tried to temper the deterministic, result-oriented elements of utilitarianism. Competing and getting and building and investing were to be considered significant not in themselves, but as a means toward a better life. On the individual level this often meant a better home, a larger carriage, more money for the advancement of one's children. Thus the pleasure associated with competition was deferred. Correspondingly the meaning of the activity was registered in something other than the effort itself: in its rewards. If value then does not inhere in the process itself, how can it be a basis for self-definition? Such a definition would by its nature be inchoate, only potentially realizable, and difficult to represent, for it is only from its termination, its closure as a social discourse, its result, that we can judge its true nature and submit it to ethical analysis. Thackeray's *Vanity Fair* (1847) provides the classic contemporary example of this dilemma, for its protagonist Rebecca Sharp embodies the entrepreneurial spirit beautifully; she is in life not for the results of her social and economic successes but for the pleasure of the game itself. She establishes her identity in the competitive process. But Thackeray, sharing the Victorian upper middle class cultural unease with such an ethos, finds himself at a loss as to how to close off his novel, and does so unsatisfactorily, where he is disconcertingly ambiguous in his assessments of Rebecca. Though he finally condemns her, she engenders, as Dickens' competitive villains often do, much of the energy of the narrative; she is where the psychic action is.

Middle class entrepreneurialism often accounts, in fact, for the "gap" with which Dickens' novels begin. The orphaned protagonists of his books, unable to find their origins, evolve in late Dickens into men, like Pip and *Little Dorrit*'s Arthur Clennam (both containing biographical traces of the author himself), who immobilize themselves with an indefinable guilt, or sense of "fault." What agonizes them is the dim apprehension that the relationships of production of bourgeois capitalism themselves have led to the social inequities and engendered the alienation of modern urban existence. As a kind of punishment for this "primal crime"—and that term has particular resonance because of the guilt associated with the usurping by the middle class male (the son) of the old (the father)—both Pip and Arthur fail in their business aspirations: Pip never finds gratification in his quest for a gentlemanly life (the "gentleman" is a code in the Victorian period for someone who is worldly, who can still operate in the experiential realm, but not in the competitive/acquisitive); Arthur ends up in debtor's prison. They must be "punished" because at some buried level, they surmise that their male class identity is bound up with the acquisitive urges of competition. This goes as much for the members of the professional class, whose position requires that they disavow it in public, as for the members of the entrepreneurial class, who are more given to celebrating publicly the virtues of competition.

In his earlier novels, such as *The Old Curiosity Shop,* Dickens tried to maintain some kind of distinction between "good" business activities and "bad" ones. Quilp, the arch-villain of that novel, engages in the undesirable activities of commerce and money lending. Similarly, James Carker stands for what has been denatured by the new economy: he represents unbridled ambition; he is a manipulator of texts—not a builder but a schemer. But both cases expose the Dickensian ambivalence, because Quilp is the source of much of the vital energy of the novel, and Carker not only fascinates us, but shares with his creator certain writerly qualities of voyeurism and artistic talent. And both are imbricated in Dickens' own repressed phantasm. Quilp lasciviously stalks the prepubescent Little Nell, who is explicitly inspired by Mary Hogarth, Dickens' adoring young sister-in-law, who died in his arms, and who became for him an ambiguous symbol as sexual object and paradigm of purity. Carker, too, embodies illicit desire and debauchery, and his death under the wheels of a steam engine is rendered in language of intense sensuality.

The traversing of images of the competitive world and of sexual desire permeates Dickens' writing and complicates the ideological contradiction that underwrites it. Figures such as Quilp and Carker epitomize desire. The objects of their lust are often implicitly commodified objects such as the idealized girl-child Little Nell, or explicitly commodified figures such as Edith Granger, who complains at one point that "I am a woman . . . who from her childhood has been . . . offered and rejected, put up and appraised, until my very soul has sickened. Hawked and vended here and there . . . until . . . I loathe myself" (*Dombey* 382). Even Lady Dedlock is commodified, on display at Chesney Wold as an elegant and beautiful possession, reflected in her expensive portraits, bound into the silence of the bought woman. An uneasy correlation exists between the commodifying and consuming of women as a form of sexual pleasure, and the aggressive excitements of the competitive world.[8]

In Dickens, then, sexuality is transposed onto competitiveness/acquisitiveness, deepening the psychic pull of the latter, but producing immense instability in the distribution of textual energies. For both these urges are repressed; they are both fraught with contradictions at the ideological level. Consequently, erratic displacements occur within the text. The sexual and economic axes are sometimes aligned, and sometimes opposed, and there is a frequent transposition of one upon the other. Women in the novels become fetishizations of economic desires; on other occasions, desire shifts away from the female human body onto economic objects; in still other instances, the association of sexual urges with competition produces a kind of displacement that has homoerotic overtones (through "bondings" with male fellow competitors, such as that between Bradley Headstone and Eugene Wrayburn in *Our Mutual Friend*).

Although such instability and conflation is to be expected when an already contradictory conceptualization is consistently elided, the crisis over male roles and male subjectivity necessarily charges these issues with remarkable intensity. The guilt and anxiety that the middle class male author registers over the social conditions of England acquire added psychic energy from the libidinal issues tied up with them. In addition, the difficulties of representing competition as a process, as a meaningful mode of behavior in itself, and the refusal to acknowledge or come to terms with sexuality, produces a set of texts in which a powerfully energized range of signifiers exist without signifieds. The excess of floating signifiers is organized through one common affect: that of desire. Desire, as we know, sustains the consumer market—it is an unfulfilled desire, stimulated by constantly substitutable objects, which are appropriated, used for the consumer's gratification, and wasted—a desire that is eroticized even on the economic level. The convolutions of this process clearly cannot be traced without close examinations of each text, which is not our purpose here, but it is enough to confirm that such a nexus of fundamental ideological contradictions militates against a stable construct of the bourgeois male subject.

By reading the ideological contradictions aroused by the competitive ethos of modern industrial society through Mayhew's *London Labour and the London Poor,* we are able to see more readily the positive and negative qualities that the ethos connoted for the Victorian middle class observer. The openness, mobility, adventure, and apparent freedom of untrammeled economic activity could be shown alongside its destructive and dehumanizing social effects. The world of the costermongers, the marginally employed, and the poor becomes a theatre in which the dynamics of bourgeois entrepreneurship and commodification in some of their most primitive forms are played out. In such an arena, class, as it is customarily designated in Victorian social discussion, is elided. Although Mayhew was one of the first reporters to give us a systematic description of significant segments of the working classes, his effort in *London Labour* to set up the new categories of nomadic and settled indicates a disposition to approach the relation between the upper and lower spheres of society on new terms. As Regenia Gagnier has pointed out, by the time he began working on Book Four of *London Labour* Mayhew was deeply into a reorientation of working relationships that jumbled the normal class hierarchies (so that pure capitalist investors along with shopmen and goods transporters were grouped together as the Auxiliary class).[9]

Certainly his groupings of occupations and types, his attention to their habitats, their work and leisure patterns, their particular customs and languages, furthers the objective of designating the street people and slum dwellers as a kind of subculture—a collective that has shared attitudes, patterns of living, and common experiential possibilities. They are portrayed as an enclave with its own internal dynamics. Such a narrative and analytical approach had sharply differentiated his depiction of the urban underworld from those largely anecdotal, largely imaginative, often touristic accounts of his predecessors such as Pierce Egan.

Mayhew himself persistently talks in terms of "class": he says he defines "those who obtain their living in the streets of the metropolis... as a very large and varied class." But given his predilection for biological terminology, it is quite likely that he is using the terms in the sense of a pseudo-scientific classification. As Gertrude Himmelfarb has shown, Mayhew is working in the midst of a general uneasiness about the appropriate terms for the poor, as distinguished from the marginal workers, the lower working class proper, and so on, and he is probably trying to impose some of his own sense of things within the welter of terms. In any event, as Mayhew represents the London poor and the street folk (as distinguished from the weavers, tailors, et al. of the earlier *Morning Chronicle* articles), he denies them that group self-awareness, that oppositional nature that E. P. Thompson postulates as the determinant of class. The elision is critical, for it means that the lowest stratum in English society will be fixed in a representation that deprives them of the characteristics of group consciousness necessary for class identity. If they are not seen as a class in the ways that the working class is, then they can be treated differently—and used differently discursively.

Nothing arrests the attention in Mayhew's book more than the capacity of the street-sellers to mimic and rework the images of the dominant culture. The street people embody, in a distorted way, some of the displaced desires for masculine freedom; they are often bizarre pastiches of the cult of individuality; they engage in a ludic extension of the mercantile competitive ethos. The engaging account of the fly-paper vendor casts an almost parodic reflection upon commercial activity. He seems to be caught up in the self-propelling replication of commodification itself, for the commodity reproduces itself endlessly, and elaborates upon itself in variations and by-products, all in the highly self-reflexive market economy, in which use value has been replaced by exchange value—an arbitrary construct of worth. Commodification fires the energy of self-parody.

In this respect, commodification at the level of the street people seems to make them a subculture of the main socio-economic system.

Subcultural movements in the late nineteenth and twentieth centuries in England share the disposition to parody or rework the patterns of behavior and production of the middle class consumer culture. We have witnessed it in recent times in the reflexive responsiveness of England's immigrants and working classes to the world of media, style, fashion, and cultural gesture. Out of the lower income neighborhoods and suburbs have come subcultural expressions of rock, mod, and punk, which are nurtured first among the lower classes as gestures of independence, even resistance (although often with a sense of irony), and are then co-opted and modified by the ever-adaptive mainstream, "respectable" culture. Subcultures give the styles and modes of the dominant culture a reflexive spin. Mayhew's street people, however, do not attain to the status of a subculture, precisely because they are not sufficiently aware of the outlook of the "establishment" to be able to parody or to form a style of ironic resistance to it. They are not sufficiently cognizant of the hegemonic values to be able to work off of them in a way that critiques them. This is significant because it leads us into what he is telling us about the problematics of individual subjectivity in this urban/commercial environment.

Specifically, the urban poor lack the capacity to conceive of themselves and to project themselves symbolically. Admittedly, we are at the mercy of bourgeois representations of the East End. It is arguable that someone like Mayhew has simply blocked out the symbolic register; in later accounts, by voices from the slums themselves, a measure of conscious mimicry emerges. Nonetheless Mayhew's most poignant or stunning accounts illustrate the limited capacities for self-conscious, reflexive awareness among the lower orders. Typical is the thirty-year-old costermonger who claims to have once served the Prince of Naples when that eminence came to London.

> "But I don't know nothing of the King of Naples, only the Prince. I don't know what the Pope is. Is he any trade? It's nothing to me, when he's no customer of mine. I have nothing to say about nobody that ain't no customers. My crabs is caught in the sea, in course. I gets them at Billingsgate. I never saw the sea, but it's salt-water, I know. I can't say whereabouts it lays. I believe it's in the hands of the Billingsgate salesmen—all of it? I've heard of shipments at sea, caused by drownding, in course. I never heard that the Prince of Naples was ever at sea. I like to talk about him, he was such a customer when he lived near here." (Mayhew I: 56)

Mayhew's costermonger's mind revolves in tight, interlooping circles, for his imaginative vocabulary is as limited as the experiential one. He lives mentally in a labyrinth that resembles the geography of his neighborhood. Without either kind of outreach, he has scant chance of transcending his immediate lot, of thinking in a symbolic register, or of achieving the kind of imaginative projection that allows him perspective on his or another social formation.

In a remarkably revelatory observation, Mayhew cautions:

> We must not in the arrogance of our self-conceit condemn these men because they are not like ourselves, when it is evident that we should have been as they are, had not some one done for us what we refuse to do for them. We leave them destitute of all perception of beauty, and therefore without any means of pleasure but through their appetites, and then we are surprised to find their evenings are passed either in brutalizing themselves with beer, or in gloating over the mimic sensuality of the 'penny gaff.' Without the least intellectual culture is it likely, moreover, that they should have that perception of antecedents and consequents which enable us to see in the shadows of the past the types of the future—or that power of projecting the mind into space, as it were of time, which we in Saxon-English call fore-sight? (Mayhew I: 101)

The difference between "classes," by this account, lies in qualities of mind. One quality is that of experiential and imaginative outreach—the appropriative mentality so characteristic of the middle class and significantly less developed in this lower class group. The other quality that Mayhew insists upon is that of culture, which by his terms, "perception of beauty . . . intellectual culture, [seeing] the shadows of the past," he designates aesthetic sensibility, cultivation, perspective, breadth of mind.

And so the urban poor are hemmed in by the limitations formulated by bourgeois discourse itself. Discourse effectively keeps alive masculine fantasy, the possibilities of adventure, mobility, and exuberant individualistic commerce, the experiential, and it even works them through parodic manifestations. By returning to the labyrinth formula, this discourse effectively preserves the possibility of intrusion by manly adventurers from the West End while denying, or making more difficult to emerge, symbolic expressions that might emerge from within the labyrinth itself. The geographic limitations that sustain the myth of manly adventure are reinforced in the picture of the mind of the poor as maddeningly self-enclosed, incapable of moving outside of tightly circuitous paths.

None of Mayhew's urban denizens quite rivals the justly celebrated "Jack Black," self-designated "rat and mole destroyer to Her Majesty." Black also goes by the name of the Battersea Otter, because he catches barrelfuls of freshwater fish with his hands. He lives in a flat decorated with stuffed birds and animals, many of them his favorite rat-hunting ferrets, and he is as domestic as you like, for Mrs. Black proudly shows Mayhew the costume their daughter wore as the "Ratketcher's Daughter," when she served behind the bar at a public house—a red velvet bodice, embroidered with silver lace. Jack bears the scars of dozens of rat bites with honor, but he has given up tobacco "since a haccident I met with from a pipe. I was smoking a pipe . . . and a friend of mine by chance jobbed it into my mouth, and it went right through to the back of my palate and I nearly dies." Here his wife added, "There's a hole there to this day you could put your thumb into; you never saw such a mouth." Jack Black is one of the voices of London's nether world that will feed a bourgeois imagination over many a sleepless night:

> "One night in August—the night of a very heavy storm, which, maybe you may remember, sir—I was sent for by a medical gent as lived opposite the Load of Hay, Jampstead, whose two children had been attacked by rats wile they was sleeping in their little cots. I traced the blood, which had left lines from their tails, through the openings in the lath and plaster, which I follered to where my ferruts come out of, and they must have come up from the bottom of the house to the attics. The rats gnawed the hands and feet of the little children. The lady heard them crying, and got out of her bed and called to the servant to know what the child was making such a noise for, when they struck a light, and then they see the rats running away to the holes; their little night-gowns was kivered with blood, as if their throats had been cut. I asked the lady to give me one of night-gowns to keep as a cur'osity, for I considered it a *pheenomenon* . . ." (Mayhew III: 17)

Jack Black is himself something of a *pheenomenon*. He is the very mimicry of life: a figure thriving on the margins, a production of his own dialogue and ingenuity, the enterprising small operator in its most bizarre manifestations. The circumstances of Mayhew's interview, in Black's domestic abode, with his proud and doting wife, his mementos of past campaigns, and his appreciation for the stories that terrorize the bourgeois imagination—the rats eating at the children's hands and feet—convert Black into almost a parody of the ordinary man. He is, after all, a working bloke, a family man, a small contractor. But, like all the Mayhew characters, Black is a specimen of a quirky kind of individuality. An individuality is all that he represents, for he like the others in the slums never cracks the bourgeois humanistic code for the subject: he never attains to that complexity, that self-awareness and self-reflexivity.

In these ways, Mayhew's opening up of the vast and exotic territory of the urban slums has imperialistic overtones. The observing culture needs the actuality of this world outside its own; it is vital that the slums be something that one can experience, if only vicariously or through a surrogate. But the crucial difference between the London netherworld and foreign colonies is the closeness: the thin line across which the imagination can travel to fantasize the reprise of a more primitive and "free" masculine life and can explore the exhilarating yet terrifying ways in which the new economic order exfoliates and degenerates at the same time. In such a relation, the distinction between literal and symbolic blurs, and the diminution of the individual subject can speak as much of the dangers facing the English middle class male as of the dehumanization of the poor. The immense evocative power of *London Labour and the London Poor* issues from its experiential, symbolic force as well as from its exposure of mid-century London's terra incognita.

The Chapters

As our discussion of Mayhew reveals, the focus of this book will be on the construction of a particular kind of urban netherworld in the Victorian age. While not all the writers we consider in these pages are biologically male, we are particularly interested in how the writings of an emerging male professional class construct the urban poor of the city of London.

In the 1860s and 1870s, the urban poor were "discovered" by journalists as a fascinating underworld. Many also used the pathos of poverty for many of their most emotionally gripping sensations. In chapter 1 we examine the rhetorical effects of this work as well as its substance. In some of the journalistic accounts, such as those of the master of disguises and intrepid explorer James Greenwood, an insulating element of culture is insisted upon as a way of keeping the reader at a psychic distance from the effects of an encounter with the Other.

But the rise of "sensational journalism" breaks down that separation, by writing private morals into public discourse, and by creating a new kind of textual effect which undermines the normative way in which the reading experience shapes the subject. The incremental construction of a centered, integral being that is the object of the realist novel is replaced by a disruptive, emotively charged discourse. And this works in conjunction with sentimentalism to dissolve the boundaries between the reader and what he or she observes. The sentimental accounts of urban poverty are particularly important to this process, for their qualities of emotional excess and their codings of private ethical and material relations expose the reader to the affect of abjection. Coded as "female," a threatening form of abject experience is constructed and distanced through the work of a number of male writers who took as their subject the urban poor. We examine here how the male writer's stance of detachment, carefully constructed, is always under threat by overpowering emotional forces that threaten to engulf him.

In chapter 2 we discuss how the discourse of "culturalism" in the 1880s attempts to contain a threat that is coded, not as affective excess, but as emotional deadening. As middle class writers, inspirited by what Beatrice Webb calls "a sense of sin," descend upon the East End to participate in a variety of "missions" ranging from the C.O.S. through the settlement movement through Charles Booth's famous fact-gathering study of poverty, the East End is constructed as a land of enervation. In the *Autobiography* of Webb, in the novels of her cousin Margaret Harkness, in the work of Walter Besant, and in the social outreach of a variety of new agencies aligned with what Donzelot calls "the social," East End life is seen increasingly as a feminized landscape, its redemption requiring not only empirical fact-gathering of the sort to be made famous by Charles Booth, but active intervention in the interest of moral and psychological reconstruction of an essentially feminized social order. The spatialized representation of the netherworld continues to favor figurations of miasma and labyrinth, but without the investment of sensationalized affect that had so marked the work discussed in chapter 1. Rather, in constructing a more "professionalized" relationship between middle class observer and lower class subject, this discourse seeks the material recuperation and cultural pacification of a social order, a redemptive mission often conceptualized as the fostering of the proper consumerist tastes. Webb's *Autobiography*, more so than other writings of the period, registers how the conditions of East End poverty constituted a threat to the integrity of the middle class subject, an ethical challenge to those who would remake this world, a spur to the development of an empirical descriptive project of large-scale dimensions, and an inspiration for a political project of "permeation" that would seek to displace the threat of personal enervation into political reform.

Nowhere is that redemptive narrative more dramatically contested than in the novels of Arthur Morrison and George Gissing, which we examine in chapter 3. Morrison, the first of the major writers to emerge from the poorer areas of the East End, portrays an underclass that cannot be culturally "improved" and absorbed, and in which its distance from the mores of the dominant society and economic order is so great that it can only be represented symbolically. The hostility with which Morrison's work was reviewed indicates that he not only irritated the nerves of the middle class, but also exposed the materialism that underlay late nineteenth-century British naturalism. Gissing's *The Nether World* shares with Morrison's work the determination to preserve the integrity of the representation of lower class life against the distortions of culturalism, and its expressions in working class popular culture. His own ambivalence toward the social resentments of the lower classes, however, articulates itself in the feverish, melodramatic portrayal of female sexuality, and in the curiously constricted, emotionally stultified personification of male desire.

Chapter 4 addresses the dominant phantasmic construction of the urban poor at the end of the century: the East End as "the abyss." Here we are concerned with the way a number of male writers (Richard Jefferies, H. G. Wells, Jack London, Charles Masterman) register the historical moment of bourgeois hegemony as a moment of intractable class conflict, resistant to amelioration. This moment in the history of the middle class male mind would see the poor reduced to threatening fantasy objects, consigned to a hell from which there is no escape. This "discourse of the abyss" is itself traced by uneasy contradictions that emerge in middle class professionalism: they become evident in the emergence of an "authoritarian" theme that pulls Wells toward celebrating the Mandarin class, London toward politically self-defeating, dark irony, and Masterman toward contempt for projects of "culturalist" philanthropy. Yet they have a productive side as well, as the discourse of the abyss rounds upon itself, exposing, at least in Masterman's writing, its own self-awareness as a production of a moment in the history of middle class thought.

- CHAPTER 1 -

Sensational Journalism, Male Detachment, and the Feminized Victim

Greenwood and Gentlemanly Detachment

*I*n the aftermath of Mayhew, representations of the urban poor become prominent features of journalistic discourse in the 1860s and 1870s. In this chapter we are particularly interested in exploring how this discourse constructs a certain type of reader, a reader poised to appreciate both the detached perspective of the male author and how he distances the threat of permeable boundaries represented by the abject poor in his representations.

The key figure is the Amateur Casual himself, James Greenwood. Greenwood had established his fame with "Night in the Workhouse," published in 1866 in the new evening paper, *The Pall Mall Gazette*, which was then edited by his brother Frederick. He moved on to *The Daily Telegraph*, where he wrote an equally notorious account of a fight in Hanley between a bulldog and a dwarf, who were chained within reach of each other in a ring, and continued his self-proclaimed "humble endeavour towards exposing and extirpating social abuses" until the end of the century, before allegedly "flickering out in police and court papers." His collected articles appeared in several books, including *The Seven Curses of London* (1869) and *Low-Life Deeps; An Account of the Strange Fish to be Found There* (1875), and he wrote children's books "of a peculiarly bloodthirsty kind," and novels such as *The True History of a Little Ragamuffin* (1866) about a street arab (Richards vi–vii).

Greenwood shares with Mayhew and many of the writers of the 1840s and 1850s an attraction to the experiential stimulation of slum reporting, rendered in a tough-minded if morally attuned, breezy, assertive manner. Yet the fascination with the economic activities of the second phase of industrialization is less marked in him; he is situated somewhere between that perspective and the more intensely moralized journalistic accounts of the 1880s. But in many ways, in tone and persona, he seems to be a throwback to an earlier version of the occasional essay and journalism writing. He is, in fact, an intriguing instance of the conflicting tenors of class and ideology at play under the cultural voice of the Victorian middle class.

For the persona of Greenwood is always there before us, establishing and sustaining a relationship with his reader that asks our complicity, but all in a deceptively casual guise. Greenwood revels in his role, and as far as his masquerades as the Amateur Casual take him, he is always in control, confident, urbane, able to penetrate the Very Deepest Rookery without losing his poise. While he disarmingly confesses at the beginning of one of his adventures, "I was young in the field of exploration then, and from all that I had heard and read made up my mind for something very terrible and desperate; I pictured to myself a band of rollicking desperadoes," such worries do not dent his bluff self-assurance. A commonsensical manner allows him to put even the worst dangers of the "moral miasma" in perspective. "Which of us can say that *his* children are safe from the contamination? Boys well-bred as well as ill-bred are mightily inquisitive about such matters, and the chances are very clear, sir, that if the said bird-lime [of criminal temptation] were of a sort not more pernicious than that which sticks to the fingers, who might at this very moment find the hands of my little Tom and your little Jack besmeared with it?" (*Seven Curses* 91). It is a disturbing thought for the middle class reader, but moderated to a certain extent by his almost jocular way of putting it.[1]

The explicit reference to a male reader ("sir") fits in with Greenwood's role as the intrepid journalist-explorer. The journalists of nineteenth-century England are seeking to establish themselves as professionals, but, as Lucy Brown notes in *Victorian News and Newspapers*, such a status is slow to come—many of the categories, such as "reporter," and "editor" (with specific reference to the newspaper position) did not enter the language until the nineteenth century (Brown 85). But journalism surely shares with the other, more established professions of law and medicine, and the emerging professions of the police inspector and the detective, those qualities that set them apart from other male roles. The professional is the figure who attempts to place himself outside of the normally fixed positions of class. He moves freely among various strata, maintaining all the while the detached, objective character essential to professionalism. He can counsel the "great," and, like Greenwood, he can descend into the very heart of East End *terra incognita* and re-emerge, unscathed, uncontaminated, his bourgeois values intact. He is, in a way, the ideal figuration of the middle class male at this stage in the establishment of that class's hegemony in England, for he symbolizes, in his own adaptability and disinterestedness, the detachment from landed property and its interests that distinguishes the middle class professional from the gentry and aristocracy. He embodies the empirical mentality of his class, and he appears to fulfill in some way the mythic self-appointed role of the bourgeoisie as "in the middle," mediating between the upper and lower spheres of society. In addition, he pretends to have nothing to do with the competitive drive that causes all those troublesome self-doubts.[2]

In Greenwood, however, there are two discourses operating at somewhat different wavelengths. What we might call the discourse of his role, of his activities as the "professional," carries all the *déclassé* connotations that we have remarked upon. His written text, on the other hand, reads as the uneasy hybrid of gentry modes and bourgeois modes that are conflated in the English middle class conception of culture. This disparity exposes the disjuncture between the image of Greenwood-as-subject engaged in action and the persona of Greenwood that is being articulated in his written discourse. The reader, presumably middle class, does not know which to identify with—and is in fact encouraged to identify with both.

In one respect the hybrid of gentry/upper class and middle class mannerisms in Greenwood's journalism can be attributed to traditions of style: resonances of the urbane, ruminative, discursive manner of the essay tradition of the *Tatler* and the *Spectator*, carried on into the nineteenth century by William Hazlitt and others. When he ventures into the underworld in *Low-Life Deeps*, for instance, he sizes up things with a gentleman's yardstick: "There was but one bedstead in the room—a mite of a place; I measured it with my walking stick and found that it was 3 sticks one way and four sticks the other, and yet it was made to accommodate mother, father and eight children" (*Low-Life Deeps* 132). Even the most searing of his vignettes, describing match-box making in Shepherd's Court, where a woman and three or four children work fifteen hours a day in the vilest of conditions, does not move him in the way that it does later writers. There are times when Greenwood seems scarcely able to keep his mind on the pathos before him: after dutifully ticking off the squalid conditions in a particularly low slum apartment, he casually digresses into the curious regulation in the boarding house against lodgers pelting each other with pillows and bolsters. In all his writing of the urban slums, he assumes a studied diffidence, as if speaking from a position of social detachment.

Greenwood's most famous newspaper base, the *Pall Mall Gazette*, was in fact conceived, the newspaper historian H. R. Fox Bourne tells us, as "a bold attempt to realise Thackeray's fancy of a paper 'written by gentlemen for gentlemen'" (Fox Bourne 274). The notion of the gentleman, in Thackeray and his followers, was itself an attempt to meld eighteenth-century gentry class worldliness and sense of privilege onto nineteenth-century middle class morality—an effort to elevate the active, socially concerned being above class struggles. The cross-class grafting did not end there, however, for the conditions of the sometime journalist, sometime literary figure in the 1840s and 1850s produced some strange combinations of political/cultural positions. Nigel Cross, in his history of *The Common Writer*, describes the rise of a generation of writers who made their living by writing occasional essays for journals such as Dickens' *Household Words*, the *Illustrated London News*, the *Illustrated Times*, and *Punch* in its early days under Mark Lemon's editorship. These men—and Henry Mayhew and Greenwood and his brother were among them—often made only marginal livings. Many were "idle young dogs that squandered away their time on the pavements of Paris or London," in the words of one of them, George Augustus Sala; many, like James Hannay, were prodigious drinkers; almost all kept irregular accounts. Their romantic term for themselves was "Bohemians."[3] For a decade or two they kept afloat because the repeal of the advertising duty (1837), the stamp duty (1855), and the paper duty (1861) unleashed a flood of inexpensive newspapers and periodicals, and vastly expanded their reading public among the middle class. Most of the Bohemians affected, however, to despise the middle class, according to Cross, and took up highly radical positions, attacking wealth, privilege, and respectability. *Arrivistes* themselves in many instances, they developed a natural sympathy for the urban poor and lower working classes because of their own frequent slips into genteel poverty. Yet what they produced was often the "dashing article from the London haunts," an account of urban slum conditions or crime that was distinctive not for its graphic realism but for its *haute-bourgeois* literary flair (Cross 90–100). Angry and disrespectful to be sure, but almost arch in its bravura, as for example, in this cutting remark from James Greenwood on government nabobs confronting social crises: "A curious exhibition of the lamentable credulity of our law makers occurred no longer ago than at the second reading of the Habitual Criminals Bill in the House of Lords. Naturally the subject was one concerning which their Lordships could know nothing, except by hearsay" (*Seven Curses* 72).

Such a medley of social positions seems to confound attempts to situate the narrating (and reading) subject in a class. It masks and ironizes ideology by playing through a range of rhetorical tonalities, some of which, like the Bohemian and the nineteenth-century gentleman, are themselves hybrids of class attitudes and postures.[4] Any analysis is further confused by the resonances of various literary voices within the text, from the eighteenth-century occasional essay to the Newgate novel to mid-Victorian radical sensationalism.

These "literary" elements in Greenwood's writing exert a certain kind of power. They situate the reader in a literary tradition, an intertextual discourse made up of the gentrified occasional essay, the middle class urban literature of Mayhew, the Newgate novel, Dickens, and the like, and their fancies about the way in which popular literature—the penny dreadfuls, for instance—influence the lower classes. The middle class reader is made aware, at some level, of his own literary sophistication and range, thereby heightening the contrast with the lower class individual, who is presumed to be hopelessly caught in the expressions and formulas of popular culture. To emphasize this, Greenwood frequently lapses half-mockingly into the florid prose of the penny dreadfuls and the "thrilling romances" that he insists shape the sensibilities of the lower orders. Of one such favorite, "Starlight Sall," he observes,

> it is evident that the [author's] mind is on his work, for he lingers over it with a loving hand. Never was there such a tender anatomist. He begins with Sall's head, and revels in her auburn tresses, that 'in silken, snaky locks wanton o'er her shoulders, white as eastern ivory . . . ' He takes her by the eye-lashes, and describes them as the 'golden fringe that screens the gates of paradise,' and finally he dips into Sall's eyes, swimming with luscious languor, and pregnant with tender inviting to Panther Hill. (*Seven Curses* 90)

Greenwood contends that such excesses of imagination shape the debauched "reality" of the London slums: "As a curse, of London, this one is worthy of a special niche in the temple of infamy, to rank first and foremost . . . Of the children who are not the progeny of thieves, but who somehow find their way into the criminal ranks, it is undoubtedly true that pernicious literature, more than once alluded to in these pages, does much to influence them towards evil courses" (*Seven Curses* 87, 112). So prevalent is the corrupting power of the thrilling romance imagination that even prison wardens believe in its efficacy. Greenwood cites instances in which sly young boys have successfully wrung the hearts of their jailors by disingenuously insisting that "it was them penny numbers what I used to take in, sir," that led them astray.

On the level of the observed objects—the urban poor—reality has become textualized, then, in a special way. It is seen as a construct in part of the slum dweller's own "literary" imagination, even by those young jailbirds who cynically exploit their wardens' credulity. The poor have ostensibly been incorporated into literary representation itself, participating haplessly in the cultural process by which they are being constructed from above. Greenwood's objective is to insert the urban poor into the continuum which has been designated as culture. The "literary" aspect of Greenwood's journalism functions, in itself, to code the expression as part of a cultural production, for the literary is identified with an emerging high culture. We shall explore the full implications of the absorption of the urban poor into the cultural continuum in chapter 2.

Suffice it to note that one immediate effect of such a construction is to depoliticize the urban condition by shifting it onto registers of artistic/cultural expression which are supposedly "outside" ideology, transcending immediate social, political, and class implications. Engels' *Condition of the English Working Class,* for instance, imbricates the poor within historical, sociological, and economic processes—ultimately political processes—in a way that contrasts strongly with the prevalent English treatment which foregrounds the middle class observer's experience. Consequently, the English response was not to address longer-developing economic and historical factors, but to call for reform and philanthropy—and to do so by appealing to the "goodness of heart" of the reader. The values attributed to the middle class reader, in other words, become the central determining elements of the representation of the urban poor.

Similarly, the recourse to the "literary" in accounts such as Greenwood's shifts the emphasis onto the reader. For one thing, the "ignorant" urban poor, as we have shown, can exercise very little power over the way in which illusions from popular literature have shaped their lot; educated and more literarily sophisticated readers such as those in the middle class have power over the literary text—the power to interpret it and dispose of it. As if it were not enough to rob the urban poor of their "reality" by saying it is partly a fictive construct, the dominant voices of representation also proceed from the conviction that the poor can never have control over fictiveness.[5]

Our culture deems the individual imagination to be a force that surpasses and, indeed, lies outside of any discursive formulation of it, especially when the imagination is attributed to the middle class reader. It is almost proof itself of the "presence" of the observer's mind at work. Thus, throughout this discussion two, sometimes contradictory, notions of "subjectivity" are being alluded to: one which is tied to a model of subjectivity as agency—the conventional notion of the "imagination" provides a good example of this—and one, a more "Althusserian" notion, which sees subjectivity in terms of signifying function: "subjecthood" is something bestowed on individuals by the dominant ideologies of their culture which "interpellate" them as subjects; the "subject" in this latter sense is a signifier, not an agent. And there is a third sense of "subjectivity" that we must take into account here: the reader's.

Since our analysis of the depiction of the urban poor has turned to the subjectivity of the reader, the Lacanian concept of suture, developed in analyses of film but valuable in the discussion of the literary construction of human subjectivity, may be helpful. Greenwood's narration foregrounds his own persona, often as a mediating factor yet also as a confusing site of ideological positions. His ostensible mission is to introduce us to the urban poor, yet his text seems at times to be principally engaged in the construction of the reading subject. As author/narrator, Greenwood is, in terms of suture, the speaking subject, enunciating a text. The urban poor are the individual subjects that he is "speaking" (writing) about; they are the subjects of the speech act (text). We, as Greenwood's readers, are the subjects who are addressed, who are spoken to. Yet a reading relation differs from everyday spoken conversation in the sense that we, too, are observing the subjects of the text, the urban poor in this case, and we are engaged in responsive relationships to them which, though controlled tightly by Greenwood's rhetoric and structure, are nonetheless felt to be determined in part by our "independent" subjectivity, as in the case of the working of the reader's imagination. We deem ourselves to be, in part, the "creators" of the representation, as if we, too, were "speaking" ("writing" or glossing) it. Greenwood has induced us to help engage in the observation and construction of the subjects of the text. But because he engineers us into our roles as interpreters and "creators," we have, in a sense, been "spoken." Thus we the readers are also the spoken subject, a term that for all its syntactical awkwardness connotes the curious position we occupy as ones induced to engage in the act of representation, but within perimeters that have been set by the author/narrator.[6] We are, in short, "inscribed readers." We are largely going to adhere to the more familiar terms of author/narrator and reader rather than speaking subject and spoken subject, but it is vital to introduce those terms to keep in mind that the reader is not just the passive recipient of a text, but that his or her subjectivity is made to construct and articulate itself in relation to the subject of the text—that it is "spoken."

"Suture" allows for a certain play of identity across the gap between spectator and actor on stage: like Hitchcock's camera in *Psycho*, which allows us as filmgoers to experience both the emotions of fear and vulnerability of the naked woman in the shower—the visible subject of the scene—and the voyeuristic pleasure of her killer (in the place of the camera eye) about to reveal her nakedness before killing her, we are sutured into these guilty scenes in ways that allow a certain indeterminacy of identification, a play across the gap between spectator and spectacle, middle class observer and lower class subject. However, the very process induces an experience of pleasure that can also paralyze the ethical impulse, as the pleasure of watching overpowers one's responsiveness to the ethical demand to act to prevent harm. In this sense, certain types of voyeurism militate against the development of human sympathy. The eighteenth-century tradition of "sensibility," perhaps best represented by Edmund Burke's *Philosophical Enquiry . . . into the Sublime and the Beautiful*, had argued just the opposite: that because we experience pleasure in the spectacle of the Other in pain we are not paralyzed but rather inevitably motivated to lend our aid to alleviate that suffering (Burke 46) However, the assumptions behind Burke's universalizing view of human suffering may well offer a more optimistic account of the process than is warranted, because powerful affective response does not automatically trigger ethical action and in fact may well work against it.

Once we are sutured as readers into the relationships with the subject of the text that Greenwood or any author has established, we are inserted into a discourse. That discourse is triangulated among the three subjects of author, reader, and the urban poor. With a writer such as Greenwood, in particular, we are acutely conscious of his presence, of his manipulation of the material, of his casting it in terms of literary and ideological texts, of his obtrusive posture as mediator (e.g., the man who ventures into the depths of the East End in our behalf). Hence we are conscious, to greater and lesser degrees as we read, that our relationship to the subject of the text is being produced by somebody (presumably Greenwood). To a certain extent, then, we occupy the site of consumption; we are induced to "buy into" the representative process. That triangulated discursive relationship is crucial because it allows us to register the complications of ideology. Greenwood, as we have noted, is himself a figure within the ideology of his time; his values and self-styled position (as journalist, "gentleman," bourgeois radical) are both produced by that ideology and propagate or reproduce it. His depictions of the urban poor construct them, and our relations to them, in terms of the ideology. To the extent that he can influence his readers, he programs them into that ideology. But the suturing operation involves more than that: it induces the reader (presumably middle class, in this case) to act as if he or she were an independent subject, imaginatively conceiving and evaluating the urban poor himself or herself. The result of that conception and evaluation, we feel, can only be knowledge rather than ideology. The triangulated relationship of the discourse enables us to feel that we are standing aside a bit from the author. Although this can be a position that allows us to resist the author's and the text's ideological construction, in most cases a successful discourse induces the reader to engage in the same ideological construction. But, of course, the reader thinks, as an independent subject, she is doing so of her own will. There can be no more compelling way to involve an audience in ideological construction than to foster the impression that it is thinking on its own as a group of free subjects. In this way, the reader is most effectively inscribed into the operative ideology.

Our analysis of suture compels us to treat the inscribed reader as a much more important element in representations of the urban poor than we might otherwise be inclined to do. Once we understand that the discourse induces the reader to conceive of himself or herself as a subject, exercising his own independence in the reading process—and when we realize at the same time that the author circumscribes or frames the exercise of that independence by what he presents to the reader, how he rhetorically manipulates him or her, etc.—then we realize that the text's construction of the reading subject is as important to examine as its construction of its ostensible object—the urban poor.

The effects of reading on readers were of course a concern of many Victorians. Throughout the first half of the nineteenth century, as

Richard Altick has pointed out, religious interests, worried about lapses in attention by the faithful to their spiritual states and ethical concerns, crusaded against fiction and sensationalist journalism. Such fervor, exercised most strongly through control over the lending libraries which were the most important source of the dissemination of literature throughout much of the nineteenth century, necessarily determined the ways in which we have defined the relation between author and reader ever since. The very forces that took stands inimical to novel and newspaper reading reconstituted that status of the reader. Admittedly, they were themselves building from more classical theories of rhetoric in reaching their sometimes hysterical pronouncements about the power of the text upon the reader, but they drastically reformulate assessments of the emotive response of the "ordinary" reader. The evangelicals in particular worked this transformation by stressing the effects of reading upon the passions. Altick quotes a contributor to the *Christian Observer*, who warns us that "We cannot . . . read continually a display of human passions and feelings, and remain wholly exempt from their contagion: no, we cannot view the war of passion with the cold and critical eye of an artist" (Altick 111). The repeated and often strident insistence upon the dangers of emotional "contamination" and stimulation creates an atmosphere in which the emotive qualities of reading relations acquire major significance.[7]

In conjunction with this, the evangelicals propagated the idea that reading effects shaped the reader's mind, and had particular consequences in his or her material relations. Altick quotes the same commentator's admonition against the results of "the continual feeding of the imagination . . . which, once deceived, becomes itself the deceiver; and instead of embellishing life, as it is falsely represented to do, it heightens only imaginary and unattainable enjoyments, and transforms life itself into a dream, the realities of which are all made painful and disgusting, from our false expectations and erroneous notions of happiness" (Altick 110). The pattern is all too horrifyingly evident: imaginative or sensational literature disables the reader from engaging in the essential material, day-to-day, operations of life—the operations that are the core of his maintenance of himself as a human being. The other significant force in defining nineteenth-century reading relationships, the utilitarian, largely reinforces this prospect, through its campaign to limit reading to what is useful, for that, too, connects reading to its consequences in material activities.

Greenwood, as we have seen, enlists the reader of his underworld accounts into a cultural tradition that attempts to sustain the values and adhere to the perspective of a worldly, relatively privileged, and predominantly male heritage—that of the gentry to which his literary manner belongs. His persona as a professional journalist accords with those intentions, for it allows him to remain psychologically and socially intact while he immerses himself in the netherworld. He performs as his upper class male model would have him do: as a worldly, urbane, publicly engaged figure. As a consequence, he seems to be telling us something about the capability of the male of his generation and social context to bridge the social classes. Even when he "loses" himself in his dramatic adventures in disguise, and seems for a moment to slip into that eerie state of transition in which the self dissolves and merges under the disintegrating conditions of underworld existence, he never achieves that breaking down of the boundaries of the self that would allow him (or the reader) to gather in and moralize the sufferings of the poor. The extension—in this case a form of dissolution—of the socially (class) cultivated self that is necessary to draw together with the lower classes in an ethical binding does not take place for Greenwood, indicating that he shares with the men of the previous generation the inhibitions that disabled them from being ethicizing agents.

Sensational journalism foregrounds the intense feeling, the emotive register, which is necessary to establishing a relationship between the classes, and brings the values so affirmed into the realm of public expression. Greenwood serves as an appropriate transitional figure, for his article "A Night in a Workhouse" electrified the London reading public, and is credited with converting *The Pall Mall Gazette* from a struggling conservative daily into the most famous of the "New Journalism" periodicals known for their sensational journalism (Diamond 25–46). So an account of exposure to the London underworld comprises a pivotal incident in the transformation of the English press. As the *Spectator* commented, when remarking on the sensation of Greenwood's account, "So utter is the dislocation of society, so complete the severance between its parts, that for a man of one caste to sleep one night in an official ward occupied by men of another has been pronounced an heroic deed. London this week feels as if it had been sleeping, like the brave author of the narrative which had awakened it, on a bed made endurable only by turning the blood which spotted it downward to the floor."[8] This is powerful testimony to the impact of Greenwood's representations, highlighting not only the evidence that writing provides of the degraded lives of the poor but the impact of his representations on the reading public. The *Spectator*'s response underlines our point that these sensational representations provided an opportunity for middle class readers to indulge a richly affective response to suffering in their midst and to do so within the context of a vague call for ethical response to the deplorable conditions the writer depicts. It is a subsequent article, however, that ushers in the new tenor of representations of the urban poor in an atmosphere of sensationalization.

Sensationalizing the Poor: Permeable Boundaries and the Abject

"In the autumn of 1883," Anthony S. Wohl writes, "a small, anonymous penny pamphlet bearing the provocative title *The Bitter Cry of Outcast London* (subtitled *An Inquiry into the Condition of the Abject Poor*) appeared in the London bookstores. Its impact was so immediate and cataclysmic that it must be considered one of the great pieces of Victorian reform literature. Alfred Spender, the editor of the *Westminster Gazette*, stated in 1913 that it was almost impossible to recapture "the sensation which such a pamphlet as 'The Bitter Cry of Outcast London' made when it was first produced." Suddenly, almost overnight, it seemed, England awoke to the grim facts of the slums. "The revelations concerning 'Outcast London,'" commented *Reynold's Newspaper*, "cause a tremendous sensation and thrill of horror through the land" (Wohl 189). The author of this bombshell was Andrew Mearns, Secretary of the London Congregational Union, and at one time a Congregational minister in Chelsea.[9] The "sensational" effect of it, as we shall see, was partly attributable to its promotion and reproduction by *The Pall Mall Gazette*, then under the editorship of W. T. Stead, the master journalistic provocateur of the Victorian age.

The material circumstances of the London poor, according to Gareth Stedman Jones, had been degenerating throughout the preceding decades, even though they had been largely put out of mind by the upper classes in the 1870s. By 1883, a severe cyclical depression had come on as the culmination of six or seven years of indifferent trade; many of the older industries in London were in structural decline; and the misplaced efforts to "clean up" the central city had simply pushed more and more marginal workers and indigents into less and less space (Jones, *Outcast London*, 281). In addition, the seeds of further anxieties were beginning to penetrate bourgeois consciousness: the specter of "collectivism" was in the air; socialism had acquired more prominence; and the working class seemed to be developing a new class consciousness. The interacting of such volatile social developments with the worsening state of a desperate underclass intensified the unsettling implications of Mearns' revelations.

Mearns follows the pattern of religious rhetoric in directing his appeal to the reader. He uses the material of slum life degradation to reinforce the middle class reader's set of values, for what is so shocking about his revelations is not the danger of some sort of socialist revolt but the spectacle of a complete breakdown of the elements of home, order, cleanliness, responsibility, and godliness that fabricate and sustain the bourgeois subject. And true to the nineteenth century evangelical construction of reading effects, Mearns emphasizes the anxiety that holds together such a subject and that poises him or her on the brink of positive or negative social actions. While acknowledging that there has been "increased attention" to the "poor and outcast classes of society," Mearns warns of peril: "Seething in the very centre of our great cities, concealed by the thinnest crust of civilization and decency, is a vast mass of moral corruption, of heart-breaking misery and absolute godlessness . . . We must face the facts; and these compel the conviction that THIS TERRIBLE FLOOD OF SIN AND MISERY IS GAINING UPON US. It is rising every day" (Mearns 82). Mearns is a far cry from the meandering, urbane James Greenwood; there is no pretense of the "high literary" here, no shifting through registers of class discourse. His tract is aimed directly at the heart of the middle class reader. Its ideological components have a coherence that we had not seen two decades earlier, and they are linked together in discourse through the very spectacle of their dissolution.

Although Mearns assures us that "so far from making the worst of our facts for the purpose of appealing to emotion, we have been compelled to tone down everything . . . or the ears and eyes of our readers would have been insufferably outraged," he subjects the reader to a set of effects that shock almost every fiber of the sensibility we call bourgeois. Having alerted us to the rising tide of sin and misery, and after telling us that church attendance is pathetically low in the slum areas, he then exposes his reader to "The Condition in which They Live." "We do not say the condition of their homes," he notes, "for how can those places be called homes . . . ?" And once again the walking tour begins.

To get into the rookeries, he says, "you have to penetrate courts reeking with poisonous and malodorous gases arising from accumulations of sewage and refuse scattered in all directions and often flowing beneath your feet; courts, any of which the sun never penetrates. . . ." Entering into the slum dwellings themselves, you must "grope your way along dark and filthy passages swarming with vermin," and once inside, "the walls and ceiling are black with the accretions of filth . . . It is exuding through cracks in the boards overhead; it is running down the walls; it is everywhere." The sickly air which finds its way into the room has to pass over the putrefying carcasses of dead cats or birds, or viler abominations still" (Mearns 94–95). Within such a sensory miasma, the people one sees, though in the most awful of conditions, seem to be little more than dry statistics. The predicament of these victims of poverty stuns the reader, yet Mearns seems to impute to them a kind of callousness; they are indifferent to the filth of their living conditions. What can we expect after all of a penniless woman in her eighth confinement, living among the pigs? One feels less of pain than of disgust and amazement. Thus, whatever emotional responses do appear come not from the lips of the destitute and suffering, but from the hearts of the middle class readers. Throughout his pamphlet Mearns keeps asking, "Who can even imagine the suffering which lies behind a case like the following?" "Will you venture to come with us and see for yourselves the ghastly reality?"—as if he were acknowledging that the real task at hand is to make the reader realize the contrast between his or her sense of values and social position and the conditions of poverty. For, after all, it is an exhortatory text, calling on the reader to act, to build bridges, to be an ethical force. It synthesizes bourgeois values associated with home and family and right action, and calls explicitly for ethical action by the middle classes to alleviate the lot of a poor whose ethical impulses are presumed to be paralyzed by the degrading conditions of their lives.

The most telling sign of this movement can be found in the reiteration of the theme of what can only be called "promiscuous" overcrowding:

> every room in these rotten and reeking tenements houses a family, often two. In one cellar a sanitary inspector reports finding a father, mother, three children, and four pigs! In another room a missionary found a man ill with small-pox, his wife just recovering from her eighth confinement, and the children running about half naked and covered with dirt. Here are seven people living in one underground kitchen, and a little dead child lying in the same room. Elsewhere is a poor widow, her three children, and a child who had been dead thirteen days. Her husband, who was a cabman, had shortly before committed

suicide. Here lives a widow and her six children including one daughter of 29, another of 21, and a son of 27. Another apartment contains father, mother, and six children, two of whom are ill with scarlet fever. In another nine brothers and sisters, from 29 years of age downwards, live, eat and sleep together. Here is a mother who turns her children into the street in the early evening because she lets her room for immoral purposes until long after midnight, when the poor little wretches creep back again if they have not found some miserable shelter elsewhere. . . . (59)

Far from describing a situation of colorful variety à la Mayhew, Mearns is here suggesting that proximity itself, a lack of proper spatial boundaries, is at the heart of the social problems associated with poverty.[10] The very enumeration of individuals promiscuously enclosed within the same small space does the job of pointing the moral itself. Vice spreads like the scarlet fever, disabling the very conditions that would make people redeemable if they lived in a Dickens novel. And he doesn't hesitate to draw the most controversial conclusions about overcrowding among the poor, convinced that if he hasn't witnessed them directly, they nonetheless must be present a priori: "Incest is common; and no form of vice and sensuality causes surprise or attracts attention" (61).

Publication of *The Bitter Cry of Outcast London* raised anew the spectacle of incest as a feature of life in the lower-class warrens, provoking discussion of the sexual proclivities of the poor by Parliamentary commission, although the issue was by no means brand new in the 1880s. As early as 1858, the medical officer John Simon argued to the Privy Council that where overcrowding exists in the "sanitary sense, . . . almost always it exists even more perniciously in certain moral senses. In its higher degree it almost necessarily involves such negation of all delicacy, such unclean confusion of bodies and bodily functions, such mutual exposure of animal and sexual nakedness, as is rather bestial than human" (Wohl 53). Lord Shaftesbury had brought the issue to the attention of the House of Lords in 1861, relying heavily on the evidence of medical officers such as Simon (Wohl 55).

However, the 1880s saw an intensification of interest in the topic, no doubt because it was that decade that saw the development of sensationalized media campaigns such as Stead's *Pall Mall Gazette*'s campaigns against child prostitution ("The Maiden Tribute of Modern Babylon") and the horrors of overcrowded slums ("Outcast London"). Picked up by Tennyson, Mearns' claim reappears in a famous line about "incest in the warrens of the poor" in "Locksley Hall Sixty Years After." In an article in *Nineteenth Century* in 1888, Beatrice Webb alleges that incest in the London slums is widespread, basing her claim on no direct evidence but simply on the assumption that overcrowding must lead to it (Himmelfarb, *De-moralization* 142).

While Mearns' report contains a fair amount of preaching against the conditions that create this state of "demoralization," what is most notable about his report is the extent to which the evidence does not speak for itself but rather is presumed by the narrator to do so. The language of the report gestures toward unspoken and unrecorded evils, most not depicted in any direct way in the pages of the report itself, but nonetheless inferred by the narrator from conditions of overcrowding that violate middle class spatial norms (and, by extension, middle class notions of bodily "decency"). In this sensationalized discourse, the very precondition for "sympathy"—spatial separation—seems impossible to achieve among the victims of East End poverty represented in the pages of the report. The poor themselves seem to press upon one with an importunate reality that threatens to engulf the reporting subject, and he forestalls the collapse of these defining differences through the enactment of a moral disgust which, while it certainly sets him apart from the people he observes, seems oddly unanchored in many observed or reported reasons for disgust. Mearns' sensationalist discourse thus presents us with people with whom it is difficult for the middle class reader to sympathize, the poor living in overcrowded conditions, for they stand convicted of a variety of crimes too heinous to be depicted in full detail by a scrupulous narrator.[11]

The invocation of middle class values of home, domesticity, proper spatial separation of people, and so on in the passages just quoted from is almost too obvious to mention, even if it does become a dominant feature of the accounts of the underclasses during this period. Its interplay in a text that created a "sensation," however, and in a newspaper, *The Pall Mall Gazette,* that came to be identified with modern sensationalist journalism under W. T. Stead's editorship, merits deeper examination. For "sensation" had become a volatile term of art in mid-nineteenth-century England, characterizing a subgenre of highly popular novels of the 1860s that dealt with bigamy, murder, incest, madness, and other assorted social maladies, usually set in upper middle class households, and often involving the intrusion of the "other world" of violence or deviance into the presumably well-ordered sphere of the English household. The major novels, infamous in the eyes of reviewers of many of the highbrow journals, included Dickens' *Bleak House,* Wilkie Collins' *The Moonstone* and *The Woman in White,* and the novels of Mary Elizabeth Braddon, Charles Reade, and Mrs. Henry Wood. They created "a national state of mind known as 'Sensational Mania,'" and comprised a substantial portion of the novelistic fare of the enlarged middle class reading public of the Victorian period (Hughes 5). The sensation novel's relationship to the press has yet to be fully examined, but there are intriguing interconnections between the so-called Bohemian journalists and the sensation novel phenomenon.[12] Many of the Bohemians published in the journal *Temple Bar,* founded by Mary Elizabeth Braddon's consort John Maxwell, and one of the chief publishers of the Bohemians, the firm of Edward and William Tinsley, owed their prominence to the astounding commercial success of Braddon's *Lady Audley's Secret,* perhaps the quintessential sensation novel (Cross 99, 101). A reviewer in the *Quarterly* also coined the term "newspaper novels" for works that drew on recent criminal reports in the daily newspapers, where "before the public interest has had time to cool," the author served up "the exciting viands in a *rechauffe* with a proper amount of fictitious seasoning."[13]

The sensation novel, as well as sensational journalism, created a generally pleasurable *frisson* through the specter of the sudden revelation of forbidden desires—of a frustrated wife, trapped in a bad marriage, losing her memory and remarrying romantically, or of a villainous spouse's dramatic demise. Such "escapism" was frequently punished, for the "villain" was often condemned to a lifetime of guilt and ostracism or shown to be mad, but it also encoded a form of resistance to bourgeois respectability.

Sensation novels, and particularly sensationalist journalism, expressed as well the anxieties that beset the newly established middle class in a modern society. The newspapers dwelt upon violent crimes, murder, rape, vicious assault, occult practices. Virginia Berridge, writing on the popular Sunday papers of mid-Victorian society, notes that "over 50% of *Lloyd's* content in 1885 dealt with murder, crime and other thrilling events. It was murder and crime, as well as scandal . . . which filled the pages of these papers" (Berridge 257). Whether it is the most notorious sensational story of the century—the Jack the Ripper murders of prostitutes in the East End in 1888—or the tales of incest and degradation that emerge from accounts such as *The Bitter Cry,* the newspapers bring into public consciousness the proximity of a world of sudden horror. Even the novels set snugly within middle and upper class environments expose the vulnerability of that milieu to "deviance" and transgression. This holds true for novels that we can now read as cries for liberation from the bonds of a brutalizing marriage or from the sterility of upper class boredom; they register the unsettling presence of needs and influences that disrupt the presumably integrated stability of the domestic bourgeois ideal. As Karen Chase and Michael Levenson argue, sensationalism is part of a much larger cultural process in the Victorian age. Its literary and journalistic forms stage a spectacle of transgression of what had been constructed by mid-Victorian middle class ideology as ostensibly a firm boundary between public and private spheres. As such, it is part of a larger cultural process that involved the perpetual interpenetration of public and private, "the thrusting outward of an inward turning, the eruption of family life into the light of unrelenting public discussion," as they put it, in which the violation of those boundaries is presumed to be transgressive (Chase and Levenson 12). Sensationalism denotes, in its very rhetorical mode, excess.

Henry James said that the defining feature of the sensation novel was its introduction into fiction of "those most mysterious of mysteries, the mysteries which are at our own door."[14] As a discourse, sensationalism always determined itself in relation to disruption, usually from the "outside": murder in the streets, degradation, scandal. Sometimes these disruptions, as in Collins' *The Moonstone,* arise from the presence within British society of foreign elements: mysterious religious fanatics from India engaging in vile "occult practices," for example. At other times, the breakdowns occur from internal passions and madness—which are always depicted as "unnatural" to the social or domestic order. Their meaning effects are generated against a background in which the norms governing bourgeois domestic relations are assumed to be locked in place.

The coding of sensational writing as a register of disruptive or invasive forces was further reinforced by the character of the sensation novel itself. In some instances the plots revolve around the incursion of the lower classes into upper class sanctuaries: Lady Audley's "real" crime is her marriage, as a lower class young woman, into the gentry; her convenient disposal of a previous husband by stuffing him down a well and her incipient madness are almost incidental to her initial presumptuousness. Perhaps of greater cultural concern were the base origins attributed to the sensation novel itself, for it was said to have derived from the penny dreadfuls and disreputable reading fare of the lower orders. Winifred Hughes quotes Braddon as admitting that "the amount of crime, treachery, murder, slow poisoning, and general infamy required by the Halfpenny reader is something terrible. I am just going to do a little parricide for the week's supply" of sensation text (Hughes 9). Thus the literary phenomenon itself mixed social spheres, dragging the crude "literary" tastes of the lower classes into respectable drawing rooms. The relationship of such fiction—which fed the mid-Victorian appetite for the kind of stimulation that comes from "news"—to the sensational newspapers only exacerbated bourgeois unease about the dangers of interclass taint, for many of the mid-century sensationalist papers, such as Reynolds's, combined their accounts of social horrors with vaguely radical attacks on established power, especially the landed gentry (Berridge 261).

The objective of the realist novel was to construct and adapt the reader's subjectivity through his or her suturing into a discourse that was materially dense, experientially rich, and elaborated through a lengthy, detailed narrative. The very process of reading a long novel such as *Middlemarch* has an accretive effect that defines the reader as a certain kind of person by constantly evoking his or her ethical and experiential responses to life-like events. Relationships to characters are developed over time; the reader has an illusion of being immersed in something called the novelistic "world." The sensation novel, and sensational journalism, on the other hand, cut off that incremental, developmental construction and adaptation of the reader's subjectivity. Although the term "sensation" seems to refer to that subjectivity, the sensation text actually accelerated the stimulation of the reader, reducing the possibilities for a complex integration of the sensational material into the reader's subject-construction. Indeed, according to the *Oxford English Dictionary*, the variations on the term "sensation" were, in this period, beginning to acquire their denotations as something evanescent and passing. The meaning of "sensationalize," for instance, as the production of factitious emotion, enters common usage in the 1860s, and generally through and in reference to newspapers.

Journalism provides the model of the process itself. Sensational journalistic material, such as that in *The Bitter Cry*, typically works through schematized formulas; it is designed to be absorbed quickly; it fits easily into certain established protocols of describing and defining behavior. This means that the newspaper reader invokes these codes almost immediately: in the case of Mearns' urban poor, the codes of sin, degradation, desperation, and so forth are instantly, and almost unconsciously, invoked. The reader responds reflexively. The thinness of "characterization" of the victims of urban poverty—the dehumanized, nonindividualized, almost categorical descriptions of the slum dwellers in *The Bitter Cry*—contributes to this effect. And once that abstraction has taken place, the distancing and reifying that we attribute to the jaded consumer of media begins to occur.

As novel-reading helped consolidate and register the distinction between public and private spheres in the nineteenth century, so sensational journalism accelerates the substitution of an already-recognized public for assumedly private values that characterizes modern life. It plays out on the public scene the ethical and emotional values that are presumably harbored and nurtured in the private sphere: compassion, pity, sorrow, moral indignation—even our innermost dreads.[15] The ethical and the emotive are publicly spread out together. The hystericized mode of such journalism imposes bourgeois ethical values on public events—and on the public consciousness—in expressions that are fraught with feeling: witness Mearns' observation that "seething in the very centre of our great cities . . . is a vast mass of moral corruption, of heart-breaking misery and absolute godlessness." The ethical evaluation cannot be distinguished from the expression of emotion; they wash together. The events or conditions that are being reported (in the ostensibly neutral guise of newspaper reporting) are thus fully saturated by feelings and moral codes. The only meaning of the conditions of the urban poor is as a site of the reader's emotional and ethical engagement, indeed, play, within a cultural context in which the distinction between "public" and "private" is assumed by the bourgeois audience. Indeed, if the "unwalled poor" of Mayhew's report lack the domestic virtues, that is because the definition of what it means to be a bourgeois family was as much "architectural" as anything else, reinforced by the structure of the middle class home and the larger geographical process of "suburbanization" that the building of railroads made the defining feature of nineteenth-century urban life (Chase and Levenson 147). In Mearns' *Bitter Cry*, the writer's own invasion of the permeable boundary separating the lower class family from the street is deemphasized by his rhetorical strategies which stress the middle class writer's imagination of what may go on behind those walls: unspeakable outrages of the domestic virtues that are constitutive of the middle class ideal of family life, the imagined domestic horrors that help consolidate notions of bourgeois comfort and respectability when they occur among others—the poor.

What we are describing is, of course, the effect of modern media, with its personalized flavor, its reflexive reaction to change and "news," and its close, even intimate, relation to our daily routines (of reading the papers, usually in private). A significant change occurs with the advent of widespread circulation of the daily newspaper, for even in its less sensationalized forms it inserts private values onto the public scene, thus creating the shock of "sensation" within a middle class culture which has already constructed the conventions by which the "private" is marked off from the "public." Thus, the private sphere is coded as the realm of affect and the feminine, but it is a realm continually subject to transgression, to an explosion of affect in the public realm or a sudden revelation of political or economic chicanery within the private sphere (as in, say, Collins' *Woman in White*): hence the shock effect of sensation. As Ann Cvetkovich has argued:

> Central to the construction of middle-class hegemony in the nineteenth century was the gendered division between the private and public spheres and the assignment of women to the affective tasks of the household. A discourse about affect represented marriage and the family as the product of natural affective bonds and individual self-expression. The construction of affect as natural, however, also meant that it might be uncontrollable; the discourse of affect thus includes the apparently contradictory construction of affect as the sources of both social stability and social instability. This contradiction is embodied in the figure of the middle-class woman, whose capacity for emotional expression at once exemplifies the domestic idea and represents the threat of transgression. (Cvetkovich 6)

The ambivalence of this discourse which Cvetkovich points to can provoke a useful rethinking of the coded oppositions which constitute the private/public dichotomy. Sexuality, for instance, as Darwin himself pointed out (and as Hardy built his novelistic career reminding us), is anything but a "private," "individual" emotion. Rather, it is an "instinct" which drives—in Hardy's case, runs roughshod over—the individual who is himself part of a larger organic whole; in that sense, it is universal, and thus, hardly "individual": the mark of "nature" on the individual rather than the effect or expression of some peculiarly "individual" and rootedly "private" desire. In other words, as creatures of instinct, we are all one.

The Victorian tendency to confine sexuality to the private sphere, however, encouraged its gradual assimilation to the individuating notion of bourgeois identity. As the critics of Victorian sexology inspired by Foucault's *History of Sexuality* have reminded us recently, the tendency of Victorians to consign sexual desire to the private sphere fostered the construction of elaborate classificatory schemas of individual desires, most elaborately evident in Krafft-Ebing's rich inventory of the "perversions" in *Psychopathia Sexualis*. In Krafft-Ebing, you are what you desire. The Foucauldian characterological "type" is thus a creature whose essence is buried in an ostensibly "inadmissibly private" realm of individual desire but who comes to recognize himself in the public category elaborated most richly by Victorian sexology: as "onanist," as "homosexual," or as "flagellant." Moreover, as Jonathan Ned Katz reminds us, the rich Victorian inventory of "perversions" even included "heterosexuality" from the time of its first appearance in the sexological discourse of the 1850s until sometime in the 1930s when changes to its definition in *Webster's Dictionary* register its loss of perverse meaning and its establishment as the name of the psychological "norm."

In the Victorian era, public figures become more and more conscious of the reaction of ordinary people—a reaction that is often couched in ethical terms, if not emotive ones.[16] Thus they become more attentive to the articulation of private values in everything they do publicly. Those private values become public ideals through reiteration, and, correspondingly, public events and affairs acquire a greater presence in private lives. An interpenetration of the two spheres, inherent from the beginning for reasons we have already discussed, becomes the norm, and thus, not surprisingly, public discussion of the "breakdown" of the "traditional family"—key institution of the private sphere—assumes its place as the arch-metaphor for all ills in the public sphere, as Jeffrey Weeks, among others, has argued (Weeks 27).[17]

The public and private spheres are grotesquely denatured by sensationalism because of its excess, which seems to cheapen not only the emotions involved, but the private ethics associated with them, and even the public events or conditions themselves. The consequences of this cheapening are more likely to fall upon the lives and sensibilities of women than men, for they are the ones who are constructed as moral guardians of the private sphere of the bourgeois home. Not only does Cvetkovich suggest that the division between private and public spheres was a gendered one in the nineteenth century, but she claims that in "naturalizing" the distinction between spheres, Victorian society was implicitly assigning to the middle class female an ambiguous (and potentially threatening) capacity for emotional expression. Thus, part of the meaning of "the private sphere" is the place for containing animalistic emotions that might otherwise routinely—and dangerously—find expression in the public sphere: the place of, to take just one example, the competitive marketplace, where presumably the nasty desire to dominate others finds bountiful opportunities to express itself. In psychological terms, in other words, the distinction between a placid, well-regulated, female-dominated private sphere and a competitive, nasty and brutish, male-dominated public one oversimplifies the cultural constructs at play by buying too uncritically into well-known Victorian overdrawings of this very distinction. Both spheres contain the psychological potentials of their opposite number latent within them. The ideal articulated by Ruskin in "Of Queen's Gardens" (1858) of the male sphere as the realm of "conquest" and the female sphere as the orderly realm of benevolent "rule" is subject to the same interpenetration of opposites that all such "ideals" are: the orderliness of the private sphere is achieved at the price of a punishing repression; rules themselves only exist to regulate behavior that answers to psychological desire. Better yet, in Foucault's view, rules help construct the very desirability of the desires they regulate. The ideal placidity of the domestic sphere is achieved only at a cost of repression which is evident in gothic literature throughout the century but especially, in the 60s and 70s, in sensation literature, which invests female characters with a capacity for violence and sexual rapacity that is contained only by being made to appear to have infected the private sphere from without.

As men and women grow more inured to the cheap and easy transposition of private values and feelings onto the public scene—as they build up a tolerance to the excess of sensationalized journalism—they come to acquire an ironic viewpoint toward it. An element of disavowal accompanies the indulgence of emotionality and morality. As a result a paradox occurs: even as public events are imbued more deeply with private values, and the public circulated more readily into private moments, the events outside one—such as the conditions of poverty and suffering in the East End—are not integrated into one's individual life. Although Mearns and those who followed him may have intensified public concern for the sufferings of the poor, he is working in a system of expression that ultimately serves to separate out and distance those stimuli that affect the middle class reader's construction of himself or herself as a subject. Essentially the sensational event has been removed to the sphere of the public, rather than integrated into the private.

We can trace this process in *The Pall Mall Gazette*'s handling of *The Bitter Cry*. As we stated, Mearns' tract became a kind of watershed for the paper under the editorship of W. T. Stead. *The Pall Mall Gazette* is particularly intriguing for our purposes in that it is preeminently a newspaper catering to the London middle class. It develops as the urban consciousness of that class develops, and it joins the new crop of afternoon dailies which cater to the changed patterns of middle class (especially professional) city behavior, to the urbanite (later suburbanite) with the leisure to read after work. One of Stead's biographers, Raymond L. Schultz, attests to the "paper's usual upper-middle-class politically oriented audience," and John Gross characterizes the readership as "cultivated well-to-do." It retained for much of its existence pretensions to cultural expression as distinct from "mere" journalism; and that interest in general readability probably contributed to its innovations in the field.

Stead helped to "sensationalize" English journalism by becoming the most notorious practitioner of what came to be known as the "New Journalism." Matthew Arnold apparently coined the term, ironically while writing for the *Pall Mall Gazette* himself, describing it as "full of ability, novelty, variety, sensation, sympathy, generous instincts; its one great fault is that it is featherbrained. It throws out assertions because it wishes them true."[18] The New Journalism's style was that of sensationalized production: it jolted its readers, as Stead prescribed, with "the startling, the unexpected, the presentation of facts with such vividness and graphic force as to make a distinct, even though temporary impact on the mind" (Schultz 31). Its changes were not limited to the writing itself, for Stead introduced and exploited, as no one had before, a variety of typographical techniques, such as multiline heads, crossheads used to break up longer pieces, maps and diagrams, woodcut drawings and portraits to supplement features, the sidebar, and news analysis articles. Some of these features existed in American newspapers, but were largely foreign to the staid formats of English dailies.

In addition, news or investigative pieces were no longer treated as isolated stories, but became, in Stead's hands, productions. The publication of *The Bitter Cry* set the pattern. Stead accompanied it with a leader entitled "Is it not time?" in which he castigated the churches for failing to attend to suffering in their midst. "Leaders and signed articles on various phases of the problem appeared; relevant articles in other periodicals were publicized and often excerpted; speeches of key figures in the ensuing debates were reported; scores of letters were printed; frequently, straight news stories on slum evils were run; and, as public interest increased, related accounts from London and the provincial press were quoted and summarized. From October 16 through November 7, every issue of *The Pall Mall Gazette* included at least one "Bitter Cry" item" (Schultz 35). Stead's method was to generate his own cultural event, whip up interest by commenting on his own story, induce readers and politicians to respond to his stories, provoke other journals to enter the debate, and then report their response as "news" items. As continual involution of the story was set into play, the coverage itself became spectacularized.

Stead's other great innovation, the personal interview, worked in the same way. The custom in English newspapers had been, especially in the handling of criminal cases and political or foreign affairs coverage, to compile a news article out of excerpts from coroner's, police, or magistrate's reports, or from speeches or official releases. Stead not only expanded such coverage through interviews with the principals, but went one step further by creating a story through an interview. His most famous case was an interview with General "Chinese" Gordon, which raised such a flap that the government was obliged to grant Gordon's proposal that he be dispatched to the Sudan to quell the disorders there (leading eventually to the slaughter of Gordon at the hands of the Mahdists). The introduction of such personal voices into English newspaper coverage contributed to awareness of the newspaper as a cultural production. An historian of the British press, J. D. Symon, observes:

> The new journalism under Mr. Stead in *The Pall Mall Gazette* introduced what is known as the "personal note . . ." It began with the interview and the personal paragraph. It remained in its fullest expression chiefly in the signed authoritative article. In the introduction of the personal note is Nemesis: insidiously, implicitly, it exposed the impersonality of the newspaper qua newspaper. The impersonal view was seen to be relatively impotent hence the change that has made the daily press an open and avowed reflection of the passing thought more than an attempt to impress impersonal thought upon the masses.[19]

The circulation of public and private elements in sensationalist journalism became a visible reality in Stead's hands. His capacity to generate moral outrage and then to influence public figures intoxicated him. "Stead was a larger-than-life crusader for democracy, morality, and women's rights, a Provincial radical who detested the London elite," Judith Walkowitz tells us. "He too believed that he had a personal pipeline to God, whom he referred to as the 'Senior Partner'" (Walkowitz 9).

The transposition of ethics from the private to the public sphere pushes as well against the gender coding of certain realms of behavior. The public sphere is essentially coded as masculine throughout the century, not only because the chief actors in public affairs (other than the Queen) were male, but because the disposition of "roles" throughout the Victorian period had assigned men to the amoral (or immoral) outer world of business and politics, and women to the site of moral upbringing and redemption, the private home. Work among the urban poor was one of the few areas in which women could be active outside the home; charity had for decades provided an opportunity for the exercise of ethical activities. As we shall see in chapter 2, the 1870s and 1880s opened the way for women such as Octavia Hill and Beatrice Webb to act upon their ethical impulses in a significantly more forceful manner than had customarily been allowed to women.

The other dominant characteristic of middle class representation of the poor in this period—its unabashed sentimentality—would also seem to push in the same direction. Sentimentality attempts to elicit a "communal" emotion, by writing large the feelings of pathos, pity, and compassion. The more excessively drawn and repeated the indulgences in emotionality, and the more clichéd they are, the more effectively they seem to function as a kind of public outpouring. Sentimentality was coded as a "feminine" discourse by the mid-nineteenth century—another indicator of the "softer" qualities of women: a good product of their sensitivity, though a dubious result of their sheltered and thus impressionable natures (this despite the continued popularity of Dickens and the publication of Tennyson's *In Memoriam*).[20] Throughout the Victorian period there is an effort to use sentimentality to create a "more feeling" nation, and thus to awaken in men, too, their latent sympathetic qualities, and the work of writers from Dickens through the journalists of the 1870s and 1880s seeks to bring that about. But sentimentalism proves to be an elusive, deceptively complex discourse, whose gender implications redound in disturbing ways, especially upon women.

The sensational appearance of *The Bitter Cry of Outcast London* had in fact been preceded by a series of illustrated articles in *The Pictorial World*, by a journalist named George R. Sims, who tries, with uneven success, to combine the dashing journalism of James Greenwood with sentimental vignettes of urban suffering. The series, under the title of *How the Poor Live,* failed to stir the public in the way that Mearns' account was later to do in part because it was not promoted through Stead's sensationalist practices, and in part because Sims degrades the

Greenwoodian gentleman-journalist manner to a kind of human interest reporter gabbiness. Sims' text contains, however, one of the classic sentimental images of urban suffering.

As is the wont of these intrepid journalists, Sims marches in and out of slum dwellings as if he had a perfect right to be there, and on one occasion, he climbs a dark, rickety staircase to an attic where "we see a picture which will be engraven on our memory for many a month to come":

> The attic is almost bare . . . In one corner, on a shelf, is a battered saucepan and a piece of dry bread. On the scrap of mantel still remaining embedded in the wall, is a rag; on a bit of cord hung across the room are more rags—garments of some sort, possibly . . . and at one side of the room is a sack of Heaven knows what—it is a dirty, filthy sack, greasy and black and evil looking. I cannot guess what was in it if I tried, but what was on it was a little child—a neglected, ragged, grimed, and bare-legged little baby girl of four. There she sat, in the bare squalid room, perched on the sack, erect, motionless, expressionless, on duty.
>
> She was "a little sentinel," left to guard a baby that lay asleep on the bare boards behind her, its head on its arms, the ragged remains of what had been a shawl flung over its legs.
>
> That baby needed a sentinel to guard it, indeed. Had it crawled a foot or two it would have fallen head-foremost into that unprotected, yawning abyss of blackness below.
>
> The furniture of the attic, whatever it was like, had been seized the week before the rent. The little sentinel's papa—this we unearthed of the "deputy" of the house later on—was a militiaman and away; the little sentinel's mamma was gone out on "a arrand," which if it was anything like her usual "arrands," the deputy below informed us, would bring her home about dark, very much the worse for it. Think of that little child, keeping guard on that dirty sack for six or eight hours at a stretch—think of her utter loneliness in that bare, desolate, room, every childish impulse checked, left with orders "not to move, or I'll kill yer," and sitting there often till night and darkness came on, hungry, thirsty, and tired herself, but faithful to her trust to the last minute of the drunken mother's absence. (Sims 9)

We find this the abiding image of the London poor. A little girl of four, in her fleeting moments of innocence, betrayed, denied childhood's freedom, and now benumbed, still, voiceless—in Sims' terms, expressionless. She is the focal point of any honest Victorian reader's pity, compassion, outrage. Sims frames that image, bringing us up the close, dark, dangerous stairs, directing the eye almost cinematically around the attic room until it rests upon a "dirty, filthy sack," then to the four-year-old girl, and holding it there upon the almost radiant icon of the girl and the baby. He tells us in his melodramatic way that "we see a picture which will be engraven on our memory," and urges us again to "think of that little child . . . think of her utter loneliness . . ." Every technique of dramatization, every rhetorical effect, is designed to intensify the reader's emotional and moral response.

As we have seen before, and as we shall see again, the object of our attention is a still-life, voiceless, expressionless—emblematized as a child. Whatever is dynamic, or articulate, lies in us the readers, not in what is represented. Sentimentality places its full weight upon the apprehension itself; indeed, its very quality of excess signals to us that only in the feeling, ethically-charged viewer can "meaning" be found. For the child is mute; she cannot be an actor; and even those who have neglected her are "away" or insensate, though victims themselves. It is thus the reader, whom we know to be middle class, who can provide the psychological and ethical coherence to interpret this vignette.

Subjective coherence, then, lies in the realm of affect. In affective responses, understanding is achieved from the emotional and psychic qualities of the scene or set of situations, rather than from what seems to transpire on the surface of them. Often, in fact, the actions or situations that are being considered are incomprehensible as events or processes, much as they are in dreams (from which the concept is derived), or, as in this case, they are mere symbols, whose meaning is discerned on the emotional level. The observer organizes the material through his or her own anxieties or desires.

In a case such as this the construction of the reading subject occupies the center of its operations: the child-sentinel, and the urban poor generally in this case, are not rendered as subjects. Peter Brooks has noted the same phenomenon in nineteenth-century melodrama: "It is important that, in talking of affective structure . . . we not be deluded into thinking we are referring to the psychological structures of melodrama's characters. There is no 'psychology' in melodrama in this sense; the characters have no interior depth, there is no psychological conflict" (*Melodramatic Imagination* 35). The concept of suture enables us to see that what is principally at stake in these sentimental renditions of the urban poor is the subjectivity of the bourgeois reader.

Sentimentality marshals a certain set of bourgeois values: cleanliness (as we recoil from the filth of the slum settings), order (as we stand aghast at the chaos and irresponsibility), morality (as we condemn the mothers who would abandon their children in drunken debauchery), and purity (as we see it threatened in the figure of the child who will soon lose her innocence). Thus subjective coherence itself is cast in terms of materialistic (and, because home, family, and motherhood are the factors here, domestic) practices. Sentimentality has the effect of reframing social issues so that they can be primarily addressed in terms of the modes of living, the material practices, of the Victorian middle class, and because of its affective qualities, it succeeds in formulating subjectivity itself in those terms. As Patrick Wright has noted in his study of the "everyday," the home, particularly as defined in the ordinary, habitual processes of living in it, "expresses the coherence of a person's self-understanding."

> Home is therefore not just evocative of the familiar (if often agonising and brutal) disposition of personalities in which so much of everyday life is experienced; it is also the interior space in which some recognition can be given to endowments and potentials which have no opportunity for realization in the world as it is outside—the space, indeed, in which disregarded potentials and needs may themselves find some limited 'home' in the world. (Wright 11)

Ironically, the excessiveness of sentimental discourse, and the imprecision with which it represents event and emotion, also contributes to the blurring of the insufficiency of bourgeois material practices. For after all, something has gone very wrong in an English society that leaves its innocents in such a horrible plight as the one Sims describes. Although the solutions offered are the material ones of better housing, better hygiene, and a more regulated environment, there is, at some repressed level, an awareness that these solutions are not enough. The uneasiness and excessiveness of our feeling tells us that.

When Brooks analyzes melodrama he finds an attempt to evoke abstract morality itself. The scene of melodrama, with its polarization of evil and innocence, its extreme states, its simplistic rendition of desires and fears, and its call for excessive emotional response, awakens something that he calls the "moral occult," a "domain of spiritual values which is both indicated within and masked by the surface of reality" (*Melodramatic Imagination* 5). Melodrama takes its characteristic shape in the eighteenth and nineteenth centuries, he argues, as a consequence of a materialistic (and bourgeois) culture's attention to the drama of ordinary life, and it registers the dearth of any relation to the sacred in the modern world. Melodrama's formulas seem to resurrect those lost, nostalgized "primary" values; Brooks describes the classic melodramatic "plot" as a representation of virtue and innocence (usually in the heroine), then the eclipse, humiliation or defeat of those qualities by evil, and finally the triumph of virtue and the reassertion of innocence. Morality in such a scheme obviously does not operate pragmatically, adjusting and refining itself to the complexities of the situation; rather, it stands as an absolute, all the more idealized because of its absence in the relativistic, quotidian reality of modern life. In many respects, the child sentinel in *How the Poor Live* symbolizes such an absolute value. Characteristically it is coded as innocence, as the state antecedent to the social contamination; it stands for the continuing myth held by the romantically-inflected English middle class of a time past that was free of competition, avarice, and politicization. Like all such mystified moments, it is frozen in tableau, emancipated from history.

The inertness, however, of this and other emblems of the urban poor, the passivity of creatures who will not be rescued from the evils around them, but will instead succumb to them, tells us that such sentimental representation requires a different reading than melodrama. Brooks' contention that the innocence portrayed represents an absolute, "occulted" morality is undoubtedly accurate, and furnishes us with a key insight into the instant and recurrent power of such excessive emotional discourses. But the awareness that our innocent figure of the urban poor is herself caught in an ineluctable pattern of degeneration, and our horrified fascination with the details of the squalor—Mearns' sensationalist pleasure in retailing each loathsome vapour and disgusting sight; Sims' seamy, crudely "knowing" relish in quoting the "deputy" of the house on the mother's "arrands;" the voyeurism that impels all our journalistic explorers into the darkest dens—all these indicate that there are other elements in play here.

Paul Ricoeur, in *The Symbolism of Evil*, his analysis of the modern refiguring of evil, attaches great significance to the imagery of impurity and its implications of defilement and degeneration of the human subject. The representation of defilement "dwells in the half-light of a quasi-physical infection that points toward a quasi-moral unworthiness. This ambiguity is not expressed conceptually but is experienced intentionally in the very quality of the half-physical, half-ethical fear that clings to representation of the impure" (Ricoeur 35). Ricoeur suggests that it awakens within the outside observer himself or herself an uneasiness, a dread, that is "half-physical" and "half-ethical"—as response to sentimentalized material always is.

Julia Kristeva's study of abjection in *The Powers of Horror* can take us further into this topic. Kristeva begins by expressing her own responses to things that disgust or sicken her—images of death, disease, filth, offal, loathsome behavior, suffering, and debasement. Her concept of "abjection" can only begin to be defined from its emotional and physical affect; it is, in her words, "a twisted braid of affects and thoughts" (Kristeva 1). What characterizes the state of abjection, however, is the ambiguous attraction/repulsion toward what disgusts the subject. It is a quality neither of desire nor of rejection, for abjection is not founded on a relation to a definable object or person, an Other. Rather, there is an insidious extension toward and identification with what is abject (which may be represented through one's fascination/repulsion with the state of another—such as the degradation of the urban poor). The relation to the figure or condition of abjection is not repressed; it is not censored or excluded through the operation of the super-ego, for there is always the insidious identification with the abject, the realization that, repulsive as it is, it is part of the subject. For Kristeva, the relation of the individual subject to abjection can be a site of resistance to the dominant social order. It sketches out the borderline between adherence to that order and the self-debauching disposition toward the perverse. "Abjection . . . is immoral, sinister, scheming, and shady: a terror that dissembles, a hatred that smiles, a passion that uses the body for barter" (Kristeva 4). Middle class representations of the urban poor would not seem to elicit such resistance (although it may come into play in the ambivalent fascination with East End prostitution, and particularly in both male and female intrigue with the more violent forms of misogynous behavior.)

Kristeva's account of abjection does, nonetheless, help us understand the psychological workings of sentimentality under certain conditions. For sentimentality produces a form of breakdown, into pathos, tears, or an angry sense of helplessness. Our consciousness at some level of the excessiveness of the emotionality, or our indulgence in it, embarrasses and demeans us. We seem to wallow in a shared moment of dissolution—and of almost lascivious fascination with degradation—which breaks down the boundaries between self and nonself. Kristeva finds the presence of the cadaver to be a particularly threatening stimulus of abjection, for it is not an abstract indicator of death, which one might be able to deal with, but the palpable presence of the defilement that is one's own physical body. We cannot help but note the fixation of George Sims with this particularly salient aspect of lower class existence. He indulges in paragraph after paragraph of lurid instances of the keeping of cadavers. In one account, the corpse of a child was left, in a decomposed state, for fifteen days in a room occupied by its parents and a thirteen year old girl, because the father lacked the means to bury it. Another body of a victim of scarlet fever lay exposed on a table in a room in which five people lived and slept, and in which the tenants did tailoring work. In a third case, the addled grown daughter of a deceased woman kept her cadaver about her for ten days while she tried to make suitable clothing for a funeral and burial. The inventory goes beyond a description of conditions; it acquires imagistic force, as of deliquescence itself.

The sharing of qualities of abjection, and the inability to cast it as the Other, causes a breakdown in the subject's construction of self. It opens up an amorphous interchange—propelled by alternating repulsion and attraction—with the other scenes of abjection. In these circumstances the categories are often spatialized—the question is "Where am I?" rather than "Who am I?"—for the demarcations are no longer fixed and sure. The spatialization has interesting implications in our discussion of the slums, for H. J. Dyos and D. A. Reeder suggest that the division into suburbs and slums in Victorian London was only "partly geographical. It was also social and psychological. The characteristic tensions being produced were not so much, perhaps, between class and class as between the individual and the mass, and between the individual's inner life and his outward behaviour. The characteristic shapes which these produced on the ground—the realities composed from their images, then and now—were of suburbs and slums" (Dyos and Reeder 360). Dyos and Reeder's analysis of the symbolic character of social organization of individual psychic relations to the urban poor suggests the ways in which discourses on several levels can reflect each other. In *Outcast London*, Gareth Stedman Jones traces the shift, over the course of the middle and later decades of the nineteenth century, from a "demoralization" thesis about the urban poor to a "degeneration" thesis. The degeneration thesis is largely an imperialistic one, premised on a post-Darwinian fantasy about the sapping of racial stock, which Victorian observers contended was shown by the physical deterioration of urban dwellers, especially those who had lived in the choked atmosphere of the inner city, and who were a generation or two removed from the countryside. Stedman Jones describes the work of one James Cantile, who in 1885 claimed to have uncovered the pure third generation Londoner: "'height, 5 ft. 1 in; age

21, chest measurement 28 in.; his head measured across from tip of ear to tip of ear, 11 in. (1 in. below the average). His aspect is pale, waxy; he is very narrow between the eyes and with a decided squint!'" (Jones 127). As a term, degeneration richly suggests the qualities of abjection that we see in depictions of the urban poor, for there was, as Stedman Jones notes, a conviction that "the savage and brutalized condition of the urban poor was the result of long exposure to the degenerating conditions of city life." The notion of demoralization, on the other hand, which was prevalent in the 1860s and 1870s, argued that "pauperism, poverty's most visible form, was largely an act of will. It had been freely chosen and was therefore sinful" (Jones 286). One can argue that the concept of demoralization, as a kind of willful, perverse, self-abasement, is closer to Kristeva's idea of abjection as a mode of resistance, but as Stedman Jones and others have noted, there was never a clear demarcation between what was the "fault" of the poor person, and what was the result of his environment. And the increased emphasis on physical as well as spiritual deterioration as a characteristic of the slum dweller intensifies the quality of abjection that they represent. It also further effaces the construction of the poor as an Other.[21]

Kristeva makes an additional point about abjection, which returns us to the issue of the gender implications of the discourse of sentimentality. She associates the feeling of an amorphousness of subjective boundaries with "what existed in the archaism of pre-objectal relationship, in the immemorial violence with which a body becomes separated from another body in order to be" (Kristeva 10). It appears to return the psyche to the anguished experience of separation from the body of the mother, prior to the formation of the Oedipal subject. As we have established, sentimentalism, with its invocation of pity, compassion, and nostalgia for innocence, is culturally constructed in the Victorian period as a feminine discourse. Those qualities are assigned to women; they are designated by the dominant symbolic order as maternal characteristics. The affective moment of sentimentalism, then, is itself a site fraught with implications of maternal care and love. Thus a kind of evocative cross-coding occurs, for both male and female readers, of the recollection of (and indulgence in) the emotions associated with the maternal (pity, compassion, etc.), and the strong psychic pull of that moment when bonding with the mother signified an undifferentiated quality of subjectivity. That cross-coding accounts for many of the classic sentimental moments in nineteenth century fiction: little Paul Dombey's decline and death in Dickens' *Dombey and Son*, for instance, in which an unformed subject is identified with the lost mother, and is characterized by instances of the oceanic feeling of the pre-Oedipal.

This is why, of course, the image of the child abandoned by her mother is so powerful in Sims' account. And yet because it is, in a sense, an emblem of innocence, of a time before entry into the symbolic order, and, as we have noted, of the "time before" industrialization's ills, it is also implicitly an unattainable state in modern life. Innocence is, by its very nature, pre-moral, and thus incapable of providing a model for a construction of an ethical subjectivity in the middle class reader. English bourgeois culture consequently replaced innocence with purity, which is a constructed ethical category. The two were consciously and unconsciously conflated in cultural discourse, and the latter was almost exclusively made gender-specific to women—by writers both male and female. Here we turn to a male writer who in the 1850s was struggling with the issue of purity and with gender construction in the context of examining poverty. In his great novel *Bleak House*, Dickens reveals a very elaborate ambivalence which charges the male imagination to construct female abjection and to associate purity only with an impossible female.

Bleak House, Purity, and the Abject

The virtuous young Esther Summerson, who is apparently an orphan, is plucked out of unhappy girlhood, and brought into Bleak House, the eccentric household owned by her guardian, John Jarndyce. Her "plot" in the novel, told in the first person in an often self-deprecating manner, is that of the "finding" of her Self, the construction of her subjectivity. But that is also tied up in her broader social role as a kind of big sister to every waif she encounters. She will embody the ostensible Dickensian "solution" to the evils of modern life; she creates around her an extended family, and in doing so symbolizes the need of the dominant classes in England to take care of the poor. Indeed, she provides a poignant connection to the lowest victims of the social order, for she befriends Jo, the homeless boy from the slums, and as a consequence, contracts smallpox from him. The symbolic resonances are quite clear: Jo embodies innocence, but it is innocence within abjection. Esther, herself an orphan, herself in a state of indeterminate subjectivity, enters into a somewhat ambiguous relationship with the abject (for she shares some of Jo's qualities), and suffers some of the disfiguring consequences of abjection. The nexus between victims is made; Esther the quintessential Victorian Angel in the House, and Jo the slum dweller, intersect conceptually. And they do so through the imagistic category that governs both abjection and the social representation of urban poverty: contagion.

Purity and innocence thus intersect.[22] Innocence, as we predicted, cannot survive in the modern social text, so Jo will die before novel's end. Purity, its construct, will struggle on, but as a highly problematical category in Dickens' hands. For Esther's confinement—and near death—with the smallpox serves in the novel as a complex rite of passage—into selfhood for Esther, and, necessarily, because female subjectivity cannot be attained without coming to grips with sexual desire, into "mature" sexuality. Esther had confessed to some sexual awakenings and disturbing feelings earlier in her story: when the impertinent young whelp Guppy proposes to her, and whenever she is around her destined husband, Alan Woodcourt (a figure of indeterminate male subjectivity). In addition, her guardian Jarndyce has spoken of making her his wife, although this creates immense uneasiness for most readers of the text, because he is a father figure considerably older than she, and there are vague, illicit, incestuous undertones.

And so the various strains of our own story about sentimentalized renderings of the urban poor come together in Esther Summerson's near fatal battle with smallpox. First of all, the pox disfigures her natural prettiness. She is violated as the innocent poor are violated. She is brought to the verge of an abject state as they are. Her sojourn on the threshold of death, however, symbolizes the rebirth that is only an idealistic promise for the urban poor. In her case, it is a birth into selfhood, a transformation into a woman who can acknowledge her own sexuality. For at the end of her narrative about her sickness and convalescence, she unexpectedly explodes with a confession of her repressed desire:

> And now I must part with the little secret I have thus far tried to keep. I had thought, sometimes, that Mr. Woodcourt loved me; and that if he had been richer, he would perhaps have told me that he loved me, before he went away. I had thought, sometimes, that if he had done so, I should have been glad of it. (*BH* 443)

As is typical of Dickens' rendering of women in his fiction, this moment of proclamation of desire, and, concomitantly, of constitution as a subject, occurs through a mystified process, through a symbolic death or near-death. Again, the reasons for his inability or refusal to portray such rites of passage consist in part of the denials associated with his personal phantasm. But they also lie in his resistance to the terms on which female subjectivity is rendered in his culture. Lest we overlook its significance, it is important to remark here that Esther's infection with smallpox in the novel marks her as a figure embodying an anti-theatrical ethos. Her invisible performance of purity somehow triumphs over her physical disfiguration—at least for those who (unlike Mr. Guppy) accord more importance to her effects on others than to the effects of the disease on her.

For Dickens' incisive account of the cultural construction of the bourgeois female subject shows that that construction relies heavily on the class's synthesis of domesticity and purity. Esther recalls part of her anxiety and delirium during her illness: she confesses her alienation from "my housekeeping duties, though at first it caused me great anxiety to think that they were unperformed." Next she seems—as a necessary step in her progress toward self-definition—to struggle free from that inscription into the familial that had up to now virtually erased her identity: "At once a child, an elder girl, and the little woman I had been so happy as, I was not only oppressed by cares and difficulties adapted to each station, but by the great perplexity of endlessly trying to reconcile them. I suppose that few who have not been in such a condition can quite understand what I mean, or what painful unrest arose from this source." And then, in a remarkable revelation, Esther exposes the oppression of bourgeois domesticity under which she had been staggering:

> For the same reason I am almost afraid to hint at that time in my disorder—it seemed one long night, but I believe there were both nights and days in it—when I laboured up colossal staircases, ever striving to reach the top, and ever turned, as I have seen a worm in a garden path, by some obstruction, and labouring again. I knew perfectly at intervals, and I think vaguely at most times, that I was in my bed; and I talked with Charley and felt her touch, and knew her very well; yet I would find myself complaining, "O more of these never-ending stairs, Charley,—more and more—piled up to the sky, I think!" and labouring again.
>
> Dare I hint at that worse time when, strung together somewhere in great black space, there was a flaming necklace, or ring, or starry circle of some kind, of which I was one of the beads! And when my only prayer was to be taken off from the rest, and when it was such inexplicable agony and misery to be a part of the dreadful thing? (*BH* 431–32)

Her difficulty in daring hint of such thoughts betrays Esther's continuing equivocation about her domestic role. Apparently only in feverish dreams can such an admission swim upward into articulation. But the imagery of trudging those endless staircases of Bleak House as Jarndyce's faithful "little woman" and keeper of the household keys, and the dramatic account of wishing to be set free from the consuming necklace of obligation, unmistakably set forth what oppresses her. The true Esther can only take shape when she is able to separate her desires from those in which she has been inscribed. Because that self-determination coincides with the quickening of sexual desire, it is fraught with anxiousness and self-doubt. Dickens' own discursive ploy of effacing the process of sexual and subjective realization in delirium and dreams and near death may, indeed, attest to the impossibility of openly articulating his critique of his culture's formations. Indeed, he may himself not be entirely conscious of the depth of his critique (and he has, of course, also transposed it in his own fantasmal economy into the illicit scenario of the older man/younger woman attraction). But this central, and dramatically intensified—libinally charged—passage in the novel lays out the conflict in graphic terms.

There are other indications of Dickens' uneasiness. One lies in the figure of the home that is the title of the novel: Bleak House. In the chapter entitled "Quite at Home," Esther devotes two long paragraphs to describing the "delightfully irregular" Bleak House in which she is brought to live by Jarndyce. She speaks of its many passageways and nooks, its "charming little sitting-room," the furniture "old-fashioned rather than old," walls laden with pictures, and of all "the moveables, from the wardrobes to the chairs and tables, hangings, glasses, even to the pin-cushions and scent-bottles on the dressing tables, displaying the same quaint variety" (*BH* 62–63). Bleak House is almost a parody of the Victorian penchant for cluttered interiors and bric-a-brac, and so self-indulgently rococo is it that the reader must be taken aback when he learns near the end of the novel that Jarndyce has built a pint-sized variation of it for Esther and Woodcourt to live in. As amused as Dickens could be with individualistic foibles, he has given us a grotesque of a home. Bleak House is, of course, an extension of Jarndyce's own subjectivity, the place in which he can exercise his private conception of it.

Because Bleak House epitomizes the Victorian bourgeois domestic excesses—and thus represents a disposition of the culture—and because it is introduced in the novel as a refuge for Esther from the cruel world of her orphaned existence, it is a symbol of the Victorian fetish for privatization. The mid-Victorian period witnessed not only an increased emphasis on private life, but also the denotation of it as a class characteristic. Donald J. Olsen has commented that privatization became, in London particularly, a distinguishing factor between the middle and lower classes, prompted by a series of considerations, such as the protection and reinforcement of morality and all the family virtues. As these values seemed to be threatened by the contagion of urban life, the separated space of living emerged as a needed zone to protect and nurture them (Olsen 265–78). Anyone could see, from accounts of the urban poor, what lack of privacy could produce in terms of temptations to incest and exposure to immorality and disease—think of an entire family living in one room, in the presence of a corpse!—and, in fact, private space became the generally recognized first step in the reclamation of the poor. Furthermore, extensive construction of neighborhoods of semi-detached villas during the second half of the century was justified as a means of sparing honest working men and women the effects of urban life. Privatization functioned as a correlative of the economic definition of the middle class, for it worked hand in hand with the replacement of the old mixed neighborhoods of shops and homes with the specialized streets of boutiques, shops selling a single specialty of goods for the middle class buyer, and private offices for professional men.

As historians such as Jeffrey Weeks have argued, the privatization fetish—especially when it comes to room divisions within houses—had a productive aspect as well: confirming middle class needs for privacy through a confrontation with the spectacle of people who seem to lack it so utterly. The so-called "problem" of incest in the warrens of the poor is itself not so much an observed problem (no social observer would confess to having observed it) as it is a logically necessary deduction compelled by the observed "fact" of "overcrowded" conditions in small flats that often housed upwards of 10 people of various ages and sexes. When the countryside practice of "bundling" was imported into the East End by immigrants from the rural countryside, it scandalized middle class reformers because it violated middle class norms of spatial separation—one might more accurately say it helped consolidate and reinforce those norms through the spectacle of their violation (Weeks 27–31; 60; 66) Andrew Mearns' *Bitter Cry* is notable for evoking the possibility of incest by compelling his readers to deduce it from the reported "fact" of overcrowded conditions, as we have already noted. A carefully constructed authorial reticence, masquerading as consideration of the moral qualms of his readers, stops Mearns well short of reporting the observation of a literal scene of incest. However, that reticence works to make the inference of incest a foregone conclusion for his readers, whose own scopophilic interest in the domestic life of the poor, which they indulge by reading the report itself, requires its own confirming but imaginary scene: a scene never directly reported but "there" nonetheless, a scene in which children of different sexes, members of the same family, couple together in the beds they share, inspired by the adults whose own enactment of the primal scene must be visible to all the rest of the family in the room they all share.

Programs to enhance privatization and then mark off private space, on the other hand, run counter to Dickens' social and emotional program. If the theme of his great novels is to awaken concern for those who live less fortunately, and to quicken the impulse for public action, then a definition of the self in terms of privatization defeats such purposes. *Bleak House* provides one of several instances of Dickens' distrust of a middle class ethos that connects subjectivity to privatization—that, indeed, confuses the two. As is characteristic of Dickens' complexity as a radical bourgeois novelist, he often engages in this critique through light-handed satire and exaggeration (although by the time of his last completed novel, *Our Mutual Friend*, the hostility is overt), and draws almost all his happy couples to happy endings in private homes.[23] Nonetheless, almost every critic registers his or her uneasiness with such "resolutions," a textual indicator of Dickens' own ambivalence, if not lack of conviction.

Finally, all "the moveables" in Bleak House catalogued by Esther signify Dickens' uneasy awareness of the relentless march of mid-Victorian bourgeois culture toward commodification. The identification of the self with one's household possessions, most of them already being mass produced, guarantees the kind of formulation of subjectivity through materiality that we have come to identify as one of the disquieting characteristics of consumer societies. Ironically, the essentialist philosophy of the individual—as something separate and unique and known only to himself and herself privately—that bourgeois humanism promotes, feeds into the commodification of the subject. Almost all that we have witnessed in the discourses of sensationalism and sentimentalism by the middle class, in their representations of the urban poor, thrusts value away from the social phenomena that are being represented, and onto the reader, as he or she is sutured into the discourse. As we noted earlier, the reader is in the position of a consumer. Reading relations, as several recent studies have emphasized, acquire, over the course of the nineteenth century, more and more of the quality of the consumption of a product.[24] The spectrum of practices, from privatization, to identification with one's purchased possessions, to the consuming of the artifacts of culture, blends into one color: that of a bourgeois ideal of womanhood.

Esther's nexus with Jo, her own experiences of defacement and spiritual violation, and the elements of abjection in sentimental renderings of the urban poor, show how problematic that Victorian construction of the middle class woman had become. For our juxtaposition of Esther Summerson and the four-year-old "child sentinel" in George Sims' *How the Poor Live* graphically illustrates a suppressed correlation in the hegemonic discourse between the poor of the cities and women. Both are defined in terms of victimization by male authors.

The concept of social victimization underwent a radical change at the end of the eighteenth and beginning of the nineteenth centuries. This is not to say that society did not produce abundant victims of its power and neglect before that time; history is replete with such cases. But a more acute—and we would say different—awareness of the effects of social victimization occurred after the last decades of the eighteenth century. The French Revolution is clearly the seminal influence, for it provokes a new sense of the presence of bodies of lower class people who can articulate their grievances, and it gives them rights, by propagating the concepts of justice and equality. At the same time, the Revolution, and the social changes arising from industrial change, denaturalizes the hierarchies of class that had previously made the lot of those at the low end of the social scale seem natural and inevitable. As the poor and the lower working classes are invested with presence as voices (or even forces), are seen—at least potentially—as human beings with certain rights, their condition in society is perceived as victimization, not as a natural consequence of their inferiority or their pre-ordained "stations" in life. Similarly, the Revolution and the struggles for class hegemony attune people to the effects of social structures upon individual conditions of living. Thus the terms "victimized" and "victimization" do not enter the language until the early nineteenth century, while the term "victim" dates from the fifteenth century *(OED)*. Indeed, a cultural narrative, such as the melodrama, which focuses on victimization, does not emerge until the French Revolution (*Melodramatic Imagination* xii), and when it does, it comes on the scene to articulate a subversive conservatism that harkens back to an earlier day of (invented) patriarchal order. As Elaine Hadley argues: "The continued representation of deferential virtue in the body of the wife seemed to many to promise the continued survival of the constitutional monarchy and its oligarchical governance in a market culture whose sudden booms and busts and whose periodic extensions of the franchise threatened central English institutions" (Hadley 139).

In her important study of the effect of women's political opposition to the Contagious Disease Acts of the 1860s, Judith R. Walkowitz shows how central the narrative of melodrama was to the efforts by Josephine Butler and others to dramatize the victimization of lower class and poor women. "The acts," she says, "and the public controversy surrounding them generated a massive documentation about the lives and actions of people such as prostitutes, who are usually missing from historical accounts. The acts also provide insight into important social and political developments in the mid-Victorian period: the rise of the institutional state; the emergence of the women's movement; changing social and sexual mores; and the problems of state intervention and deviance" (*Prostitution* vi–vii). The urban poor, particularly young women, and the social and political restrictions on women generally, rise to the forefront of public consciousness at the same time: the 1870s and 1880s. The agitation over repeal of the Contagious Diseases Acts, complemented by the "sensationalizing" of the injustices to and frustrations of women in the sensation novels, illustrate the centrality of victimization in certain practices of the patriarchal social system.

In a later essay, Walkowitz analyzes W. T. Stead's series of articles in *The Pall Mall Gazette* on the trafficking in virgin little girls, called "The Maiden Tribute of Modern Babylon" (*Dreadful* 81–120). The accounts, epitomizing the new "sensationalism" in English journalism, caused a furor. As Walkowitz notes, moreover, they were a natural extension of his publication of "The Bitter Cry of Outcast London." In both instances, the journalist takes a moralistic but also voyeuristic approach toward the victims of social poverty. In the "Maiden Tribute" articles, Walkowitz argues, Stead relies heavily upon the narrative of pornography, with a particularly lascivious/moralistic stress upon the despoliation of female purity. The cross-coding of representations of the poor and of victimization of women is electric. Under such circumstances it is inevitable that the psychological identifications that we found in the discourse of sentimentality will occur.

Dickens had discerned and exploited the power of that cross-coding decades before it became notorious in the 1870s and 1880s, but that only goes to show that the association between the urban poor as victims and women as victims had been present in nineteenth century social discourse for some time. Its prevalence raises questions about the language of Victorian social analysis, for it indicates that many of the positive values—such as redemption—of the middle class must come from the victims and the powerless, from the children and the little people of no economic or apparent social consequence—or at least from the relations between the women in the middle classes and the poor. The very code of middle class values is being synthesized from the bottom up. While that relationship does not establish women as victims in the Victorian period, it does show how they became especially sensitized to the effects of victimization, and how they serve as conduits and arbiters of ethical values that are awakened by social injustice. We have for some time been aware of the way in which the assigned domestic roles for women have created a certain passivity and instinct for self-denial. Dickens' account of Esther Summerson's dream shows how that domestic position is wedded in the larger social order to the breaking down of personal and class borders that takes place in the sentimentalizing of the poor. We have seen as well how sensationalism draws the integral private values of which women were supposed to be exemplars into public expression, and how the urban poor become the focal point of this process. As our analysis indicates, the representations of city poverty have a crucial part to play in the social construction of middle class female subjectivity in the Victorian period.

In our next chapter, we will examine some of its individual effects at the very time the social order is putting in place countervailing means to render it impersonal. As we look at Beatrice Webb and Margaret Harkness, we can perceive the mixed psychology of social and political work among the poor—how it both ennobles and enervates. In addition, our approach in the chapter, through studying the affect of sensationalism and sentimentalism, underscores the extent to which the issues surrounding urban poverty were cast in terms of feeling, thus mystifying and obscuring the concrete relations and practices of mid-Victorian ideology. Values of a highly emotive register, associated with pity and an intensely moralized sense of justice, dominate the debate, producing a disproportionate emphasis on a cultural and social system—such as middle class privatization—that will sustain them. However, this discourse struggles with another emerging one founded on reification and detachment: a professional, scientific analysis of poverty that seeks to lower the emotional temperature in discussions of poverty.

- CHAPTER 2 -

Culturalism, the Feminized Poor, and the Land of Deadened Affect

Beatrice Webb, the "Social," and the Loss of Affect

*I*t may seem odd to focus a chapter in a book like this on a woman—in this case, a very prominent and unusual woman. However, Beatrice Webb is an important figure in this text for a variety of reasons, and her dilemma is one that is emblematic of that facing many male professionals in the nineteenth century with a concern for solving the problem of poverty. She exemplifies, in more than one way, both how the hope of fighting urban poverty fired the imaginations of an idealistic generation and how those hopes were menaced by the threat of enervation. As her writings reveal, she felt both inspired by the mission and menaced by its seeming hopelessness, her own desires and wishes undercut by the intensity of abject experience. Nonetheless, she, more so than others, reinterpreted the central ethical challenge of outreach toward the poor as the duty of those with power toward those without it. Moreover, she contributed mightily both to a richly ruminative diary that details the psychological impact of her developing sense of mission and to the larger, more detached, public scientific projects—in particular, Charles Booth's large-scale study of poverty in London to which she made a significant contribution—that marked a significant change in the professional stance toward poverty in the City. In her diary she illuminates both how the mission to grapple with poverty threatens the bourgeois subject with engulfment by the abject, and how that threat is distanced and contained through a strategy that employs detachment in the interest of culturalist philanthropy.

A sense of sin, says Beatrice Webb, drove middle class reformers into the East End in the 1880s with unprecedented fervor. No longer passive toward the problems of urban poverty and crime, the bourgeoisie found for itself a new mission to regulate health, morals, and education among the destitute, to "humanize" them with culture, and to submit them to a vastly more intense social surveillance. Some of the apparatus for social intervention had been building for decades, in the creeping penetration of sanitary and housing regulations, in health inspection, and in laws requiring school attendance by the children of the poor. This was state intervention—the extension of the policies of nineteenth-century liberalism in opposition to the *laissez-faire* tradition. There had also been citizen intervention, primarily by charitable bodies and by the churches and their missions. In the 1880s, however, these forces acquired a heightened intensity, fired by a new zeal to rehabilitate the human sensibilities of the downtrodden who endured lives of meanness and futility, and haunted by a consciousness of a crisis in the capitalist social order.

That crisis is what Beatrice Webb meant by a sense of sin. "The origin of the ferment is to be discovered in a new consciousness of sin among men of intellect and men of property;" she wrote in *My Apprenticeship* (1926), the first volume of her partially completed autobiography, "a consciousness at first philanthropic and practical—Oastler, Shaftesbury and Chadwick; then literary and artistic—Dickens, Carlyle, Ruskin and William Morris; and finally analytic, historical and explanatory—in his latter days John Stuart Mill; Karl Marx and his English interpreters. . . . When I say the consciousness of sin, I do not mean the consciousness of personal sin. . . . The consciousness of sin was a collective or class consciousness; a growing uneasiness, amounting to conviction, that the industrial organization, which had yielded rent, interest and profits on a stupendous scale, had failed to provide a decent livelihood and tolerable conditions for a majority of the inhabitants of Great Britain."[1]

Webb's autobiography, one of the most compelling works of the nineteenth century, addresses the social and economic structure of England itself, those essential relations and processes that had been elided in the sensationalizing and sentimentalizing accounts of the poor. The dysfunctions of gross inequality are, in her view, symptoms of laissez-faire capitalism. Written from her perspective, in later life, as one of the most prominent figures of the Fabian Socialist movement, as a proselytizer for repeal of the Poor Law, and as an uncompromising member of a Royal Commission on the problem, Webb's autobiography records what she calls the "Time-Spirit" of the 1880s which brought to the amelioration of urban poverty a new set of sociological and "scientific" methods and, in her hands, an awareness of the roots of destitution in capitalist excess and classism.

"Sin" is a term of personal spirituality rather than of collective responsibility. It is not surprising to encounter it in Victorian social analysis, of course, for the chiefly Protestant religious ethos resounds through English political discourse, from Carlyle and Ruskin to the voices of imperialism. Beatrice Webb appears to have adopted the term from the remark of Samuel Barnett, rector of St. Jude's, Whitechapel and founder of Toynbee Hall, who said, "the sense of sin has been the starting point of progress" in the fight against poverty. But it has a deeper resonance in Webb's vocabulary, for it touches the vital nerve of her personal relation to capitalism, class, and social duty, and to her struggle for self-definition as a woman.

Webb's story of her life cannot be told without elaborating the influences on her from a childhood in the most secure realms of mid-Victorian capitalism. The first chapter of *My Apprenticeship*, entitled "Character and Circumstance," begins with the contention that "the sociologist . . . is in a quite unique manner the creature of his environment. Birth and parentage, the mental atmosphere of class and creed in which he is bred, the characteristics and attainments of the men and women who have been his guides and associates, come first and foremost of all the raw material upon which he works, alike in order of time and in intimacy of contact" (1). These influences, for her, are her grandfathers who "rose rapidly to affluence and industrial power, one as a Manchester cotton warehouseman, the other as a Liverpool merchant trading with South America," classic tales of the formation of the English middle class in the late eighteenth and early nineteenth centuries. Beatrice's parents, Richard and Lawrencina Potter, initially set themselves up in life as rentiers, living off inherited income, devoting themselves to leisure, culture, and community good works. The financial crisis of 1847–48 wiped away the major portion of Richard's inheritance, so he was obliged to enter into a career as "a capitalist at large." Impatient with everyday office work, he instead flourished as a man with "a taste for adventurous enterprise and a talent for industrial diplomacy" (3). Starting by acquiring a franchise to sell depreciated timber in his lumber yard for wooden huts for soldiers in the Crimean War, he entered a career of financial speculation and the administration of public companies—many of a highly romantic nature, such as the Grand Trunk Railway of Canada, and an abortive scheme to build a Grand Canal through Syria to compete with the Suez Canal (which would have entailed submerging of scores of holy places). "Memory recalls a maze of capitalist undertakings of which he was director or promoter; undertakings of every degree of rank and permanence, of success or failure," writes Beatrice. Richard Potter epitomized "advanced Capitalism," the speculator and deal maker, the manager of enterprises put together with venture capital, the man with the political and financial contacts to secure franchises and to operate beyond the scope of conventional trade or manufacturing. And Beatrice adored him.

She confesses a pull at times toward the attractions of privilege. Raised like her sisters to combine the best of a young woman's education with the attractions of the London season, herself a beautiful woman of wide intellectual interests, and clearly a stimulating conversationalist, she is candidly conscious of her ingrained disposition toward the life of moneyed security that is enjoyed by the upper middle class. The young woman who will serve as a rent collector in one of the worst slums of the East End as part of a systematic attempt to record and scientifically analyze conditions there must always take into consideration the degree to which her own "character" is molded by such "circumstances."

Her inner struggle accounts in part for the highly personal terms—of "sin"—by which she defines social problems. At various points in her autobiography a dialectic is set up between her two "Egos"; she speaks of "the deep-lying controversy between the Ego that affirms and the Ego that denies, upon the issue, which was continuously present in my mind: Can we have a science of society, and if so, will its conclusions be accepted as a guiding light in public policy?" (187). *Egoism* alludes not only to the divisions within a Self that is fighting to establish its role in the world; it is a catchword in the mid-Victorian period for the evils of rampant individualism in a laissez-faire economy. For Beatrice Webb, the principal evil of capitalism appears to be excessive individualism. The "empirical Socialism" that she and other Fabians later espoused would work to curb those excesses through regulations and social awareness. The "annual increments of Socialistic legislation and administration," inspired by the gathering of evidence of social ills and an ongoing debate in pamphlets, books, and reports, would produce "the slow but continuous retreat of the individualist forces" (178). Webb advocates, in other words, a conjunction of socialist legislation and moralistic reformism that will modify capitalism, curbing its "individualistic" or "egoistic" excesses while leaving the basic structures of production and consumption intact. The personal "circumstances" of her own milieu, her life with Father-the-entrepreneur, can be sustained psychologically through this compromise—but only, as we shall see, at considerable psychic cost to herself. For she has transferred the site of contradiction away from the capitalism that her father embodies and onto herself as social mediator.

Science serves as the means by which Beatrice Webb can try to efface the mental and spiritual strains of this contradiction, and she grasps at it passionately as a neutral force that will submerge strife-torn human qualities in its objectivity. She devotes herself to Charles Booth's great cataloguing of the "Life and Labour of the People of London," in the comfort that "Charles Booth was, within my circle of friends, perhaps the most perfect embodiment of what I have described ... as the mid-Victorian time-spirit—the union of faith in the scientific method with the transference of the emotion of self-sacrificing service from God to man" (214). The scientific method, particularly the empirical gathering of data, constitutes, as her comment indicates, a circuit for the directing of emotional energy. It channels the social and psychological conflicts that arise from Webb's personal position, so that she is able to say of her commitment to Booth's work that "the impulse came neither from politics nor from philanthropy, but from scientific curiosity; from the desire to apply the method of observation, reasoning and verification to the problem of poverty in the midst of riches" (209).[2]

As crucial a role as the scientific spirit plays in Beatrice Webb's early career when she was intensely involved with the urban poor of the East End, it is a deeply troubled concept. Her long devotion to the prominent social scientist Herbert Spencer, who was a close family friend and something of a mentor to her in her youth, her skeptical puzzling out of his *First Principles* and other theoretical works, the poignant account of her attendance at his bed during his last decline—all furnish a narrative of the problematic quality of science as a human guide. Spencer is for her an object lesson of the limitations of belief in science. He dies alone, unfulfilled, in her mind: a man who had devoted his life to an impersonal, abstract force that canceled out his own full subjectivity (30–31). Although she can pass off Spencer's sad case as an instance of a man who had denied himself love and family, who was a flawed thinker, and who tried to fit everything into a predetermined thesis rather than work inductively, Webb is aware that science itself performs a problematic function in the displacement of the underlying contradictions of the social order. In retrospect she is able to write, "it is hard to understand the naive belief of the most original and vigorous minds of the 'seventies and 'eighties that it was by science, and by science alone, that all human misery would be ultimately swept away" (126).

For social science, she realized, simply changes the terms—but not the nature—of the essential exploitations of bourgeois power. In her effort to probe the contradictions of her relation to her privileged family background, Webb asks, "This ignorance about the world of labor, did it imply class consciousness, the feeling of belonging to a superior caste? A frank answer seems worth giving. There was no consciousness of superior riches.... The consciousness that was present, I speak for my own analytic mind, was the consciousness of superior power. As life unfolded itself I became aware that I belonged to a class of persons who habitually gave orders, but who seldom, if ever, executed the orders of other people" (42). And later in her autobiography she asserts that "deep down in the unconscious herd instinct of the British governing class there *was* a test of fitness for member-ship of this most gigantic of all social clubs, but a test which was seldom recognized by those who applied it, still less by those to whom it was applied, *the possession of some form of power over other people*" (49).

A less personalized power is the primary element in what the Foucauldian social theorist Jacques Donzelot calls the "social." The "social" comprises that set of institutions, discourses, and practices that developed in England, France, and the United States in the nineteenth century to regulate the health, education, familial relations, and living conditions of the working and lower classes. It embraces the panoply of social work, sanitation and health inspection, child care and care for expectant mothers, educational systems, counseling, family courts, and reformative and rehabilitative services that penetrated nearly every aspect of the family lives of the middle and lower strata of society. It is in many respects the great pride of the modern social order, for it has been responsible for the mitigation of ills and the improvement of life of those who have been most disempowered by the inequalities of the competitive system. But it necessarily causes a massive and systematic intervention by the state and the dominant classes into the everyday lives of the poor and the working class.[3] Donzelot describes how educators, the family court judge, the psychologist/counselor, and the doctor, usually working in conjunction with the wife/mother, gradually strip the husband/father of much of his authority in the family and marriage. The shift in patriarchal power is vividly illustrated in the tableau of the stern male judge interrogating and disciplining a wayward lower class child, while the father stands silent and impotent, cap in hand, in the courthouse audience.

The net effect of such an expansion of social intervention is to circumscribe the loose, clan-oriented, life of the lower classes, and to attempt to organize them into nuclear family units that can be more easily fitted into a bourgeois social system. The lower orders are compelled and induced to adopt the values of the middle class (although we will see in the next chapter how strong the resistance could be), ranging from reverence for the sanctity of the family and the nurturing of the child to the emulation of consumer desires. Although the laissez-faire capitalist system put into place a number of laws and social institutions that would eventually constrain its own freedom to operate, it nonetheless established moral and social authority over potentially disruptive classes, and began to ingrain in them a belief in bourgeois values of education, social order, obedience to state authority, and the family as an ethical center. And it did so in the name of values and principles that seem to lie outside of class and politics. Social regulations for health, education, family preservation, and so on are rarely seen as instruments for the preservation of the dominant economic and social order; they seem to address "universal" needs and aspirations of all people for a decent, comfortable existence and a chance for individual improvement. This is not to say that they do not, in most cases, have those positive effects, but the depoliticizing of the exercise of power constitutes one of the prime advantages of the "social" for the hegemonic class. It was a concept that could be, in fact, embraced in principle by all ranges of the political spectrum, from the conservatives to the socialists. Depoliticization was further enhanced by the application of "scientific methods" to the sphere of social intervention, chiefly in the rise and reorientation of the social sciences such as sociology, psychology, and economics.[4]

As Amanda Anderson has recently argued, the aspiration toward detachment that underwrites these efforts is far from a wholly negative phenomenon. Whether in the form of Dickens' cosmopolitanism, evident in his novels of the 1850s and 60s, in the argument for exalted feminine social and moral agency offered by Ruskin in "Of Queen's Gardens" (1864), or in the ironic detachment of Matthew Arnold or Oscar Wilde, the attempt to stand outside self-interest brings the ironic form of cultural critique together with the nonironic forms. Both articulate an aspiration toward detachment that cannot be easily reduced to ideological situatedness. That said, though, it is nonetheless difficult not to see, from the perspective of the present, at least some, if not all, of the more earnest attempts at cultural redemption of the poor in the late nineteenth century as taking significant steps beyond mere scientific description to coercive behavioral modification on a grand scale. No matter how pure the individual motives that drove them, no matter how necessary amelioration might have been, these efforts amounted ultimately to an unprecedented interference of middle class reformers in the lives of lower class people.

That the East End became a site of significant social surveillance is beyond question. The writer Thomas Burke, who grew up in Limehouse, notes in his somewhat nostalgic autobiography *The Wind and the Rain* (published the year before Webb's *Autobiography*) that the panoptical gaze was ever present to the East London poor of the late nineteenth century:

> We were like private soldiers, whose whole lives are spent in public. Every moment of our days was known to the officials, and if one of the old men asked, 'What has Brown or Smith been doing to-day?' he would have been supplied with a detailed report of Brown's and Smith's bodily activities from eight to eight. (*The Wind and the Rain* 71)

Burke's awareness of the reality of social surveillance is convincing evidence of its presence, as he was neither a socialist committed to documenting the grounds for class warfare nor an Arthur Morrison committed to an aesthetic project of constructing a landscape of hopeless violence and misdirected resistance. There is little question but that the Education Act of 1870 required an acceleration of social surveillance unprecedented in English history.[5] In fact, a later book of Burke's (*The Real East End*, 1933) is dedicated to challenging the commonly-held "legend" of East End life by presenting an alternative picture of his own experience of ethnic and class diversity, supportive, clan-based families, and positive social relationships founded on different, more "elemental," interpersonal exchanges. However, to discuss the relationship between the middle classes and their representations of the urban poor requires one to hold in mind these antithetical theses: (1) that these middle class representations were often high-minded, and sometime noble, attempts to understand poverty and to ameliorate its effects and (2) that they often reflect the coercive nature of middle class philanthropy and scientific understanding embodied in state institutions and private philanthropy—the power of the "social." The two assertions wash together.

In England, the social sciences came of age—took on the shape and principles that essentially defined them in the twentieth century—in response to the specter of urban slum conditions. Something so dreadfully wrong with the social order as the suffering, unemployment, brutishness, and apathy that one witnessed in the East End and elsewhere signified an infirmity in the body politic, and in the analysis and theorization of modern societies. Among the most influential of the new social theorists was the economist Alfred Marshall, Professor of Political Economy at Cambridge, author of the *Principles of Economics* (1890), and the seminal influence on economic thinking and teaching from the 1880s to the 1920s. His students are said to have filled half the chairs in the field in the United Kingdom, and he and they exercised immense influence on government and business. Marshall, who had originally intended to enter the Anglican clergy, and who "had come into economics out of ethics," according to his own account, essentially discarded the old economics of Malthus, Adam Smith, and Ricardo, with their theories premised on the distribution of wealth (Soffer 72). Marshall was moved by the challenge of poverty—its waste of human potential—and called first for a systematic *empirical* analysis of economic conditions: the fact-gathering that Beatrice Webb calls the scientific method. Accumulation and examination of data was not enough, however, for it must be pursued by a set of policies that will redeem the lost human resources of society, that will provide a rational means for opportunities to bring those people into the work force and the consuming public.

Marshall's redirection of economic thought and practice aligns it with the "social" in Donzelot's sense. For the impetus behind his beliefs is the exercise of ethical power: a determination to bring the treatment of the downtrodden into the ethical continuum of the English middle class. While his work constitutes a critique of the malformations of the capitalist society, it is in no way a rejection of that society. On the contrary, for Marshall the objective of economic reform is to bring the lower classes into the capitalist orbit. A firm devotee of the work ethic, he argued that labor was the primary means for achieving dignity and self-respect; social "good lies mainly in that healthful exercise and development of faculties which yields happiness without pall" (quoted in Soffer 78). Post-Darwinian biology had taught that environment and circumstances shaped development, so economic policy should create an opportunity for those who were less fortunate to realize themselves. Realization, Marshall believed, would be in middle class terms achieving a "standard of Comfort" that he equated to the life of a middle class "gentleman" (Soffer 75–79). Indeed, she suggests that Marshall, perhaps in keeping with the shifts of capitalism in the late nineteenth century, considered people more in terms of consumers than of producers. Donzelot argues that, in fact, one of the consequences of the emphasis on family and on bourgeois values generally in the reforms of the "social" is to create the mentality of the twentieth-century petit bourgeois: that marginal segment at the bottom of the middle class which is characterized by its overinvestment in family life, its narrow sense of economy, its fascination with education, its slavish envy of the upper class, and its frantic consumer desires (Donzelot 93).

Marshall advocated a more general redress of the conditions of poverty, but in many respects his emphasis on realizing the potential of the faceless poor shares some of the selectivism of the program of the Charity Organization Society, the largest and most well known of the private restoration efforts of the period. Headed by Octavia Hill, the COS was designed to put an end to "indiscriminate" almsgiving. Hill and others argued—and it was a venerable doctrine in English debates on charity—that open-handed giving to the poor corrupted both the receiver and the giver. It cultivated "deceitfulness, servility and greed" in the poor, demoralizing them and their families, and robbing them of the incentive to improve themselves. It not only frittered away the resources of the giver, but created false virtue and false comfort. The COS set itself up to weed out the deserving and undeserving, and to regularize the distribution of charity. Beatrice Webb saw through the hypocrisy of the COS almost immediately. First, it was foolish to attribute, as many of its spokespersons did, the persistence of poverty to indiscriminate and unconditional doles. Secondly, the COS policy of giving only to those who were most "deserving" broke down almost at once, because the most deserving were often those who suffered from chronic illnesses or injuries which prevented them from working. Since helping them would entail expensive and prolonged medical treatment, or unending support in many cases, the COS decided to put its money elsewhere. The criterion was changed: "the test is not whether the applicant be deserving but whether he is helpable" (195). The "unhelpable" were thrown back onto the Poor Law.

The social interventions into the world of urban poverty were always beset with these contradictions, in part because most of the schemes were candidly designed to shore up competitive capitalism, and in part because many of the most impassioned workers among the poor were torn by their own doubts about the order—or at least troubled by their ambivalence toward it. In summarizing the failure of the COS, Beatrice Webb writes, "By rudely tearing off the wrappings of medieval almsgiving disguising the skeleton at the feast of capitalist civilization, they had let loose the tragic truth that, wherever society is divided into a minority of 'Haves' and a multitude of 'Have Nots,' charity is twice cursed, it curseth him that gives and him that takes.... For human relationships, whether between individuals, groups or races, do not thrive in an emotional vacuum; if you tune out fellow-feeling and the common consciousness of a social equity, you tune in insolence, envy and 'the wrath that is to come'" (196–97). Those emotional, almost spiritual, registers of the experiences of Webb and others in social work in the London slums must be gauged, for what is at stake is self-definition, the construction of a certain type of subjectivity.

Beatrice Webb's autobiography and her diary are significant documents because they not only record the agonies of such self-construction with great insight and honesty—and because, as we have noted, she recognizes the implication of her capitalist origins in that process—but also because they are the expressions of a woman. As we discussed in the first chapter, the male construction of poverty emphasized the threat of a feminine abject in sensationalized accounts. Beyond that, however, women become pivotal figures in the discourse of the "social" that we have identified. The focal point of the intervention of social services and regulations is the family. Donzelot argues that the family is the site at which the dominant social order enacts its transformations, and yet it is also the object of criticism by that order (Donzelot 53). Its "failures" and inadequacies elicit the involvement of social services. Increasingly over the course of the century an ideal of the nuclear family becomes a "normative" unit against which everything is measured. Donzelot and others see in this the influence of the rising middle class, whose relations of production and consumption are organized around the family and its gendered division of labor, and which ethicizes and emotionalizes the family for the purposes of class preservation and control (as we observed in the principle of privatization), of gender discrimination, and as a means of reproducing itself through the nurturance and education of children. Indeed, Donzelot argues that the family is essentially *constructed* as a social organism throughout the century; it is given a hallowed status retroactively, enhancing its status as the "natural" state of human relations.[6]

At the heart of the family is the woman. Donzelot observes that "the transformation of the family was effected with the active participation of women, for they disseminated the principles of the medical and teaching professions into the home, helped win adherence to new norms, and produced a revaluation of power relationships between men and women."⁷ All the areas that were woman's domain—child raising, hygiene, moral education—in the bourgeois code of the nuclear family were made into pressure points for the intervention of the state. She served as the means for the interchange of private and public values. She was, after all, the ethical figure through which the ethicizing of the "social" could occur. As social intervention became more professionalized later in the century, the woman acted as the mediating element; it was she who took the children to the doctor and who dealt with the school authorities, and it was she who was often favored in family counseling and family courts later in the century.⁸

But the relative empowerment of the woman was not without its costs. The woman was often the target of social intervention. Her practices in raising children and maintaining a decent home were examined, criticized, and "reformed." A recurrent pattern in accounts of urban poor and working-class life presents us with a slovenly or dispirited wife and mother, sometimes a casually immoral one, and one of the silent premises of social reform is that the father and husband is held less responsible for home values. The woman thus occupies an uneasy double role: as mediator of the public efforts at reform, and as object of that reform. To the extent that the "social" is a feminized discourse—a feminized space, as Denise Riley notes, because its concerns are those of health, education, hygiene, fertility, demography, chastity, and fecundity—the woman functions as interrogator of her own role and being. "'Women' both come under and direct the public gaze in the later nineteenth century as sociological subjects in a double sense,'" Riley observes. "Studies of poverty and of family life, of 'social conditions,' are from the 1880s to the 1930s frequently explained as the ravages of deprivation on the family whose pivot and heart is 'the working-class woman,' who may also be represented as its ignorant saboteur" (Riley 50). Finally, the "social" generally, and what is known as "social work" specifically, are often set out as appropriate vocations for women: activities in which an enterprising middle class or upper class wife, or one of the growing body of unmarried "odd women" or spinsters in nineteenth century England, might engage.⁹

Beatrice Webb's description of her work in the East End, principally as a rent collector for the Katherine Buildings, a housing project designed for the poor, illustrates the ambiguous state of a woman—in this case an upper middle class woman—who acts as mediating figure in the sphere of the "social." She is not, of course, a direct target of the social intervention, but she is deeply affected by her role as an instrument of it. Webb, in fact, welcomed the depersonalizing, instrumental qualities of it. For one thing, it seemed to channel energies that otherwise would go into unproductive, wayward directions of high society life, desultory study, specific attachments: "There is so much spare time in my life, it must be filled somehow. If I were, in a fit of discouragement, to throw up everything (for if I gave up my aim it would mean this with me, I couldn't do purposeless work) I should become miserably restless, probably give way to some strong feeling and find my own nature too much for me" (*Diary* 114). Work among the poor substitutes for the religious faith that she has discarded. She shares, it seems, like many others of her generation, the faith that the "scientific method," the gathering of data on the conditions of urban poverty, will have ethical value in itself. One of the allures of empiricism in the nineteenth century was its apparent capacity to be more than simply a method. Empirical observation and fact-gathering by a dispassionate "professional" established a base for ethics. The more one knows about other people, their feelings, needs, and lives, the greater is the potential enlargement of one's own sympathetic powers. Behind the fetishization of empirical study of the poor in the nineteenth century lies, one suspects, a vestige of the belief that the acts of knowledge and appropriation themselves enlarge and transform human nature. The empirical observer becomes a better person.

The model for such social investigation was, for Webb, the work of her cousin-in-law Charles Booth, whose monumental multi-volume survey and classification of the strata of the metropolis, *Life and Labour of the People of London*, was begun with the East End, the subject of the first volume, published in 1889. Webb worked as a researcher for Booth's project during her stint in the slums. Booth categorizes the people into eight strata, listed A through H: "A. The lowest class of occasional labourers, loafers, and semi-criminals. B. Casual earnings—'very poor.' C. Intermittent earnings and D. Small regular earnings, together the 'poor.' E. Regular standard earnings—above the line of poverty. F. Higher class labour. G. Lower middle class. H. Upper middle class." He calculated the percentage of the total city population of each group—Class A he reckoned at 11,000 or 1¼ percent of the population—and provided a wealth of data about marriages, jobs, housing situations, class mobility, and so on.

Booth was an eminently humane man, and cross-verified his figures and observations through sources such as health inspectors and education officers who regularly worked in the East End. But his project also contributes to an abstraction of the condition of the poor. We understand, of course, that Booth is not attempting to provide a full picture of urban life, of the causes of poverty, of class relations. His is only data-gathering, a preliminary work as it were, toward other forms of representation, although Philip Abrams points out that when Booth began his project he was interested in more than the collection of data; he was concerned with the structural processes of poverty (Abrams 84). It aids in establishing, nonetheless, a vision of urban life that Jameson and others identify as one of classification (Jameson 190).

Representations of the urban poor in a novel such as *Bleak House* cannot be separated from the anxieties of the bourgeois male over his social role, the displacement of the competitive ethos, or the construction of the middle class female subject. In the classificatory mode of 1880s social science, there is an attempt to divide out such factors, to make the issues independently addressable, even if the impetus in men like Alfred Marshall and Charles Booth is reformist. Booth's scientific method, in its effort to purge the topic of the distortions of other forms of representation, has provided us with an incomplete representation. It lacks the totalizing quality, to use Georg Lukács' term, of the Dickensian version, and, as we shall see, it paves the way for the reification of the poor in late nineteenth-century science fiction and tales of the "abyss."

Beatrice Webb plunges herself into a relentless, punishing round of work in the slums of the East End. "Working hard," she records in her diary on June 4, 1885. "May have some rough work to do, but am gaining experience. When over-tired, the tenants haunt me with their wretched, disorderly lives" (*D* 134). On September 14, she sighs, "Oh so tired. Struggling through the end of my work with painful effort. The old physical longing for the night that knows no morning" (*D* 138). And, indeed, this account for November 15 chronicles a life in which she is giving herself no quarter:

> 15 November. Worked well. Monday, Katherine Buildings, one to nine o'clock. Afterwards saw over Whittington Club.... Tuesday at Katherine Buildings book, 4 hours. Wednesday Albert and Victoria Docks from 10 P.M. to 6 A.M. Thursday, idle morning castle-building—afternoon, Katherine Buildings. Friday, 7 hours' work at Katherine Buildings book. Saturday, Katherine Buildings 12 to 7 o'clock. Forty hours' work including railway journeys. (*D* 143)

Webb's life of duty would be difficult enough to sustain physically, but it is also undermined by the self-doubt that keeps reappearing in her early self-confessions and that makes it such a compelling account. "Shall I always disappoint myself and others when my strength comes to be tested; or will my strength increase and enable me to carry out what I intend?" (263). Her social work is more than a test of endurance to her; it is a test of character. "I have a much greater show of ability than reality," she decides, "arising from my audacity of mind and plausible way of putting things. My dear old Father, I am a sort of weak edition of you!" (266). She examines her motives: "Earnestly hope I shall never get conceited again, or look upon my work as more than the means for remaining contented and free from pain. Relief to be alone . . . Trust I shall never make social capital out of my work. That with me is a danger . . . and the 'vanity motive' comes in to strengthen desire" (256). Her scientific approach to her task, always trying to keep a book describing the individual cases, so that work will not simply be a routine, but will be the base for social scientific observation—the self-imposed rigor of this sustains her while the actual encounters with another sphere of life, with the poor, prompts only (as we have seen hinted) a confused distaste and sympathy.

For this representative of the middle class urban social worker battles between a determination to bring science, will, and intellect to bear on the major social ills of the day—an effort that she deliberately abstracts into an impersonal empirical/analytical operation—and her own attractions toward the upper middle class sphere from which she comes. The choice often appears to her to be one between social scientific work, and love and marriage. At the end of her stint at Katherine Buildings, Webb has reached a nadir of despair. It is compounded by her father's stroke and invalidism (for she devotes herself to nursing him), and her younger sister Rosy's *anorexia nervosa,* but it is also a resignation to spinsterhood. "It will be a sad life; God grant it may be a useful one, that I may dedicate myself earnestly and without trembling to search after the truth which will help my people. There is no inflation now. I have not despised the simple happiness of a woman's life; it has despised me and I have been humbled as far down as a woman can be humbled" (D 160). In her autobiography, in a section headed "The Dead Point," she states, "The sympathetic reader may have noted a black thread of personal unhappiness woven into the texture of my observations on East End life. From the entries in my diary I gather that I saw myself as one suffering from a divided personality; the normal woman seeking personal happiness in love given and taken within the framework of a successful marriage; whilst the other self claimed, in season and out of season, the right to the free activity of 'a clear and analytic mind'" (270). Here we have the ideal of detachment—implicitly associated with masculine activity in the public sphere—juxtaposed against the ideal of a "normal" emotional life for a woman. In Webb, the two ideals have come to seem incompatible with one another.

My Apprenticeship makes almost no reference to any unhappy experiences in love for the young Beatrice Potter. But from the diaries we learn of courtship by Joseph Chamberlain, the charismatic Radical-Liberal leader who was one of the principal figures for social reform, and whose split with Gladstone in 1885 over the issue of Irish Home Rule led to the break-up of the Liberal party. The romance, or at least negotiations relating to it, stretched on in an unsatisfactory and desultory fashion over many months, but in her diary entry for January 12, 1884, Beatrice Webb, by her account, at least, had concluded that it would be a destructive match for her. After dinner,

> By a silent arrangement we find ourselves in the garden. "It pains me to hear any of my views controverted," and with this preface he begins with stern exactitude to lay down the articles of his political creed. I remain modestly silent; but noticing my silence he remarks that he requires "intelligent sympathy" from women. "Servility, Mr. Chamberlain," think I, not sympathy, but intelligent servility; what many women give men, but the difficulty lies in changing one's master, in jumping from one tone of thought to the exact opposite—with intelligence. And then I advanced as boldly as I dare my feeble objections to his general proposition, feeling that in this case I owe it to the man to show myself and be absolutely sincere. He refutes my objections by reasserting his convictions passionately, his expression becoming every minute more gloomy and determined. (D 102)

Webb went on in the entry to analyze correctly the limitations of Chamberlain, those which led to his eventual failure as a leader: "He is neither a reasoner nor an observer in the scientific sense. He does not deduce his opinions by the aid of certain well-thought-out principles, from certain carefully-observed, ascertained facts. He aims, rather, at being the organ to express the desires of those he believes to be the majority of his countrymen" (103). Disappointment in love may be a factor in this analysis, but we would be doing a disservice to Webb not to appreciate the intellectual and philosophical terms on which she premised their relationship—and saw their incompatibility of natures. Her principles, and her convictions about the necessity of adducing them from "carefully observed, ascertained facts," turn this from a Jane Austenish account of pride and prejudice into a decision that demonstrates how much those ideals have come to constitute her essential self-construction. This is even more than the case of a young woman making a choice between a career and a marriage that would subordinate her; it is a decision affirming a thoroughly and rigorously thought out set of methods and purposes. The gender distinctions she is implicitly making here are complex and have no necessary relation to biological sex, as her critique of Chamberlain's failure to achieve the ideal of detachment is measured by her own yardstick—as a woman who is fully aware of her own ability to do just what Chamberlain cannot.

Yet, under such circumstances, how can work in the slums not serve in some way as a surrogate for feminine desire, a suppression or rerouting of it? Webb keeps circling back in her reflections on this time to the effects upon a woman of a life given to social work among the destitute. She muses about her fellow workers:

> But it is no use shutting one's eyes to the fact that there is an increasing number of women to whom a matrimonial career is shut, and who seek a masculine reward for masculine qualities. There is in these women something exceedingly pathetic, and I would do anything to open careers to them in which their somewhat abnormal but useful qualities would get their own reward. . . . At the best, their lives are sad and without joy or light-heartedness; they are now beginning to be deeply interested and warmed with enthusiasm. I think these strong women have a great future before them in the solution of social questions. (266–67)

She ponders the kinds of qualities—"feminine" and "masculine"—that are required for such service, and the limitations that each entails.[10] Of Emma Cons, a philanthropist who showed qualities as a "governing and guiding woman," she writes:

> Unlike the learned woman, the emotional part of their nature is fully developed, their sympathy kept almost painfully alive. Their eyes are clear of self-consciousness and bright with love and the pity from

which it springs. They have the dignity of habitual authority. Often they have the narrow-mindedness and social gaucherie of complete absorption, physical and mental, in one set of feelings and ideas. The pure organizer belongs to a different class. She is . . . to a certain extent unsexed by the justice, push, and severity required. Not that I despise these qualities; the former is indispensable in any work, but with the manager it is more moral; with the organizer more technical justice. Push and severity are not prominent qualities of the governing and guiding woman. For the guidance of men by personal influence, feeling more than thought is required. (D 136–37)

For a woman to persevere in the East End some stiffening of nature and refocusing of elements of one's mind and feelings is required. The daily encounter with such appalling wretchedness, with the shiftlessness and evasion and dispiritedness, acts in disorienting ways upon the woman who binds herself to fulfill the missions of an upper society that is ethically committed, yet frustrated, impatient with the almost hopeless tasks before it. Webb cannot always contain her revulsion. She writes in her diary on November 8, 1886:

But this East End life, with its dirt, drunkenness and immorality, absence of co-operation or common interests, saddens me and weighs down my spirit. I could not live down here; I should lose heart and become worthless as a worker. And practical work does not satisfy me; it seems like walking on shifting sand . . .
 Where is the wish for better things in these myriads of beings hurrying along the streets night and day? Even their careless, sensual laugh, coarse jokes, and unloving words depress one as one presses through the crowd, and almost shudders to touch them. It is not so much the actual vice, it is the low level of monotonous and yet excited life; the regular recurrence to street sensations, quarrels and fights; the greedy street-bargaining, and the petty theft and gambling. The better natures keep apart from their degraded fellow-citizens and fellow-workers, live lonely and perforce selfish lives, not desire to lead their more ignorant and unself-controlled neighbors. (267)

At times she is coldly critical: "We all designate them as on the whole a leisure class; picking up their livelihood by casual work, poor in quality; by borrowing from their more industrious friends, and by petty theft." The beggars are "as a class, in a purely business relationship in which no other moral principle enters than that of fulfilling contracts—hopelessly unsatisfactory" (261). These encounters produce in her a withholding of feeling, perhaps a disavowal of it, that she finds deeply troubling. She admits in her autobiography that she was described as "'a rather hard and learned woman, with a clear and analytic mind,' so records a brilliant journalist." Her defense is that "to me 'a million sick' have always seemed actually more worthy of self-sacrificing devotion than the 'child sick in a fever' preferred by Mrs. Browning's Aurora Leigh" (249–50).

Webb's moments of attachment always have that abstract, principled cast to them, for social service tied to scientific investigation partakes of some larger dispassionate spirit that is also heavy-handed in its manner. This is so, even in affirmations of the ethical obligation itself: "One thing is clear to my mind, it is distinctly advantageous to us to go amongst the poor. We can get from them an experience of life which is novel and interesting; the study of their lives and surroundings gives us the facts wherewith we can attempt to solve the social problems; contact with them develops on the whole our finer qualities, disgusting us with our false and worldly application of men and things and educating us in a thoughtful benevolence" (*D* 85). The leap of sympathy never quite seems to occur; rather, Webb looks on with curiosity not only about these pathetic specimens of social and self-ruin, but also in a bemused way about her own ambiguous and strangely muted, depressed responses:

> 20 May. Visited this morning Pavey (C.O.S. case), Had been dispenser, took to opium eating, now unfitted for work. Wife earning 15s a week, has to support him and three children . . . Still clings to her baby, poor woman. 'Why should I be separated from my children as if I were a bad woman? What will they think of me? . . . I cannot bear it much longer; I must give way.' The wretched man, standing sulkily in the corner, twisting his thumbs, cursing the existing order of things, talking of his better days and good education, could write well, talk and translate French, had a smattering of Greek and Latin. All to no purpose! One is tempted to a feeling of righteous indignation against the man, but did he not make himself wretched and is he not on the whole more pitiable? Look at the two faces. An expression on the one of dogged discontent and misery, ever present disgust of the world and himself; marking the woman's face, deep lines of unselfconscious effort, of perhaps agonizing struggle, agonizing in those moments when she felt herself face to face with the fact that in the end she must succumb; but still she loved, and the little one for whom she is giving away strength,

and maybe life, smiles sweetly and stretches its tiny arms longingly towards her. *(D 86)*

Such distanced despair, and such a scene of enervating desolation, acquires in the workers among the netherworld of the 1880s the quality of experience in an almost alien landscape. East London was often, during this period, likened to a colonial land, but nowhere more luridly than in William Booth's *In Darkest England and The Way Out* (1890). Booth (no relation to Charles) was the founder and leader of the Salvation Army, one of the most energetic organizations in the slums. He begins his book on the problems of urban poverty by invoking the highly popular newspaper reportage by Henry Morton Stanley of his trip through the densest jungles of Africa. The expedition was an exhausting, terrifying trek through treacherous undergrowth, where no sunlight reached the ground, and the only sounds were those of falling trees and the appalling thunder-bursts and their echoes, a realm of dampness, gloom, chill, and disease—and of ever-present danger, from snakes, insects, wild animals, and perhaps from the cannibalistic pygmies. Booth then draws a parallel with the East London slums:

> The Equatorial Forest traversed by Stanley resembles that Darkest England of which I have to speak, alike in its vast extent—both stretch, in Stanley's phrase, "as far as from Plymouth to Peterhead;" its monotonous darkness, its malaria and its gloom, its dwarfish de-humanized inhabitants, the slavery to which they are subjected, their privations and their misery. That which sickens the stoutest heart, and causes many of our bravest and best to fold their hands in despair, is the apparent impossibility of doing more than merely to peck at the outside of the endless tangle of monotonous undergrowth; to let light into it, to make a road clear through it, that shall not be immediately choked up by the ooze of the morass and the luxuriant parasitical growth of the forest—who dares hope for that? At present, alas, it would seem as though no one dares even to hope! It is the great Slough of Despond of our time. (W. Booth 12–13)

Booth echoes, although in a grandiloquent way, the despair that Beatrice Webb expressed in the midst of her venture into the slums. The waves of defeatism that engulf even the most "stout-hearted" of the workers among the urban poor record not only the immensity of the task before them, but the alienation that lies at the heart of the entire relationship. "Darkest England" is a figure of speech, a metaphor, for the extensive disavowal of the inter-relations of class identity and personal self-definition, and of economic structures and individual effects, which only can provide us with an integrated and "total" representation of the condition. The parallel to Africa is a pure gesture of reification, containing perhaps traces of the male middle class fantasy discourse that we discussed from the 1840s and 1850s, but essentially displaced from the dynamics of middle class self-definition.

Culturalist Philanthropy and Its Civilizing Mission

William Booth, like Webb, was a figure caught up in attempted class mediation, and, like her, he sought to efface it by asserting an overriding ethical imperative. Even here, though, the difference is telling, for Booth's religious mission is itself reified, bound up in his design of the Salvation Army itself—the discipline, the self-denial, the uniforms, the religious fervor. And his "solution" to urban poverty was to evacuate the poor into work camps in the country or to transport them abroad—to bundle them off as one would a cartload of broken objects.

In both William Booth and Beatrice Webb the ethical imperative, undertaken in full conviction of its necessity and (in Booth's case) its righteousness, engenders a withering of enthusiasm as it encounters the bleak prospects of real poverty. Both employ imagery of the deadening of sensibility—in Webb's case explicitly linked to the sacrifices of womanly desire that are the price one pays for social service in the East End. Booth's sensationalized vision of Darkest England, which was apparently touched up by none other than W. T. Stead, projects its morality with militant Christian energy, but even in his account there is a stultification of spirit in both the reformer and the figure of urban poverty. The personal self-image of the middle class social worker falters at this moment, and the class's imagination dwells on a picture of desolation. This permeation of affect into both the upper class observer and the scene of his or her effort is best embodied in a novel by Margaret Harkness, entitled *A City Girl* (1887).

Harkness was Beatrice Webb's second cousin and very close friend; the two went on a trip to Austria in 1884 after Webb's emotional crisis over Chamberlain, and Harkness introduced Beatrice to Sidney Webb, who became her husband and intellectual partner. Harkness actually lived in the Katherine Buildings during the 1880s, and wrote a series of novels about the slums under the pseudonym of John Law. Relatively little is known about her, and even about her political positions, for although she was a socialist during the 1880s, and helped in the Dock Workers' Strike, she was often critical of socialists in her fiction, and apparently turned against socialism in the next decade. John Goode, one of the few literary critics who have given her any notice, remarks, "what we don't know is whether she was a woman of consistent ideas who worked opportunistically in a series of alliances (her own image of herself), a radical feminist converted to socialism in the mid-1880s and disillusioned by it in the early 1890's, or simply a neurotic of wide but volatile sympathies vacillating between seeing herself as a journalist in pursuit of 'cold-blooded copy' and a rejected saviour of the working class" ("Harkness" 49). She is perhaps most famous for the letter Friedrich Engels sent her after reading *A City Girl*, in which he discusses his preference for Balzac over Zola, and praises her for the "truthfulness of her presentation" of the conditions under which the proletariat suffer.

Her neglect as a literary figure is understandable on reading *A City Girl*, for it is a strangely spare, uninflected novel. The story is a familiar, almost starkly symbolic one, of a pretty slum girl named Nelly who aspires to a more romantic existence. Nelly is casually seduced by a West Ender named Arthur Grant, made pregnant, and ruined in health and spirit. It is, as Engels noted, the classic rendition of the exploitation of the poor by the callous rich—yet there are unsettling little differences: Nelly's father was probably a West Ender himself; she aspires to pleasures and beauty that are normally thought to be beyond the ken of dispirited slum dwellers; Arthur Grant is a socialist and a novelist and, ironically, a devoted family man, not your ordinary roué; and her eventual rescuer is himself a man with a respectable military service background, someone who nurtures his resources in order to better his condition. Nelly shadows the sensibility of a victimized young woman from a higher social class—perhaps of Harkness herself. The novel, however, thwarts such subliminal readings, by denying Nelly any but the most melodramatically stereotyped mental characteristics. Grant reflects that "she was no psychological study, this little Whitechapel girl, only something pretty to look at" (Harkness 76). Spoken, to be sure, by a philandering seducer, who thinks that "'hands' have no hearts," but crudely true to the limitations with which she has been rendered by Harkness.

For Nelly's is a limited subjectivity in a realm of a limited scope, inhabited by limited beings. *A City Girl* paints a landscape of spiritual desolation, but one that cannot be quickened into dark nights of the soul. The figure of religion, Father O'Hara, a Catholic priest who had suppressed the demon of unbelief by repressing his intellect and his feelings, represents the utter devastation of mind that one encounters in the East End. Whitechapel "is the land of dumb thought and dumb feeling" (Harkness 99), the narrator asserts, and this is what it truly is, a "land" of benumbed thought and feeling, a landscape of affect, the spatialized depiction of a state of mind. Scarcely a breath of vitality is stirring in our mental image of the novel; the characters are enervated and passive—even Nelly—and they are largely types, uninflected into particularity; the action is desultory and fatalistic; the underlying impulses of the text are stolidly repressed—Nelly's pregnancy and the birth of her baby are only obliquely referred to, and sexuality is a casual diversion to the upper class and a wretched miscalculation for the poor.

The spatialized representation of the netherworld continues, in a sense, the figurations of miasma and labyrinth in which it had always been rendered: a combination of atmosphere and of physical setting that correlated well with theses of degeneration, and later naturalist notions of the effects of environment on character. But Nelly's story is, in another sense, the story of Harkness' and Webb's alienation and depression, of the banking of their own fires of desire—and yet the stirring of them with the ghostly wisps of romances with men from their middle class backgrounds—and of the spiritual stultification that seems to set in upon those who sacrificed in these seemingly barren fields. The sparsely psychologized, relatively unmodulated figure of Nelly—almost as purely symbolic as the little girl sentinel of George Sims' *How the Poor Live*—articulates the constriction of sensibilities, perhaps even the narrowing of the protagonist's subjectivity that Georg Lukács described as a symptom of character driven by abstract ethical imperatives that cannot be realized in the exterior world (Lukács 65–66).

This landscape of affect was recast into the dominant public image of the East End in the 1880s by the most influential novelist on the subject, Walter Besant. Besant was one of the most popular and eminent novelists of the period, although he is mostly remembered now as the catalyst for Henry James' essay on "The Art of Fiction."[11] The prominence of Besant is what prompted James to make him the object of his dialogue in his seminal essay on the principles of aesthetics and realism, and Besant's prominence was in turn built on his presidency of the Society for Authors, his activity in seeking fairer contractual terms for writers, and his involvement in bringing the conditions of the East

End, as he saw them, to the attention of a vast middle class reading public. As Peter Keating has observed, Besant was as much a reformer as an artist, but the two aspects make an intriguing combination (*Working Classes* 94).

Besant characterized the East End as a vast desert of monotony and "meanness." He uses "mean" in the sense of lowly, abject, and ignoble, lacking any elevating qualities. For him, then, as well, all the communities and subcultures of the urban netherworld are characterized in terms of the affective nature of the quality of existence within them. When he writes *East London* in 1899, he transforms that quality of existence into a descriptive landscape, opening with a visual panorama of the area, a sort of walking tour, in which he defines it through what is absent:

> It is a city full of churches and places of worship, yet there are no cathedrals . . . ; it has a sufficient supply of elementary schools, but it has no public or high school, and it has no colleges for the higher education and no university; the people all read newspapers, yet there is no East London paper except of the smaller and local kind. . . . In the streets there are never seen any private carriages; there is no fashionable quarter . . . (*East London* 8)

The East End is flattened, a cultural prairie, with no vital connection to its past, no sense of citizenship, no vitality. "Unlovely City," he hails it, "City of Dreadful Monotony."

Besant's characterization of the East End as a place that parches the spirit is echoed by other observers, including, as we shall see in the next chapter, one of its inhabitants, Arthur Morrison, in his short story "Mean Streets." But Morrison's larger picture is one of vitality, and that is confirmed by the Reverend A. Osborne Jay, who spent years in the worst sections, and who writes in his memoirs, *A Story of Shoreditch: Being a Sequel to 'Life in Darkest London,'* (1896), "I recollect once talking with a somewhat superficial observer as to the difficulties of work in East London, and being told that its chief feature is monotony. This, at least, is not characteristic of Shoreditch: to the uninitiated, life there, provided that they survived, would surely assume the appearance of a chronic surprise, and even to those fairly seasoned, there is never any lack of uncertainty" (Jay 47).

Besant may not have intended to deny the East End its manic violence, but he nonetheless presents to the "uninitiated" middle class reader a picture that omits all the local color, the busy culture of the nether world. He provides his audience with a landscape of dull, unmotivated, shiftless grey figures, inured to poverty, slipping below the fully human. We are in a world of vacant subjectivity, a terrain in which very little desire stirs. While we could find links between this picture and the psychological states of women such as Beatrice Webb and probably Margaret Harkness—and thus could reasonably designate it as a site of affect—there is no such inflection of Besant's sensibility. For the positive-thinking Besant, the subjective emptiness speaks not of him, nor of the ambivalences of his class, but of a social challenge: the need to create and nurture a subjectivity within the underclasses, to bring them into the hegemonic formation by providing them with cultural "being." His mission among the downtrodden is to resuscitate desire, but within stipulated perimeters: a socially constructive, ethically bound, and materialistically realizable desire. He wants to foster the individual potentiality of the deprived worker in the East End. He wants, as he puts it in his *Autobiography* (1902), to show "the romance that lies beneath its monotony" (*Autobiography* 243).[12]

In this project, Besant is more in line with the other great pattern of middle class intervention into the slums that took place in the 1880s. While Webb, Charles Booth, and their associates were trying to bring a systematic analysis to urban conditions, another wave of socially conscious upper middle class figures moved in (literally) to the East End with the mission of establishing individual human connections between the classes and of bringing culture to the poor. They were part of what became known as the settlement movement, or the Toynbee Hall movement (after the most famous settlement project). It was inspired by the ideas of a number of prominent academic figures, such as the philosopher T. H. Green, the cultural scholar Benjamin Jowett, and the historian Arnold Toynbee at Oxford, who argued that only through a more personal, individual contact between the upper classes and the underclasses could the urban poor and the lower working class acquire those traits of character that would enable them to improve themselves. In 1884 a Universities' Settlement Association was set up, with the goal of establishing a series of residences in the East End, in which a select group of University men would live among and attempt to exert a personal influence upon slum dwellers and workingmen, through example and through cultural uplift. Within the next four decades 46 settlements were to be established in the United Kingdom, reaching an estimated total of 100,000 working class people (Rose, *Edwardian Temperament* 57).

The young men who joined in the initial forays of the settlement movement were the cream of the English upper middle classes. They were ready to devote themselves to public service, and many of them were out of the tradition of Thomas Arnold's Rugby School, which aimed to prepare boys for a life of civic action and responsibility. They responded strongly to the dangers of social disintegration that had been brought on by some of the excesses of capitalism: the unequal distribution of wealth, the growing class resentments, the divisions between social strata. East London symbolized a social pathology: the loss of an English sense of community. They were chosen for this task because of their own aspirations to realize the best in themselves; here would be a cadre of dedicated and disinterested leaders who would teach workers how they might become part of the larger English community by cultivating their own higher qualities. This was bourgeois class mediation at its most explicit.

The spiritual leader of the settlement movement was T. H. Green, who could address the elements of religious doubt in many of the young men at Oxford in the 1870s, because "he had himself abandoned Christian orthodoxy in the 1860s," the historian Standish Meacham tells us. Green argued that loss of belief in the outward manifestations of divine power did not require one to forsake the principles of Christianity. God was immanent in each man, "'present in the believing love of him and the brethren, a Christ within us, a continual resurrection,' which could be manifested in the subordinating of self to the needs of fellow human beings." The doctrine of immanent divine qualities assigns to each individual an inner core of being that realizes itself in social duty. To serve the needs of social harmony is to be. Green's ability to conceptualize ethics as being in this way attempts to prevent it from taking on the nature of an exteriorized duty, as it so often is for Beatrice Webb. Theoretically, class mediation and essence are melded together. And the terms of being are correlated more directly to bourgeois values in Green's dictum that God was "the possible self."[13] Although the "possible self" evokes Arnoldian cultural theory, the "best self" that is altruistic, cultured, and idealistic, transcending materialism, it employs terms that are intrinsic to the middle class projective mentality that thinks ahead, that speaks of its own potentiality.

The ethos of the settlement house movement tries to correct one of the chief infirmities of other upper class interventions into the East End: the impersonality of it, the reifying qualities that attach to the treatment of individuals as objects of aid or of social interrogation. The organizer of Toynbee House, the Reverend Samuel Barnett, had been an associate of Octavia Hill in the Charity Organization Society, and had for some years served in Whitechapel as rector of St. Jude's, and he well appreciated the need for what he called a "one by one" approach to the poor. The young men from the universities who came to reside at Toynbee Hall were expected to develop personal relationships with members of the lower classes, and to provide them with living examples of the development of character and intellect. In such a relationship, Barnett proclaimed, the East Londoners "take in knowledge which they do not tabulate; they absorb thought as air, they consciously become more sympathetic, and lose the narrow views which kept them as a class apart. . . . The habits and tastes, therefore, which lie at the root of Poverty, Ignorance, and Sin, may best be met by the formation of other habits, which come through the example of persons, by the contact of man with man."[14]

Barnett's theory of improvement by emulation, of "raising the buried life" that lies within even the most blighted of individuals, sounds very English in its individualistic emphasis. It purports to elide class distinctions by arguing that men are shaped by the limitations of circumstances. Yet the selection of Oxford and Cambridge men for the role of mentors reinforces a hierarchy of breeding and acculturation, even if it is a potentially mobile one. Indeed, many of the Oxbridge devotees to the settlement house project complained that they were made constantly conscious of their special backgrounds. And Meacham's study indicates that the vast majority of the Londoners who attended settlement house events and profited by them were not of the poorest group but from upper working and lower middle classes (Meacham 58). Whitechapel itself was particularly resistant to the movement because it was made up of many transient workers and had a high level of the unskilled. Furthermore, the predominantly male composition of the settlement house movement identifies culturalism as a strategy with patriarchal overtones when used in dealing with the lower classes. We saw similar tendencies in the writing of journalists such as James Greenwood, whose "literary" rhetoric placed it squarely within the tradition of the patriarchal eighteenth century essay and whose partially gentrified class sensibility diminished the possibilities of the male journalist acting as an effective ethicizing force among the lower orders. Bringing cultivation to the heathen is, in certain respects, a moral mission, but for all of T. H. Green's efforts to link culturalism and ethics, the movement has imperialistic overtones. Partly because of this, and partly because the movements toward cultural improvement did not work, Arthur Morrison and George Gissing treated the settlement houses with contempt, as we shall see in chapter 3. Gissing, in particular, also recognized the potentially rigidifying self-contradictions that the strategy of culturalism caused in the middle class male.

The settlement house movement could also be faulted for its depoliticizing tendencies. The issues were not those of class conflict, supposedly, but of individual self-development. In such a scheme, anyone could realize his potential, given the right examples and opportunities, and political action or unionization by the underclasses only disrupted community and ruined the chances of one-on-one interaction and self-improvement. Of course, as we have noted, the effort was far from apolitical. The middle class desire for mediation prompted it, and the inculcation of upper class values and desires in the lower classes could only conclude in subjecting them to hegemonic control. The concept of hegemony is central to the success of the Western European and American middle class control over their social orders, for that control is achieved not through repressive force, but by convincing those who lack power and privilege to share in the values of those who have it. As long as the individuals in subordinate positions believe in the dominant social order's rightness and naturalness, and only want to be part of it themselves, they will abide by its prescriptions. The problem was becoming equally acute with respect to the urban poor, for the emphases on the atavistic natures of these dwellers of the underworld, of their degeneration into less than full human beings, denied them individuality in this sense. At some level, the settlement house approach attempted to address this very crisis.

The writer Thomas Burke, whom we have already discussed, captures well the prevailing sense that the settlement house movement, as well as the work of all the other disciplinary agencies concerned with alleviating the social effects of poverty, actually undermined the autonomy of the poor through their invasive activities:

> No pious youth from college ever seemed to think of doing a little Settlement work in Curzon Street or Portman Square. Always it was the defenceless, voiceless poor who were the victims of the whims and theories of the educated; and what with the District Visitor, the Provident Visitors, the School Board man, the curate, the Infant Welfare Visitor, and the Settlement Worker, our homes were far more public than any public-house. (*The Wind and the Rain* 26)

A self-proclaimed member of "the poor," Burke, who depicts an East End far more open to the outer world than Morrison's, was nonetheless dogged in his early life, not only by persistent hunger, but by constant reminders that the poor were always objects under surveillance by the well off—a source of potential danger to the people who employed them as servants or for day work. An exemplary East End figure who made a name for himself as a writer after years of struggle in dire poverty, Burke conveys a vision of East End life as more hopeful than certainly Arthur Morrison, whose work we will discuss in chapter 4, and far more energetic than the enervated landscapes of Harkness and Besant. It is also interesting to note that Burke's interest in art and his opportunities to advance his writing skills were enabled, not by the efforts of exogenous middle class cultural philanthropy, but by an indigenous cultural institution with a close connection to the lives of the urban poor and working classes: the music hall.

And thus we are brought back again to Walter Besant, for in his vision the terms are most sharply drawn. From the desolate East End of meanness and monotony, from a site of absence—absence of churches, absence of places of recreation, absence of history, absence of subjectivity—we set about the task of constituting a "being" for the underclasses, or etching on that template the cultural sensibility that can replicate itself in the hegemonic order. This, for Besant, is the Great "Romance" that lies beneath the City of Dreadful Monotony. His widely read novel, *All Sorts and Conditions of Men* (1882) dramatizes that Romance as a romance, for at the heart of it is the love story of Angela Messenger, a graduate of Newnham College and heiress to the fortune of the Messenger Brewery, and Harry Goslett, a native of the East End, who was raised by an aristocrat as if he were a member of the upper classes, and who returns voluntarily to the slums to work as a joiner.[15] Harry is an example of settlement house philosophy in action, for his lowly origins do not prevent him from attaining to all of the knowledge, personal style, and good breeding of the highest order. As his guardian, Lord Jocelyn puts it, "I expected you would take a rough kind of polish only—like nickel, you know, or pewter—and you turned out real silver. A gentleman, I thought, is born, not made. This proved a mistake" (*All Sorts* 160). Angela Messenger tries to prove out the best, most altruistic of the mediating impulses of the upper middle class, for she takes another name—Angela Kennedy—and establishes a dressmaking firm amidst the sweatshops on Whitechapel Road. This is no ordinary dressmaking establishment, however, for the working conditions are elegant but simple, the girls break at intervals to play tennis in the specially built courts, or to exercise in their private gymnasium, then they are fed a hearty, healthy meal with real roast beef, they are read to as they work, and after a shortened day by East End standards, they are invited to stay on to dance in the ballroom, read in the library, or entertain their friends. In addition, they share in the firm's profits.

The goal is to civilize these girls. By refining them, by exposing them to the pleasures of life, by teaching them to appreciate music and literature, and by surrounding them with pleasantness, Angela intends to make her employees aspire to something beyond their mean existences. "Unless they are discontented, there will be no improvement. Think . . . what it is that lifts men out of the level of the beasts. We find out that there are better things, and we are fighting our way upwards" (95). And after some initial suspicion, the cure works miracles: it even affects the working girls' speech—"my girls can talk without angry snapping of the lips, and without the 'sezi' and 'sezee' and 'seshee' of the omnibus" (130)—and their demeanor—"all their faces during the last few months had changed for the better: not one among them all bore the expression which is described by the significant words 'bold' and 'common'"(328–29). Note that it is women who are being remade here. The work of higher culture chooses the female as its object for reconstruction, although the assumption of acculturation, in the minds of Besant and the settlement house advocates, had been that men as well as women would be the objects of change. The choice of women is, in fact, symbolic for Besant, for they represent the essentially "feminized" status of the lower classes in the discourse of culturalism, and underscore the similarity between the position of the lower classes and that of woman in modern consumer society who is both programmed consumer and object of appropriation and consumption.[16] The role played by a woman, Angela Messenger, in the acculturation process does not contradict this reading, for Angela, a student of Newnham College in Cambridge, is introduced to the reader as a new, less "feminized" woman. When her female companion vows never to let love sway her from her idealistic purposes, Angela responds, "Nor will I. . . . Marriage spoils a woman's career. . . ." (4). One of the most difficult balancing acts that Besant faces, in fact, is to keep alive the "feminine" characteristics of Angela and to justify her ultimate retreat from the dominant figure in her relationship with Harry to a more traditionally passive, "womanly" one.

Such a romantic transformation occurs here in the lowest, most exploited forms of production in English capitalism: the sweatshop. Angela has, by her own admission, flouted "every precept of political and social economy" (128). Aspects of her project recall the paternalistic factory settings of the early industrial revolution, although the novel essentially denies the value of the competitive ethos. This is, as we saw in Dickens, a common strategy among English novelists, and as in Dickens the excesses of the capitalist order are laid not at the feet of the rich but of the grubbing commercial figures: the villain of the novel is a real estate speculator who tries to cheat Harry Goslett out of his property. But the significant change in Besant's 1880s vision is the effort to deny the realities of production. Angela subsidizes the high costs of the "work place" that would price her dresses out of the competition, and in fact there exists no real market for the goods, because they are bought up by Angela herself, in the name of Miss Messenger of the West End. Production has been effectively effaced. The "romance" at this later stage of English capitalism is with consumption.

Although the girls in Angela's dressmaking shop learn to be happier workers, they are really being taught the joys of the life of the consumer. They develop taste; they appreciate the finer things that work can furnish for them. The "discontent" that Angela instills in them is not so much discontent with working conditions, but with their "mean" and limited aspirations, which will settle for beer and a stroll around the slum streets and worse. When Harry Goslett rouses the Stepney Advanced Club, a group of Whitechapel working men who had been foolishly agitating for radical political action, he tells them politics is useless until you know what you want: "[One] thing that you want is pleasure. Men can't do without it. Can government give you that? . . . You do not know how to enjoy yourselves. You don't know what to do. You can't play music, nor sing, nor paint, nor dance; you can do nothing. You get no pleasure out of life. . . ." (247). It is not so much the promise of affluence, nor the lure of specific goods that Harry and Angela hold out for the lower classes, because they insist that the best things in life are free, like music and art and the enjoyment of beauty. Rather they—and by implication Besant and the likeminded settlement house missionaries—are attempting to reform the lower class individual, giving him and her expanded possibilities for fulfillment, giving them desires—"know what you want. And this is what you want . . ." The hegemonizing operation is going at full tilt, instilling into a new segment of society less the work ethos (although their higher aspirations will presumably convince them of the value of better work) than the value of proper consumerist desires.[17]

More than the elision of production is occurring here, however, for Besant is marking a broader shift in England from a production-oriented society to a consumer-oriented one. Lawrence Birkin, in *Consuming Desire*, a study of the relation of this shift to the development of sexology, points out that the driving forces of England's economy were being transformed, from the 1870s on, from production as the measure of value to consumption. Such a change was being openly theorized by marginalist or neo-classical economists who contended that "value was neither the objective result of social labor nor of social need for products, but was simply attached to objects by the subjective desire of consumers" (Birkin 32). The changeover was manifested in a variety of ways: through a spectacular increase in advertising in both England and the United States, the growth of brand names, the advent of department stores and specialty shops and the notion of "shopping," the markedly increased circulation of currency (especially among women), and the exploitation of a significant expansion of leisure time and leisure values.[18] A consumer driven economy, Birkin argues, shifts the locus of influence from the engines of production onto the desires of the buyer.

This, in turn, makes the construction of desire a more critical factor in the management of the economy, and one can see Besant, the settlement workers, and the social work establishment unconsciously shaping that desire at the lower ends of the social scale through their interpellation of a subjectivity that seeks to emulate upper bourgeois tastes, that is "discontented" in Angela Messenger's words, and yet materially based in family and home. The panoply of operations that we have designated as the "social" prove particularly influential in the latter case, as they strengthen the ideas of home and its material values. In addition, the ethicizing functions of the "social" attempt to control the lower orders in a particularly insidious way, for the working classes and the poor are told to mute their desires through ethical constraints; they are invited to find substitutions for frustrated aspirations toward political and social power—and, need we say, revolution—in the consolations of the consumer products of ordinary material living. The channels for "improvement" are education and orderliness, which will inscribe in them the hegemonic values of the middle class, or products, those surrogates for social values. The "social" thus works hand in hand with the burgeoning consumer state, both of them constructing the carefully limited and unthreatening lower class subject that we see emerging from the settlement house, social worker, and Besantian schemes.

Jean Baudrillard has argued that consumerism in modern capitalist societies operates as a system of signs that assures middle class domination. Consumption inaugurates a process of discrimination, with products as both the means to discriminate between class strata and to compensate for social class differences. Once an individual is caught up in the sign system, he or she succumbs to its values, which always legitimize the class at the height of power. The aspirations are thus converted into terms of legitimation. As the English middle class begins in the last decades of the century to feel more comfortable about itself—to shed or repress many of those anxieties we observed in the 1840s and 1850s—it establishes legitimacy through its own material insignia (the appurtenances of comfortable living and disposable income), and almost mockingly invites the lower classes to strive for the same. And one of its most effective tools is culture, which by putting an arbitrary value on art, certain leisure activities, and education, those spheres primarily under the control of the upper middle class, introduces the worker into a system of desire that cannot be grounded in usefulness or even exchange value.[19]

The definition of culture as "high culture," that is, the cultivation of the arts, the study of perfection, the devotion to the best thoughts and models of action that Matthew Arnold articulated in *Culture and Anarchy* (1868), entered the idiom, as Raymond Williams has noted, in the 1860s and 1870s (Williams 80). It informs, clearly, the settlement house movement and Besant's novel, and it is a particularly useful formulation for controlling the lower classes. Among other things, it incorporates the ethical idealism that one sees in the Oxbridge young men who entered the settlement houses and that grounds Arnold's thought, and it also lends itself to the development of certain patterns of behavior—life styles, if you will—that emblematize the highest reaches of consumerism. High culture drew the domains of the middle class and the aristocracy closer by exalting an appreciation for the finer things that ranged from the arts through disinterested public responsibility through gracious living among fine houses, sumptuous decor, elegant dress. The material appurtenances of a cultivated existence were not often differentiated in kind from the more properly aesthetic.

In addition, culture both dehistoricizes and historicizes.[20] These antithetical properties are very much in evidence in the role of culture in *All Sorts and Conditions of Men*. For not only does Angela conceive and put into place a dressmaking operation that civilizes her young ladies, but she and Harry dream up and erect a Palace of Delights, to be built in the East End slums. Funded through Angela's largesse, it emerges as an opulent, tapestry-hung, marbled palace, in which, as Harry announces to the gaping crowd, "Here you will have music, dancing, singing, acting, painting, reading, games of skill, games of chance, companionship, cheerfulness, light, warmth, comfort— everything. When these things have been enjoyed for a time they will become a necessity for you, and a part of the education for your young people" (411). But more wonderful still is the fact that Besant's book inspired an actual Palace of Delight, built by Sir Edmund Currie in 1887 and eventually called the People's Palace. Besant describes it in his autobiography:

> It was built and furnished with a noble hall, a swimming bath, a splendid organ, a complete gymnasium, one of the finest library buildings in London, a winter garden, art schools, and a lecture room. Unfortunately a polytechnic was tacked on to it; the original idea of a place of recreation was mixed up with a place of education . . . We started with all the things mentioned above, and with billiard-rooms, with a girls' social side, with a debating society, with clubs for all kinds of things—cricket, football, rambles, and the like; we had delightful balls in the great hall, we had concerts and organ recitals, the girls gave dances in their social rooms; there was a literary society . . . nothing could have been better than our start. (244)

Culture, as conceived for the working class, is as many parts recreation as it is art. In the last decades of the nineteenth century, concerted attempts were made to "rationalize" the leisure activities of the lower classes, to head off rowdiness and worse by disciplining play just as work was disciplined.[21] Acculturation of the working class, in the schemes of someone like Besant, was thus a program of mixed high culture and popular culture activities; it concocted something that could be tolerated in the lower orders as a "working class culture," which incorporated what was recuperable of the old amusements of the lower classes, and added onto them attractions, or distractions, that would draw the worker into the consumption patterns and ideals of their superiors. As part recreation, this culture would keep the working class in an ideologically passive, readily amused, and presumably orderly state.

Unfortunately the People's Palace did not live up to expectations— or maybe it did. The men, Besant complains, started betting on the billiard games, the literary club proved a failure, and the polytechnic detracted from the pleasurable aspects of the venture. Ultimately, the Draper's Company took over the day-to-day management of the Palace and neglected the library, closed the winter gardens, and stopped the baths. But no matter; the Palace was symbolic anyway: symbolic of the notion that class difference could be erased by culture, which, because in its now recreational aspects it addresses universal ideals of beauty, the highest forms and the highest ideals, rationality, a "best self," and a secularized spirituality that transcends narrow creeds, exists outside of historical conflict. The earnest denizens of Whitechapel could leave all class envy and class spite behind them, as they entered a cultural continuum from the lowest to the highest in England.

But the antithesis holds as well: for the very notion of a continuum suggests a process by which the lower classes can become acculturated. The People's Palace, and the settlement house cultivations, begin the rough working man or woman on his or her ascent toward a higher, finer community. It was understood as a tonic reality that East Enders could not be changed overnight, nor should they aspire to that. It might, in fact, be a matter of generations. For it was through an historical process that they had been stunted in their development, and it would be through an historical process that they would be changed.

The passiveness and enervation of the urban poor in many of the renditions we have of them, the landscapes of deadness, and the mood of defeatism and despair in the accounts, contribute to the impression that this is a natural phenomenon that we are witnessing. Indeed, the arguments for a degenerated urban dweller, atavistic, several stages below the fully developed Englishman, reinforce the naturalization of their condition. We are beyond the passionate awareness of Dickens that something the upper and middle classes have done or neglected to do has created this abysmal mess. For all the "sense of sin" that activates the 1880s, the general view is that urban decay has become a nearly intractable problem because generations of people have grown up, and adapted, in a Darwinian fashion, to its deadened life. The reformation will be a process of changing nature.

Changing nature through culture. Here, too, we sense that we are at something of a conceptual watershed, for implicit in this "nature"/culture opposition lies the conviction that the individual subject can be constructed (or reconstructed) culturally. Daniel Cottam's excellent analysis of the cultural assumptions governing George Eliot's fiction delineates the many ways in which cultural construction undergirded her theories of characterization and social interaction—the foremost and most powerful being education. For, as Cottam notes, the assumption behind educational reform is that one has not reached his full human potential—has not become a full subject—unless he or she educates himself or herself.[22] In many of the horrific accounts of melodramatic degeneration among the poor, we witness the reverse movement: the disintegration of the individual as a result of life of failure and meanness. In Margaret Harkness's second novel, *Out of Work* (1888), the narrator describes such a case:

> The man had a very barren mental history. He was one of the many people crushed out by our present competitive system. He might have been a statesman or a judge if he had been born in more favorable surroundings. . . . His crude, narrow ideas were fast crystallizing. Years had slipped by while he painfully and slowly gathered crumbs of knowledge. His brain was losing its power of gathering from fresh sources, beginning to exercise itself upon the small stores of knowledge stowed away in its cells. Personal experiences had made him bitter. He had only seen one side of life, and he did not believe in what people call 'happiness'; unless, perhaps the rich enjoyed it. (*OW* 59)

Even "pleasure" in this account is viewed as a construction. This may account for the conflation of pleasure and cultivation in the program of the People's Palace. Billiards and concert-going comprise parts of the same constructive intervention. The curative course, in any event, lies within the realm of broad cultural interpellation; it is no longer principally a task of improving the economic conditions of production, or even of reforming or moderating competition, as it had been in Dickens' time.

The final antithesis in culture is that of materialization and dematerialization. The latter has been, of course, asserted most strenuously, for Matthew Arnold's call upon his countrymen and women to rise above "doing as one's ordinary self likes"—field-sports and pleasure activities among the Barbarians or upper class; business, money-making, and indulgence in comfort among the Philistines or middle class; and beer-drinking among the Populace or lower class—beckons them to the qualities of a non-material existence. Catherine Gallagher has brilliantly argued that the Arnoldian discourse of high culture elevates itself above material representation, to a plane on which it constitutes its own determining reality, without attaching itself to a realm of spiritual value, without becoming symbolic.[23] On the other hand, the spatialization that dominates culture's representations at least at the level of the urban conditions should warn us that the terms on which it will be formulated (and here, again, it works hand in hand with the rise of consumerism) are material terms. The nexus between the expansion of the consumer society and the high culture movement confirms the relation.

Yet the imagination of the middle class in the 1880s, as we saw in Webb, Harkness, William Booth, and Besant, depicts a world of emptiness and enervation. This is the East End from which certain strata of the lower working classes can be recuperated through Besant's and the settlement house schemes of cultural uplift. It is vital that these salvageable workers be redeemed, for they must be plucked out of the dangers of contamination from those below them—those who would degrade them into violence and radicalism. The rest, the residuum, classes A ("the lowest class of occasional labourers, loafers, and semi-criminals") and probably B ("Casual earnings—very poor") in Charles Booth's classification, are consigned to desolation.[24] They are outside any possible cultural continuum, and they are essentially outside of the power of materialist ethics to refashion their appetites and self-images. The urban poor, or at least a segment of it, has now been exiled from the social strategies of the middle class, but not, as we shall see in the next two chapters, from the middle class imagination or its nightmares.

Finally, implicit in these writers' construction of a landscape of deadened aspirations complexly connected to their own failures of aspiration, we see operating a newly gendered East End, implicitly configured as passive but receptive. It is one that associates the East End with the failure to differentiate itself, the failure to emerge from its undifferentiated state of deadened aspiration. A more active East End, however, was also the subject of attention from writers at the end of the century, an East End characterized by the virulence of criminal violence or threats to the integrity of the journalistic subject, as we shall see in the next two chapters.

- CHAPTER 3 -

Morrison, Gissing, and the Stark Reality

Morrison's Vital Misogyny

*I*n the early 1890s a stark vision of life in the East End emerges from the pens of two writers with a close acquaintance with life there: Arthur Morrison and George Gissing. Morrison was born in Poplar in 1863, the son of an engine fitter who worked on the docks. His father died of consumption when Arthur was a boy, and his mother raised the three children by running a haberdasher's shop in Grundy Street. Arthur himself took a job early as office boy in the architect's department of the School Board of London at a weekly salary of seven shillings, and moved up to junior and then "third class" clerk in 1886, when he left to become secretary of the Beaumont Trust, which administered Besant's People's Palace. There he started a Dickensian kind of journalistic ascent, publishing pieces on the East End in the *Palace Journal*, honing his journalistic skills at the evening *Globe*, and finally attracting attention, like Boz, with the publication in *Macmillan's Magazine* (October 1891) of his sketch of "A Street in the East End."[1]

Morrison underwent, as his brief biography might suggest, an *embourgeoisement* that takes him beyond his East End roots, and the dialogue that his writings create is with a middle class reading audience. But he saw himself as an authentic voice of the urban slum experience, and his early works provide such a strikingly different version of the East End that they immediately created a small critical sensation. They are unlike the representations of the poor that had dominated the literature for half a century; Morrison rejects the sentimental and the melodramatic for a laconic, unmodulated prose that rarely rises to a dramatic climax. He portrays a world of gratuitous violence and enervating degradation which offers up no meaning to the middle class reader; it cannot be integrated into the systems of value, psychology, or material relations of the middle class. Morrison's world seems to be of a different order altogether.

The bourgeois feminine sensibility, which we had seen to be the site of affective connection between the middle class and the urban underclass, through the discourse of sentimentality and abjection, no longer provides a focal point around which to construct even the effect of subjectivity. In "Lizerunt," the most famous story in Morrison's first book, *Tales of Mean Streets* (1894), the protagonist, Elizabeth Hunt, differs significantly from the pure and "unexpressive" young women who became the channels for middle class ethical projection. As the corruption of her name to "Lizerunt" signifies, she has scarcely any chance to assert her own integrity and separate identity. Her time as a saucy young flirt, playing the boys off against each other, proves short; she attaches herself to Billy Chope in spite of his viciousness, and descends quickly into a life of steadily increasing degradation, in which she becomes coarsened. Morrison graphically renders the relationships of East End existence that are missing from the earlier journalistic and sociological accounts. They are not uplifting.

> ... Billy, rising at ten with a bad mouth, resolved to stand no nonsense, and demanded two shillings.
>
> "Two bob? Wot for?" Lizer asked.
>
> "Cos I want it. None o' yer lip."
>
> "Ain't got it," said Lizer sulkily.
>
> "That's a bleed'n' lie."
>
> "Lie yerself."
>
> "I'll break y'in 'arves, ye blasted 'eifer!" He ran at her throat and forced her back over a chair. "I'll pull yer face auf! If y' don't give me the money, gawblimy, I'll do for you!"
>
> Lizer strained and squalled. "Le' go! You'll kill me an' the kid too!" she grunted hoarsely. Billy's mother ran in and threw her arms about him, dragging him away. "Don't Billy," she said, in terror. "Don't Billy; not now! You'll get in trouble. Come away! She might go auf, an' you'd get in trouble!"
>
> Billy Chope flung his wife over and turned to his mother. "Take yer 'ands auf me," he said: "go on, or I'll gi' ye somethin' for yerself." And he punched her in the breast by way of illustration. (*Mean Streets* 37–38)

Billy later tries to abuse Lizer within hours after she has given birth to their unwanted baby, and he has to be thrown out of the house by the attending medical student, who is then roundly attacked by both Lizer and Billy's mother for interfering. The medical student is an outsider who clearly does not understand the code of East End life, which follows its own brutal logic. When Billy's mother dies from overwork, too poor for a decent burial because he has stolen all her savings, Lizer then feels the full brunt of his meanness. And the story ends with his forcing her into prostitution:

> It was more than Billy could bear: so that, "'Ere," he said one night, "I've 'ad enough o' this. You go and get some money; go on."
> "Go an' git it?" replied Lizer. "O yus. That's easy, ain't it? 'Go an' git it,' says you. 'Ow?"
> "Any'ow—I don't care. Go on."
> "Wy," replied Lizer, looking up with wide eyes, "d'ye think I can go an' pick it up in the street?"
> "Course you can. Plenty others does, don't they?"
> "Gawd, Billy . . . wot d'ye mean?"
> "Wot I say; plenty others does it. Go on—you ain't so bleed'n' innocent as all that. Go an' see Sam Cardew. Go on—'ook it."
> . . . He pushed her into the passage. "Go on—you git me some money, if ye don't want yer bleed'n' 'ead knocked auf."
> There was a scuffle in the dark passage, with certain blows, a few broken words, and a sob. Then, the door slammed and Lizer Chope was in the windy street. (47)

"Lizerunt" follows Rudyard Kipling's remarkable story, "The Record of Badalia Herodsfoot," in detailing the "creed and law" that governs slum life. Badalia is recruited into service by the local curate to help distribute alms because she is streetwise enough to spot a fraudulent claim, and because she is not above smashing the face of any woman who tries to steal food or money meant for those in need. The story tells of her struggle between maintaining the trust that has been placed in her, and her adherence to the slum code of womanhood that says she will be faithful to her drunken husband to the end. The struggle proves fatal; her husband beats her mercilessly in an attempt to get the alms-money out of her. Yet even on her deathbed she refuses to accuse him—thus keeping both "trusts."

Morrison and Kipling sketch out an East End that is more complexly—and fatalistically—coded than that of earlier accounts. It is no longer a land of shadows cast by the projections of middle class subjectivity, no longer a terra incognita to be read in line with the dominant class anxieties and desires. It constitutes its own social order: a subsystem of gender relations that exert a power within their own domain that cannot be interpolated into bourgeois categories of self-agency. The slums of Morrison and Kipling acquire a density of customs and personal patterns that had rarely been observed in earlier accounts, as if, in Morrison's case especially, there were an effort to say that the East End is not simply an object of upper class anxiety or domination, but an entity in and of itself. At the same time that he suggests this, Morrison also insists upon the enclosed, immobilizing fatality of that world; its immersion in violence, its deadened submission to poverty, its constricting social containment. The vicious circularity of the poor is symptomized by the frequent set pieces of Amazonian brawls between women, such as this one from a later Morrison work:

> Down the middle of Old Jago Street came Sally Green: red-faced, stripped to the waist, dancing, hoarse and triumphant. Nail-scores wide as the finger striped her back, her face, and her throat, and she had a black eye; but in one great hand she dangled a long bunch of clotted hair, as she whooped defiance to the Jago. It was a trophy newly rent from the scalp of Norah Walsh, champion of the Rann womenkind, who had crawled away to hide her blighted head, and be restored with gin. (*Jago* 64)

For all the efforts of social services to confirm the woman as the ethical center of lower class life, she turns out, in many of these stories, to be as uncontrollable as the men, at her worst, or too passive to resist her own victimization, at her best. Morrison always insisted that the code of respectability was strong among the lower orders, yet his writings often show it to be a fragile creed. In the haunting tale in *Mean Streets* entitled "Behind the Shade," a woman and her daughter try to maintain a respectable life in the East End slums, keeping a neat, private little house, symbolically set off from its neighbors by the well-dusted shade of fruit in the front window. "They are known at once for well-to-do, and are regarded with the admixture of spite and respect that is proper to the circumstances. They are also watched" (75). The two women offer piano lessons, but no one signs on, and gradually, ineluctably, they sink down the social scale, taking in cheap shirts for sewing, then sneaking out in the dark of night to pawn their belongings, spied on and resented all the while by the vengeful neighborhood.

Finally, they are not seen to emerge from the neat little house at all, and dust begins to accumulate on the shade of fruit. When the landlord comes to collect the rent he finds that "in the front room with the striped blind and the short curtain there was a bed of rags and old newspapers; also a wooden box, and on each of these was a dead woman. Both deaths, the doctor found, were from syncope, the result of inanition; and the better-nourished woman—she on the bed—had died the sooner; perhaps by a day or two. The other case was rather curious; it exhibited a degree of shrinkage in the digestive organs unprecedented in his experience" (81–82).

In a state of economic stagnation and social isolation such as Morrison's East End there is no larger economic and social context in which to project their aspirations or into which they can integrate their activities. All the economic forms available to them, such as rent gouging, fencing of stolen goods, counterfeiting of coin, and prostitution, are unproductive, and almost parodic of generative commercial and capitalistic activity. They are, in fact, in only a tangential and marginal relationship to the dominant economy of the city, serving to keep slum dwellers out of any paths for economic or social improvement, caught instead in the circularity of exploitation of themselves and others. Counterfeiting, one of the most lucrative of slum activities during this period, is symbolic of the incapacity of the lower orders to introduce themselves into the real, larger market and labor economy; they can only create false coin. Hence the urban poor do not have any referentiality with respect to the middle and upper classes. It is interesting to compare Morrison's accounts of life in the East End in the 1880s and 1890s (and, as we shall see, the similar account by another denizen of the worst of these slums, Arthur Harding) with Robert Roberts' recollections of life in the Manchester slum of Salford in the twentieth century, recounted in *The Classic Slum*. Roberts, who grew up in poverty, depicts the subculture as one with certain petit bourgeois characteristics, particularly a closely bonded home life—a kind of lower class privatization—that integrates their experience into middle class norms in ways that are absent in *Mean Streets*. Richard Hoggart's portrayal of twentieth century lower class life in *The Uses of Literacy* also reflects a substantially greater involvement in the material preoccupations of the upper classes, almost a kind of measuring of slum life by the standards of middle class life, in a well-defined "us" and "them" mentality.

The conditions of Morrison's East End not only diminish the capacity of women to act as ethical forces in family and neighborhood; the economic isolation of the slums also eliminates the woman as a figure of commodity desire. Ironically, the objectifying in the upper classes of women into fetishes of style, beauty, even spiritual worth, transposes them into symbols of social and economic status and advancement. Clearly this is a form of dehumanization, but it has the effect of masking or finessing whatever subjection of the women that is occurring. In a subsociety, such as Morrison's urban slums, in which women cannot be conceived as icons of aesthetic or ethical value because there is no role for such values in the social order—no possibilities for women to be the means of financial or social improvement, no function for them to fulfill as the conservers of money and ideals—their status will be severely reduced. They lack especially the openness to emotional experience which grounds their relative moral superiority to males, according to the complementary gender codes constructed for the middle class household (Tosh 44).

Correspondingly, the diminishment of women refigures the literary form, for the heroine as the register of morality, and as the focal point at which aesthetic and social ideals were brought together, had been essential to the mainstream English novel itself. The great experiment in the naturalist novel of the lower classes—Emile Zola's *L'Assomoir*, Edmond and Jules de Goncourt's *Germinie Lacerteux,* and George Moore's *Esther Waters*—had been to dramatize the moral and emotional issues of poverty and struggle through women whose victimization, and in some cases, personal weaknesses, stripped them of much of the auratic power of the conventional heroine. Moore, in particular, compensated by sentimentalizing his heroine, and it is telling that the prominent English example relies on the bourgeois ethos of feeling to sustain a measure of attraction to his protagonist. Morrison will have none of that, and, as a consequence, his writing in *Mean Streets* has different rhetorical rhythms; it resembles in many respects the uninflected, neutral style of Margaret Harkness' *A City Girl*.[2]

The circumstances of life in the slums affect the possibilities for writing a traditional masculine text as well. The wave of optimism that prevailed at the beginning of the Victorian period, and which allowed the writers of Mayhew's generation to balance all their misgivings about the rapaciousness of the new competitive order and the loss of scope for mythicized action in men's lives against the excitement of change and social mobility (some of it based directly on those new competitive possibilities), has disappeared from the scene of lower class London. The dynamism that converts the somewhat puerile fantasy of masculine adventure and power into a vibrant, if often bizarre, scene of small entrepreneurialism and vivid sensory impressions, is gone. In its place is misogyny. The lower classes had always been depicted as misogynist, and we are quite aware how poverty leads to abuse and the self-hatred that goes with it, but the East End of Morrison's and Kipling's streets is the logical deterioration of the propensities of the illusory, gender-fixed compensations of the 1840s and 1850s representations of an alternative underworld. The failure—or perhaps the word is reluctance—of the male imagination to bring into play any ethicizing spirit to its imaginative penetrations of the urban depths leaves its later versions bereft, Morrison shows us, of means to reconceive the relationships of the poor. The misogynist social texts that we get of the slums thus also undermine any attempt to construct a generative male subjectivity. Morrison's male protagonists are to a man unfulfilled, fated to frustration. Economic and social conditions force this upon them, but the inchoate natures of all the characters indicate that a full, mutually interdependent code of subject construction is absent.

A system such as that of the middle class, in which a female ethical subject balances and validates the agency that is granted to the male, is missing in the nether world. This is, after all, the primary reason that the myth of a realm of primarily male adventure and "freedom" cannot be represented except in the hermetic form of the boys' adventure story, in which the protagonist never has to come of age. There is something of the same limitation in Morrison's novels about the slums, all of which focus on boyhood and young adolescence. It is only natural, in a way, that Morrison should turn to some form of the *Bildungsroman* for his accounts of life in the East End, since the likely course that the slum culture would take would be to imitate the middle class in its effort to establish for itself a masculine-based, if not patriarchal, order. The *Bildungsroman* is the form that epitomizes that effort, and we can surmise that Arthur Morrison had in mind, as a kind of model, the century's best known book about poverty, Dickens' *Oliver Twist*. Morrison's most famous and most compelling book on East End life, *The Child of the Jago* (1896), and his later novels touching on the urban slums, *To London Town* (1899) and *The Hole in the Wall* (1902), focus, therefore, on the issue of the formation of the male in the slums: the classic patriarchal story. Tellingly enough, the protagonist in each of these novels is a boy, as if to indicate that mature or "full" subjectivity is either never attained or difficult to imagine in lower urban existence. Morrison selected as his setting for *A Child of the Jago* one of the most anarchic and violent quarters of the East End, the Old Nichol area in Bethnal Green, a nest of streets just to the East of what is now

Shoreditch High Street (about ten blocks north of Liverpool Station). The Old Nichol (which Morrison calls "The Jago") was known as the warren of some of the most impoverished and depraved wretches in London, a pocket of narrow streets and courts that was on the verge of being demolished by the London County Council in the 1890s. Morrison spent 18 months there, gathering impressions under the tutelage of the Reverend Arthur Osborne Jay, a well regarded and intrepid slum minister. In a later interview with *The Daily News*, Morrison contended that the "majority of the Jago people are semi-criminal, and an ordinary respectable working man would quickly be hounded out . . ." ("The Children" 6).

Morrison's Jago denizens eke out an existence in robbery, burglary, picking pockets, or "coshing" unwary strangers (a "cosh" is an iron bar); the women survive by making match boxes or through other marginal activities. The men and women entertain themselves with massive and bloody brawls between rival gangs, and *A Child of the Jago* has several unforgettable accounts of the pitched battles between the Ranns and the Learys, which rage back and forth throughout the novel, including one titanic boxing match involving the protagonist's father, Josh Perrott. There is no quarter given to delicate Victorian sensibilities in *Jago* and the popularity of the novel was only matched by the critical outrage over its alleged grossness. Yet the violence is so spectacular, and so emblematic of the ferocity that comes out of lives of depravity and idleness, that the pathology becomes symbolic. The opening chapter establishes an atmosphere in which the specific details—of the restlessness in the Jago on a typical night, as a victim is coshed and robbed—are transposed into a symbolic setting: "Old Jago Street lay black and close under the quivering red sky: and slinking forms, as of great rats, followed one another quickly between the posts in the gut by the High Street, and scattered over the Jago" (45). Even the violated human body auratically conveys a social pathology:

> Out in the Jago the pale dawn brought a cooler air and the chance of sleep. From the paving of Old Jago Street sad grey faces, open-mouthed, looked upward as from the Valley of Dry Bones. Down by Jago Row the coshed subject, with the blood dry on his face, felt the colder air, and moved a leg. (52)

The ostensible protagonist of the story is the Child of the Jago, Dickie Perrott, who roams its streets, participating in its random violence, its crime, and its occasional play. He is a lad of strong familial instincts, attached to his younger sister, but he shares some of the community's meanness, especially toward a crippled boy, Bobby Roper, who becomes Dickie's nemesis and stands for the perverse crippling of Dickie's own conscience. Under the influence of Father Sturt (modeled after Arthur Osborne Jay), Dickie makes one effort to go straight and work his way out of the Jago, but it is condemned to failure. Indeed, any effort to get out of the Jago, by virtuous work or by crime, is doomed, and the "moral" of the story is intoned by "old Beveridge, regarded . . . as a trifle 'balmy,' though anything but a fool," who points to a gathering of the super-criminals, the High Mobsmen, and tells Dickie,

> "Now, Dickie Perrott, you Jago whelp, look at them—look hard. Some day, if you're clever—cleverer than anyone in the Jago now—if you're only scoundrel enough, and brazen enough, and lucky enough—one of a thousand—maybe you'll be like them: bursting with high living, drunk when you like, red and pimply. There it is—that's your aim in life—there's your pattern. Learn to read and write, learn all you can, learn cunning, spare nobody and stop at nothing, and perhaps—It's the best the world has for you, for the Jago's got you, and that's the only way out, except gaol and the gallows. So do your devilmost, or God help you, Dicky Perrott, though He won't: for the Jago's got you!" (95–96)

If the only way out of the Jago is to emulate the High Mobsmen, it is a route through a parodic Jago-vision of the "better world" of money and power. "Those of the High Mob were the flourishing practitioners of burglary, the mag, the mace, and the broads, with an outer fringe of such dippers—such pickpockets—as could dress well, welshers, and snidesmen. These, the grandees of rascality, lived in places far from the Jago, and some drove in gigs and pony traps" (95). The Mobsmen and their circle mimic and exaggerate upper class clothing and upper class airs—those with their gigs and pony traps—and parade before their inferiors a bizarre parody of privilege and grand manners. Their affectations transmit the felt presence of upper class power—they play out a crude image of another realm of life—but they have the upper class codes all wrong. Such mimicry attests to the force of upper class cultural expression, but it does not connect with it, surely, in the ways that Besant and his fellow "improvers" had in mind. For its exaggeration spectacularizes the styles and practices of the dominant social order. In the twentieth century such mimicry will, in the hands of some lower class groups, provide an oblique means of resistance, for it will denature the higher culture and continuously pull it down into the realms of popular culture, which is itself spectacularized and often split free from any authentic social and psychic context. In Morrison's Jago, however, mimicry only confirms the inaccessibility of the upper class life. The best the poor can do is parrot it (hence the name Perrott) without comprehending it. The life of the classes above cannot be imaginatively grasped in its reality; emulation of it in such terms only produces a travesty.

Here, once again, the absence of a vital counterdiscourse through which to contextualize the urban slum dweller's sensibility is telling. Jean-Paul Sartre describes the process by which the middle class in France initially used reflection and then mimicry to set themselves literarily apart from the upper classes. Bourgeois figures attached to the Court and the nobility in the seventeenth century began with a body of literature, Sartre says, that served essentially as a flattering mirror for their patrons in the aristocracy. Seeing themselves rendered positively, however, compelled the upper class to stand "outside" themselves, and even the bourgeois "writer, though completely assimilated by the oppressing class, is by no means its accomplice; his work is unquestionably a liberator since its effect, within this class, is to free man from himself" (Sartre 91). Middle class court writing evolved over the course of the next century from a reflective and complimentary art to a form of mimicry and then of satire, developing into a powerful tool for the assertion of bourgeois consciousness and its resistance to aristocratic forms. That evolution took place, however, in the broader context of developing middle class moralism, and of the complex social discourse that we call the formation of the middle class, with its own values, social and economic relations, and philosophy. Mimicry served as a means of appropriating the manners and exercises of power into bourgeois discourse, and it opened up a literary space within which a subordinate class could insinuate its critiques and could assert its differences.

Morrison is uncompromising in rejecting these possibilities for the urban poor. The "mind" of the East Ender, Morrison wrote in *Mean Streets,* "is unfavourable to the ideal" (28). Its capacity for imaginative projection is distorted by its paranoia toward the upper classes and by the restricted mentality of slum existence. Father Sturt, as a man from that outer world, is regarded as something of a "toff," and thus as a man of awesome power. He embodies the force of the hostile upper class social order. "[I]t was the way of the Jago that its mean cunning saw a mystery and a terror where simple intelligence saw there was none" (83). Swept up in the centrifugal vortex of its ignorance and self-violence, the Jago denizen cannot conceive of the alternative world in a way that would allow him or her discursive access to it. It is as if the two spheres—the urban slums and the social world above it—are sealed off from each other, psychologically, socially, and economically.

Nor has the Jago male the experiential dimension to allow him to transcend the limitations of his own existence in the world of Morrison. Josh Perrott, desperate to make a "click"—a good robbery—takes a train out to the northern suburbs in order to find choicer prospects. It is a hapless adventure, for Josh cannot "read" this alien territory; it is uninterpretable. Tired and footsore from tramping about strange neighborhoods, he breaks into a suburban house, slugs the old man who lives there and steals a watch. The heavy hand of irony slams down upon him, for his victim is the highest of the Mob, a man who has clothed himself in respectability but actually finances much of London crime. The word goes out to every dealer in the City to be on the lookout for the stolen watch, and Josh is nabbed the minute he tries to fence it. The poor fellow could not even spot an arch-criminal among the suburban fauna; he is totally unable to interpret the society that lies outside his own narrow realm. Again and again we witness the inability of the slum dweller to understand the outside world, and this deprives him of the knowing quality, and of the capacity for irony, that would turn his mimicry of that other world into something other than parody.

Josh himself can be seen as a projection of Dickie; he is the grown Child of the Jago, a living illustration of the futile impotence of masculinity within the nether world. After serving time for the theft of the watch, Josh takes vengeance on the man who betrayed him, the conniving Jago fence for stolen goods, Aaron Weech. Josh slits Weech's throat and takes almost no care to do it quietly, so he is cornered by police and vengeful citizens, chased through the maze of back alleys and darkened streets, and hunted down at last in an excavation where part of the Jago is being torn down for Council buildings. His hallucinatory efforts to find his way in the confusion of the Jago landscape, being hemmed in on all sides by pursuers, is further emblematic of the inability to "escape" the Jago, as the text dissolves into nightmare in order to communicate that the entrapment is psychological as much as physical. There is no way to get out of the Jago, as the crazy Beveridge warned, except through death, and Dickie Perrott falls soon afterward by flinging himself suicidally into a gang fight where he is stabbed from behind by his alter-ego, the hunchback Bobby Roper. The symbolic image of the inward torque of the Jago—and by extension the vast realm of the urban underworld—is manifest.

In addition, the nether world is spun around—tempted and betrayed by the regressive economic forms of the consumer economy. Josh Perrott is tried and sentenced to death by hanging for the murder of Aaron Weech, but his last days are all mental confusion for him, during which he finds himself curiously detached from his circumstances. As he sits in the courtroom at his trial,

> The judge stopped a witness to speak of a draught from a window. Josh Perrott watched the shutting of the window—they did it with a cord. He had not noticed a draught himself. But pigeons were flying outside the panes and resting on the chimney-stacks. Pud Palmer tried to keep pigeons in Jago Row, but one morning the trap was found empty. A poulterer gave fourpence each for them. They were ticketed at eighteenpence a pair in the shop, and that was fivepence profit apiece for the poulterer. Ten-pence a pair profit on eleven pairs was nearly ten shillings—ten shillings all but tenpence. They wouldn't have given any more in Club Row. A man had a four-legged linnet in Club Row, but there was a show in Bethnal Green Road with a two-headed sheep. It was outside there that Ginger Stagg was pinched for lob-crawling. And so on, and so on, till his head buzzed again. (194–95)

Josh's head buzzes with the financial complexities of the pricing of stolen birds: the profit of the fence who resells the pigeons for a vastly greater sum, the implicit swindling of the thief who takes all the risks, and so on, and so on. For the economic order of the Jago revolves among the trapping of an animal (a bird, whose connection with Perrott is of course clear), the theft of it, the fencing of it, the reselling of it at an exorbitant mark-up. There is no production in this system; it is a round of exploitation. Nothing is created or enhanced in such an economic order, for fencing and pawning, the chief resources of the lowest margins of humanity, involve a kind of complicity in the exploitation of one's self, the paying out of one's economic entrails. The apparently illogical association of the story of the pigeons with the displaying of two freaks, a four-legged linnet and a two-headed sheep, in the "upper class" Club Row connects the economically abasing order of slum existence to its parodic conception of the outside world. The relation of the Jago to the dominant order is that of a freak show.

As can be seen, a world such as that of the Jago can only be represented symbolically. It cannot be accommodated to the middle class program of representation of the urban slums because it presents us with a subsociety that is almost totally alienated from the mores that underlie that representation. Morrison's Jago is not a part of the cultural continuum proposed by middle class observers such as Besant and the settlement movement reformers; the denizens of the East End are almost to an individual cut off from the possibilities of the transformation of one's status that is central to the ideal of acculturation. Similarly, they do not share the ethicizing ethos that informs English middle class practice, for that ethical conviction is directly related to the possibilities of economic security and advancement—possibilities largely denied the poor. Bourgeois ethics presume the potential for self-improvement, and they are calibrated in Victorian society to the exercise of power, both as the mediating element determining the appropriate (and just) exercise of power, and as the hegemonic discourse that instructs those who are powerless in ways that make them orderly and content with their lot. When, as is the case with the Jago, the economic order produces no transformative (and potentially ameliorating) effects, when it exists only in a self-reflexive, regressively parodic version of itself, then the impulse to ethicize one's relation to it is minimal. The Jago, then, proves intractable to the programs of upper class "reform."

A social formation so detached from the prevalent order can, however, be conceived symbolically. This was, as it turned out, the very thing that Morrison's middle class reviewers refused to allow him to do. The minute they read the disquieting book, they called it a "realistic" novel. And by "realism" they meant the English literary establishment's conception of "naturalism," a literature that dealt with lower social orders, with distasteful and debasing material, and that was characterized by graphic detail, violence, and physicality.[3] Emile Zola's philosophy of naturalism, after all, had been predicated upon the inscription of the lower classes into the prevalent economic order, even if the working classes and the marginal poor were to fail to succeed in that order. "Man is not alone; he lives in society, in a social condition," Zola insists in his seminal essay, "The Experimental Novel." "And this is what constitutes the experimental [naturalist] novel: . . . finally to exhibit man living in social conditions produced by himself, which he modifies daily, and in the heart of which he himself experiences a continual transformation." The Rougon Macquart series depicted lower class individuals in a wide range of factory and lower commercial work of the modern industrial society, and was designed to interpret "scientifically" the relationship of the lower spheres to the upper. In his conviction that "in this way we shall construct a practical sociology, and our work will be a help to political and economical sciences," Zola clearly facilitates the appropriation (and thus the hegemonizing) of the lower classes by the middle class. He gives the novel a "use value," as it were. "The social circulus is identical with the vital circulus; in society, as in human beings, a solidarity exists which unites the different members and the different organisms in such a way that if one organ becomes rotten many others are tainted and a very complicated disease results" (Zola 12, 15, 16). Arthur Morrison may share that aspiration to some extent in unfolding the traumatized condition of the worst urban slums, but he confronts his audience with a society that cannot be readily appropriated within the conventional ethical schemes; the voice of the slums is disturbingly alienated; its economy cut off from the larger economy; its denizens geographically isolated.

The late nineteenth century English debate over realism and naturalism, then, involves much more than literary taste and style: it embodies the effort by the cultural establishment to assure that all depiction and expression of lower class life will be kept within the power of the middle class to assimilate it and represent it. One of the major pitched battles occurred between Morrison and the prominent literary critic H. D. Traill, and it is worth pursuing briefly because it focuses the issues at stake. Remarkably enough, Traill perceives at some level that *Jago* is a symbolic text, and it makes him so uneasy that he rushes to dismiss the possibility. He acknowledges that what "has most astonished" him "is the impression of extraordinary unreality which, taken as a whole, [the novel] leaves behind it. To a critic opposed to the theories and methods of so-called realism, this is naturally rather disconcerting." Girded to show that the realism of *Jago* has sacrificed art for a false and exaggerated naturalism, Traill "comes out from the Jago with the feelings, not, as he had expected, of a man who has just paid a visit to the actual district under the protection of the police, but of one who has just awakened from the dream of a prolonged sojourn in some fairyland of horror. This, to be sure, may be the effect which Mr. Morrison desired to produce: it is certainly not difficult, I think, to show that his methods are distinctly calculated to produce it; but then those methods cannot be exactly the methods which the realist professes to employ, nor that effect at which he is commonly supposed to aim" ("The New Fiction" 9–10). Traill insists that Morrison's work be treated as realism, that it be measured by representational fidelity, and be shown to be untrue to actuality. "But I will make bold to say that as described by Mr. Morrison—described, that is to say as a place of which, with [a] half-dozen exceptions ... every single inhabitant out of 'swarming thousands' is either a thief, or a harlot, or a 'cosher' or a decoy, or a 'fence,' or a professional mendicant—it never did and never could exist ... If it is not what you would have actually found in exploring the Jago, it is no doubt what you might have found if all London had happened to pour its manifold streams of corruption into that particular *sentina*" ("The New Fiction" 13–14).

Several things bother Traill here. First, he rejects Morrison's premise that the urban slums constitute a fully fleshed out subsociety, with its own set of codes antithetical to bourgeois norms for the lower classes. Second, he recoils from the notion that there might be a place where people live who cannot be reached and redeemed by either sentiment or economic "logic." Realism for Traill (and others of his time) means that characters will always stand in for human subjects, and by this he means figures whose sensibilities are registered on terms readily associated with middle class values: who desire what we desire. And finally, Traill's determination to categorize Morrison as a "realist" will assure that Morrison's vision will always be grounded in material terms. An apparent paradox exists here, for we would assume that any literature so graphic and mired in gross physical details as Morrison's is, would be materialistic. Yet we have observed his insistence on a symbolic register for works such as *A Child of the Jago*. What he is resisting is an absorption of the nether world into the specific materialistic program of middle class representation. For we have seen that the dominant class can, in its scheme of representation, categorize and organize the urban poor through material criteria, specifically spatialized criteria. By the last quarter of the nineteenth century, the slums were being dealt with primarily through demolition of their neighborhoods, installation of their inhabitants in Council housing, and regimentation of their places of habitation (see Wohl 92–108). While Dickens tried to create a nexus between rich and poor on emotional terms, his successors did it through their insistence that the poorer classes will improve only if they live like their betters, in clean, well lighted rooms, in cheaper versions of middle class space. Within those spaces they should then begin to accumulate furniture and goods that will introduce them into the material consumer system. As the lower classes share those material desires, they will enter into the prevalent value system.[4]

Morrison's Jago is not accessible to that scheme. The physical details in his novel attest, paradoxically, to the estrangement of the lower classes. Amy Kaplan has noted this in American realist works, saying that they "often assume a world which lacks solidity, and the weightiness of descriptive detail—one of the most common characteristics of the realistic text—often appears in inverse proportion to a sense of insubstantiality, as though description could pin down the objects of an unfamiliar world to make it real" (Kaplan 9). The spareness of Morrison's prose, its starkness—held in place only by a half-Dickensian ironic narrative commentary—constitute not realism, at least as the English and French middle class literary culture knew it, but a symbolic text. So disturbing is his version of slum existence, so alien, so intractable is it to middle class representation and hegemonizing, that he has to contend with the charges that what he describes isn't there.

Consequently, an almost absurd exchange took place between Morrison and his supporters and Traill and his. The publication of Traill's essay on Morrison in his book, *The New Fiction*, was accompanied by a letter from a Mr. Woodland Erlebach, "who speaks from a thirty years' acquaintance with the district (Mr. Morrison's Jago)," and who writes, "I boldly say that the district, though bad enough, was not even thirty years ago so hopelessly bad and vile as this book paints it." Traill then appends the names and addresses of eight other people who had written letters protesting Morrison's picture of the East End (Traill 25–26). Morrison, for his part, rallied Arthur Osborne Jay to his defense, and argued his bona fides in *The Daily News* interview. In a separate article titled "What is a Realist?" in the *New Review*, he summed up all the strategies used against him:

> There is a story current in the East End of London, of a distracted lady who, assailed with a request for the loan of a saucepan, defended herself in these words:—"Tell yer mother I can't lend 'er the saucepan, consekince o' 'avin lent it to Mrs. Brown, besides which I'm a-usin' of it meself, an' moreover it's gone to be mended, and what's more I ain't got one." In a like spirit of lavish objection it has been proclaimed in a breath that I transgress:—because in the first place I should not have written about the Jago in its nakedness; next, that my description is not in the least like; moreover, that it is exaggerated; further, that though it may be true, it was quite unnecessary, because the Jago was already quite familiar, and everybody knew all about it; beyond this, that the Jago houses have been pulled down; and finally that there never was any such place as the Jago.[5]

Ironically, one of the strongest testimonies to Morrison's accuracy in representing the Old Nichol and the East End appeared in print a few years ago, when the historian Raphael Samuel published *East End Underworld: Chapters in the Life of Arthur Harding*, described as a first hand account by the "last man alive to have been brought up in the 'Jago.'" The volume grows out of a series of interviews with Harding, told in his own voice. Harding confirms that "the Nichol was something like a ghetto.... The whole district bore an evil reputation and was regarded by the working-class people of Bethnal Green as so disreputable that they avoided contact with the people who lived in the Nichol." His family could have fitted easily into a *Mean Streets* sketch, for his mother was crippled with a hip injury and was for a long time an alcoholic; his father, sometimes known as "Flash Harry," was generally shiftless, a ladies' man, picking up odd jobs. "Victorian husbands of the working class were very ignorant and brutal in their treatment of their women, and during my early years I often saw the results of a row upon my mother's face" (21). Early childhood was a time of petty mischief and of shameless begging: "The writers of that period, even Dickens never made proper use of children—how clever children are. Some children are born actors, there's no argument about it, they can cry at will. All they had to do was see someone well-dressed coming along and they'd turn the tap on: 'I've had nothing to eat all day'" (47). Harding himself graduated quickly to crime, moving from pick-pocketing to armed hold-ups, protection rackets, and territorial wars. He served a good deal of time in prison, and Samuel quotes a 1907 report of the Royal Commission on the Metropolitan Police describing him "as the 'king' or 'captain' of the Brick Lane van-draggers—'a most slippery and dangerous criminal' (according to the testimony of a local police inspector)" (vii). One of his later haunts, Brick Lane (now a flourishing Bangladeshi restaurant district), is possessed by all the horrors of Morrison's Jago: "In the back alleys there was garroting—some of the brides [prostitutes] would lumber a seaman while he was drunk and then he would be dropped—'stringing someone up' was the slang phrase for it" (107). "May I say that [two men he knew] were more like animals—and wild animals at that—than human beings. They inflicted terrible injuries on each other. China Bob had many scars and half-healed cuts upon his body, he smelt of decaying flesh." Even Sally Green lives again:

> Another character who haunted Brick Lane at that time was Biddy the Chiver. She and China Bob were natural enemies—he inflicted injuries

upon her with his little hatchet what he carried about in his inside pocket. Biddy would have a go at anything, 'lumbering' a man and all the rest of it.... She'd terrorise all them people who got a living from lumbering sailors and that kind of thing. Men as well as women were afraid of her. With her, you couldn't be sure you would get away with superficial wounds. (107)

Harding survives into the late twentieth century because he is ultimately able to penetrate the world outside the slums. Although his excursions into respectable neighborhoods are often repelled, as Josh Perrott's venture was, Harding thrives over the long stretch of time by his wits, unscrupulousness, and a certain wily caution, becoming a figure recognizable to readers of cockney working class fare. He emerges in Samuel's record as something of a "colorful character," in contrast to the fatalistically depressed lot of Morrison's *Mean Streets* and *Jago*. In part this reflects the evolution of the East End itself in the twentieth century: the First World War not only absorbed the surplus of lower class young men—decimating that class in the trenches—but it also brought home a brief wave of prosperity through soldier's salaries. That prosperity was to end with the hungry 'thirties, but it was enough to set up Harding as a wardrobe dealer and later a gold and silver dealer. The journalist Clarence Rook tried to follow in the line of Arthur Morrison in his book *The Hooligan Nights* (1899), a reputedly first hand account of the life of a young criminal named Alf, from the slums of South London. Rook seemed prepared for some of the same objections to his "realism," for he stresses in the Preface that "This is neither a novel, nor in any sense a work of imagination. Whatever value or interest the following chapters possess must come from the fact that their hero has a real existence...." Rook goes on, however, to paint a picture of a slum career with a romance to it that is a long way from Dickie Perrott's existence:

> When the *Daily Chronicle* published portions of the history of young Alf early in the year the editor received numerous complaints from well-meaning people who protested that I had painted the life of a criminal in alluring colours. They forgot, I presume, that young Alf was a study in reality, and that in real life the villain does not invariably come to grief before he has come of age. Poetic justice demands that young Alf should be very unhappy; as a matter of fact, he is nothing of the sort. And when you come to think of it, he has had a livelier time than the average clerk on a limited number of shillings a week. He

does not know what it is to be bored. Every day has its interests, and every day has its possibility of the unexpected, which is just what the steady honest worker misses. (Rook vi–vii)

Young Alf is something of an original: he was trained as a boy by an acrobat to be able to creep about in absolutely complete silence; he modeled himself after South London's Patrick Hooligan, with whom, "as with the lives of Buddha and of Mahomet, legend has been at work" (14); and he apprenticed himself to the celebrated Billy the Snide, the most accomplished passer of false coin of his time. He lives a life along the undersides of society that often approaches, in Peter Keating's term, the "pastoral" in its freedom from moral self-doubt and in its removal from the harsh realities of the economic system. Alf glides in and out of Rook's view at times like a phantom, losing himself in back alleys, stairways, and the crowded stalls of the South London slums. He insinuates himself upon victims through his charm, and eludes capture by the same means: in one bold house burglary he saves a baby from choking to death on its nightdress, and is toasted with wine by its grateful parents, the burglary victims. The Artful Dodger lives again.

A similar romanticism creeps into another Morrison-inspired novel, W. Somerset Maugham's early work *Liza of Lambeth*.[6] Liza, though a product of the margins of the slums and the lower working classes, charms the reader in ways that no denizen of the urban depths had done before her:

> It was a young girl of about eighteen, with dark eyes, and an enormous fringe, puffed-out and curled and frizzed, covering her whole forehead from side to side, and coming down to meet her eyebrows. She was dressed in brilliant violet, with great lappets of velvet, and she had on her head an enormous black hat covered with feathers. . . .
>
> Liza had been so intent on her new dress and the comment it was exciting that she had not noticed the organ.
>
> "Oo, I say, let's 'ave some dancin," she said as soon as she saw it. "Come on, Sally," she added, to one of the girls, "you an' me'll dance togither. Grind away, old cock!" (Maugham 8, 9)

Spirited, genial, fun-loving, engagingly flamboyant in dress and gesture, Liza is perhaps the most affecting figure in late nineteenth century representations of the poor. Yet the dark futility of the slums quickly casts its shadow upon her. She proves vulnerable to the charms of a married man, who will not leave his family to marry her, and she is turned into a pariah among the Lambeth lower working class. Caught up in an awful determinism, she slips into social ruin, finally beaten so severely by her lover's wife, in one of those celebrated fights among women which seemed to have become staples of the novel of the lower classes after Zola and Morrison, that she miscarries the child she is carrying, and dies of the attendant complications. The paradigm is similar to that of a *Mean Streets* story, but the difference is that a winsome, vital figure emerges briefly in the portrait of Liza. A personality is created, and possibilities for self-definition are suggested, as if in an effort to open up a space for a gentler, happier experience among the lowest of the working classes and the urban poor. Liza has time to dream, to fall in love, to play cricket in the streets with the neighborhood children, to go off with her boyfriend on a lively, pleasurable bank holiday excursion. Maugham, who observed many of the conditions of Lambeth poverty during his years there as a medical student and clerk to physicians, shared some of Morrison's pessimism about the bridging of social spheres—and Liza's death symbolizes the futility of it—yet the tenor of *Liza of Lambeth* differs greatly from that of "Lizerunt." A new element has been infused into the line of slum novels so dramatically begun by Morrison. Just as Alf's *joie de vivre* absolves us from the depressing fatality of poverty and petty criminality, so we can find solace in Liza's sharing of the same desires that any lower middle class girl might. Her instinctive good-heartedness can pass for a lower class version of ethics; she is potentially redeemable, transformable within the system. The fact that she cannot rise above her blighted circumstances may make her, in an odd way, more comforting to the reader, for she enacts the myth that the lower classes share bourgeois English traits and are resigned to exercise them in even the most unpromising of circumstances.[7]

Rook's and Maugham's novels belong to the line of late-nineteenth-century literature that Peter Keating categorizes as the cockney school of novel. These novels generally dealt with the urban lower working class, and only occasionally with the hard core poor, but they proved to have a greater influence on the nature of the fiction of the lower class than Morrison's graphic accounts, largely because they provide a means of constructing lower class life in formulas recognizable to the upper strata. The writers of the cockney school, such as Henry Nevinson and Edwin Pugh, created an individual subject that could be brought within the hegemonizing of middle class English culture. "Because of [the cockney's] determination to remain free," Keating writes, "he has developed the ability to take whatever life has to offer without complaint; take it wittily, cheerfully or philosophically. Such a man is of inestimable use to a democratic society. So long as his wit, drunkenness, violence, sentimentality and love of freedom are expressed in individual terms, he is socially harmless; so long as these qualities are viewed from a distance he is even attractive and picturesque" (*Working Classes* 221). He epitomizes, in Regenia Gagnier's words, the optimistic liberal view that the lower class individual is "an apparently autonomous and universal human spirit."[8] The cockney is typecast as the English "common man": individualistic, spirited, jingoistic, hard-playing, blunt, beef-eating, beer-drinking, and for all that, ultimately law abiding. Certainly the portrait has its truth value—all the visitors to the working class areas in the East End attest to its vital popular culture and to the remarkable resilience of the people—but one is reminded of the critique by the Frankfurt school that mass culture transforms originally realistic accounts into representations that one can read as repetitive diversions which present no danger to the dominant system.[9] More recently we have seen further evidence of how the jingoism of the turn of the century working class was produced through careful stage-management by middle class writers, editors, and political leaders. In her recent book on the Boer War, Paula Krebs discusses how the arrival of news of the relief of Mafeking precipitated a carefully stage-managed jingoistic celebration designed to confirm the existence of the very thing it was held to be a spontaneous symptom of—mindless working class patriotism. As Krebs puts it, "In the events of Mafeking Night we see the emergence of a British public that observers had been assuming existed all the while that they were creating it" (Krebs 4).

The separation of depictions of the lower orders of London that we noted before thus takes place. On the one hand, the cockney novel reiterates the redeemable nature of the working class. While the culturalistic programs of Besant and the settlement house workers sought to absorb working class popular culture into a more refined expression, the cockney novel makes use of the rawer versions of that culture to achieve the same ideological objectives. On the other hand, Morrison's *Jago* and *Mean Streets,* Harkness' depiction of a desolate East End, and George Gissing's *The Nether World* confront the reader with an essentially alienated domain. To a certain extent, this division is strategic, as we have noted; it carves off the salvageable working class from the residuum.

Yet it does not entirely banish the lowest of the poor from the bourgeois imagination, nor end their role in the ideological construction of the middle class. Morrison's refusal to ameliorate his graphic picture, nor to make it possible for the dominant social order to reach down in material ways to the Jago, tells us that there are limits to cultural appropriation. The deepest slums in London stand outside the hegemonizing imagination, but as his symbolic rendition of their life insists, they speak to us of a severe, almost untranslatable alienation. They are like voices from an entirely different cultural order. And they speak also of a disarray of gendered energies that is highly disturbing. For the social workers deeply committed to a mission among these people, the desolation of the scene becomes an affect of their own repression. Beatrice Webb, Margaret Harkness, and the women Webb describes all lose themselves at times and split off from themselves at others. For the men, the slum life unleashes a scenario of misogyny, often abusive, that is symptomatic of their erratic efforts to find focal points in action and in self-expression for energies that the perversely operating economic order and the closure of experiential outreach has created.

Gissing's Emotionally Constricted Male and the Cultural Externality of the Nether World

George Gissing's powerful novel of the London slums, *The Nether World* (1889), directly confronts the insidious integration of the London poor into the social discourses of popular culture, and like Morrison's work, it resists the easy representation of slum life that facilitates such an appropriation. Indeed, as we shall see, Gissing resists the absorption of the "experience" of the East End into any of the forms of culture—high or low—that we have seen to have been the social strategy of the 1880s. Gissing himself came to the slums from a lower middle class background, driven into poverty by a dishonorable act and by his tortured fidelity to Nell Harrison, a prostitute and an alcoholic, whom he married in order to save, and who added to the misery of years of a dreary existence in wretched rented rooms in lower class London neighborhoods. *The Nether World* is the greatest of a set of four novels Gissing wrote about the working classes and the slums, and it appears to confirm Morrison's abiding sense of the futility of the struggles of the underprivileged to rise out of their circumstances. The protagonist of the novel, Sidney Kirkwood, marries a woman who has been ruined in looks and spirit, and who burdens him with her near suicidal despair and her self-spiteful selfishness. The young woman he should have married, Jane Snowdon, resigns herself to celibacy and poverty, and when they come together in a scene at the close of the book, the narrator can find hope only in their courage and determination: "Sorrow certainly awaited them, perchance defeat in even the humble aims that they had set themselves; but at least their lives would remain a protest against those brute forces of society which fill with wretchedness the abysses of the nether world" (*Nether World* 392).

Long before then, however, the reader has learned that there is no passage from the nether world to the spheres above it. To move across it in a train is to travel "over the pest-stricken regions of East London, sweltering in sunshine which served only to reveal the intimacies of abomination; across miles of a city of the damned, such as thought never conceived before this age of ours; above streets swarming with a nameless populace, cruelly exposed by the unwonted light of heaven . . ." (164). A place called Shooter's Gardens epitomizes the heart of the nether world, and the narrator snarls that it is "needless to burden description with further detail; the slum was like any other slum; filth, rottenness, evil odours, possessed these dens of superfluous mankind and made them gruesome to the peering imagination. The inhabitants of course felt nothing . . . here was . . . the liberty to be as vile as they pleased. How they came to love vileness, well that is quite another matter, and shall not for the present concern us" (74). Charity cannot redeem such creatures: "of all forms of insolence there is none more flagrant than that of the degraded poor receiving charity which they have come to regard as a right" (253). Indeed, none of the apparatuses of the social order have any effectiveness in this dismal land. The novel seems for awhile to turn upon the device of charity, for Jane Snowdon's grandfather, having come into wealth, and haunted with guilt for his past omissions, concocts a scheme to turn Jane into an angel of mercy; since she grew up as a poor, abused servant girl in the slums she would be, he thinks, the ideal figure to administer a charitable project. This would be no visiting lady from the upper classes come to pass out alms, but a woman who knows the true contours of need. Unfortunately, the scheme is as impracticable as any of the others, and it is thwarted in the plot of the novel, as if Gissing were bent on exposing the fecklessness of the entire concept of such wish-fulfilling, guilt-dispelling interventions. It is thwarted because the grandfather's desire for reform is traced by the contradictions that are, in Gissing's view, unresolvable: one cannot make people "better" without exercising a kind of manipulative power over them that constitutes a well-meaning tyranny, but tyranny nonetheless. The very desire to escape such tyranny is valorized as heroic individualism; here it is at war with the desire to make people better.

The settlement house movement had already been ridiculed in an earlier novel, *Thyrza*. As John Goode has pointed out, the London of Gissing has become a territory of sealed-off zones, across which classes cannot move. "The social space of the city, insofar as it is created space (which is more and more true as the city stops serving the country and becomes an end in itself, enclosing its own production and consumption), is partly organised to keep class relationships to an abstraction—suburbs, ghettoes, thoroughfares are all ways of keeping the possibilities of direct confrontation at bay" (*George Gissing* 100). Mobility through acculturation is illusory; the conditions of life in the slums and lower working class districts grind the inhabitants into a fatalistic struggle to survive. In turn, the vision of the observer adjusts itself to the discrete separation of social groups, and adopts the naturalistic devices of classification and categorization by activity and social position that only intensifies the reification that it is trying to describe (Jameson 190). Gissing's later literary works will, in fact, focus on specialized groups and figures, such as the hack writers in *New Grub Street*, who seem to be defined more by their particular functions or social positions than as free-moving agents in an open continuum.

Yet in *The Nether World*, the isolation of the lower classes seems to provide for an integrity of experience that Gissing values. In his rejection of all the efforts of philanthropy, social intervention, and acculturation of the poor and marginal workers, Gissing asserts—albeit ambivalently—the authenticity of the qualities of suffering, struggle, and anger that he has discovered among the disenfranchised. This integrity of experience is embodied in Jane Snowden and Clara Hewett, the two women whom Sidney Kirkwood loves.

We first encounter Jane when she is an abused servant girl: pale, thin, constitutionally weak, intimidated by her cruel employers, slavishly attached to Sidney, the only man who is kind to her. Her grandfather liberates her, and gradually we see her develop into a quiet figure of determined compassion, with a muted but solid sense of social justice. As she comes upon the poor, "With wide, pitiful eyes, Jane looked at each group she passed. Three years ago she would have seen nothing but the ordinary and the inevitable in such spectacles, but since then her moral and intellectual being had grown on rare nourishment; there was indignation as well as heartache in the feeling with which she had learnt to regard the world of her familiarity" (130). But for all the philosophy Jane imbibes, and all the strength of character she acquires, she is still indelibly marked—indeed debilitated—by her earlier suffering:

> Two effects of the time of her bondage were, however, clearly to be distinguished. Though nature had endowed her with a good intelligence, she could only with extreme labour acquire that elementary book-knowledge which vulgar children get easily enough; it seemed as if the bodily overstrain at a critical period of life had affected her memory, and her power of mental application generally. . . . The second point in which she had suffered harm was of more serious nature. She was subject to fits of hysteria, preceded and followed by the most painful collapse of that buoyant courage which was her supreme charm and the source of her influence. Without warning, an inexplicable terror would fall upon her; like the weakest child, she craved protection from a dread inspired solely by her imagination, and solace from an anguish of wretchedness to which she could give no form in words. (135–36)

As we shall see again, the body, as a site of material being, asserts itself to complicate the ideological solutions of the text. In Jane, it recalls the fear of past wretchedness, the inexplicable terror of abuse, and it disfigures the rational consciousness indelibly. Jane signifies the real suffering, the psychic injury of poverty, the humbling that precludes rebellion. Hers has been an experience that provides its own probity, which depends in large part upon her being a witness to the social injustices of the nether world. And it assures that, for all her improvement in learning and manners, she will never be assimilable into the higher culture of the middle and upper classes. She cannot be appropriated into her grandfather's charitable project—her mind and body rebel against it whenever he demands it of her. She cannot be philanthropized. Although in many respects she is the idealized, cheerful, industrious little worker among the poor that brighten many popular cultural accounts of life in the lower classes, she cannot be commodified. She is damaged goods. In almost perverse terms, she represents the nether world's message of social inequality and political failure.

Sidney Kirkwood recognizes this significance in her. When he is deeply attracted to her, the narrator recounts, "of a sudden he experienced a kind of shame, the result of comparison between himself and the simple girl who stood before him; she was so young, and the memory of passions from which he had suffered years ago affected him with a sense of unworthiness, almost of impurity" (168). While the specific, conscious impulses of his sense of shame are the comparisons of his own worldly desires with her innocence, he unconsciously associates Jane with the social suffering of the nether world, for the text has so deeply implicated her in the conditions of her class that she has come to represent the essentiality of that experience to her being—and to those whose lives she represents. For him to love Jane, and to be a party to elevating her out of the slums, would be in some way to break faith with his mission—really Gissing's mission—which is to assert the integrity of the message of that suffering. The logic of the book, as well as the logic of the social conditions it depicts, dictates that Jane will remain as the troubled victim and consciousness of the nether world.

While Gissing respects the endurance of the lower classes, he is scarcely an unqualified admirer of the life that they live. He can be as unsparing as Morrison in sketching the meanness, the wanton brutality, and shiftlessness of slum dwellers and the lower working classes. His account of the leisure activities of such people seethes with contempt. Several of the characters take a bank holiday excursion to the Crystal Palace, the emblem of popular diversions:

> How they gape, what listless eyes most of them have! The stoop in the shoulders so universal among them merely means over-toil in the workroom. Not one in a thousand shows the elements of taste in dress; vulgarity and worse glares in all but every costume. . . . Mark the men in their turn; four in every six have visages so deformed by ill-health that they excite disgust; their hair is cut down to within half an inch of the scalp; their legs are twisted out of shape by evil conditions of life from birth upwards. (109)

Gissing is no more disposed toward the cockney novel hegemonizing of the lower orders than Morrison is. Although he perceives the growing separation of the classes in London that was taking place late in the century, he is conscious that they are mediated through the discourse of consumerism, leisure, and nationalism that is subsumed under popular culture, and he deplores the kind of identity that is being constructed among the lower working classes. Furthermore, long years of semiobscurity scribbling for little recompense had hardened Gissing against the mercenary nature of writing in a popular vein for a mass audience.[10] Not only is the popular culture vision of the working classes and poor untrue to their conditions, but it is actively implicated in the propagation of a mindless, animalistic hedonism symbolized in the Crystal Palace itself.

Gissing's antagonism to the consumerist aspects of both popular culture and the literary marketplace explains as well the particular nature of his own relationship to culture, a relationship that in a sense governs Kirkwood's characterization in *The Nether World,* and the animus that book contains toward the programs of acculturation of the lower classes taking place in England. Clearly the confluence of the Arnoldian "high culture" movement and the rise of consumerism produced among Gissing's generation a certain amount of uneasiness. Since the very notion of higher culture was to establish a body of thought, art work, and activities uncontaminated by commercialism, a conscious effort was made to reconceive culture as a discourse that lay outside the marketplace. Culture was made to reside in the realm of the sumptuary, outside use and exchange value. Needless to say, this realm is one that has been traditionally occupied by the upper reaches of the middle class and by the aristocracy, for it requires a certain degree of immunity from the exigencies of a market economy in order to assign arbitrary worth to objects of art and to a cultured style of living. Gissing confirms this in his own writing and thinking, for the realm of art for him was explicitly associated with a higher class, all the more intensely because of his resignation to the fact that he would never inhabit that world (although he frequently visited it). This defines him in his concept of himself as an exile, as a man who is of the "unclassed."

For Gissing, as well as others of his generation and social position, the symbolic registers of high culture are the classics and philosophy. In the former, in particular, he was a relatively learned man, supporting himself, in fact, in his twenties as a tutor of Latin and Greek. Sidney Kirkwood, although a lower class artisan, enjoys a certain immunity from the effects of near-poverty because of his reading and his philosophy. When Jane's grandfather attempts to "educate" her out of her sphere, into the class position from which she can exercise philanthropy, he does so through readings in philosophy and classical ethics. "In spite of the humble powers of her mind and her narrow experience, she had learned to think on matters which are wholly strange to girls of her station, to regard the life of the world and the individual in a light of idealism and with a freedom from ignoble association rare enough in any class" (226–27). Specific texts or bodies of thought are not identified, for that very obscurity connotes the detachment of mind that a classical education embodies.[11]

Gissing shares with other artists and intellectuals of his generation—Samuel Butler, W. H. Mallock, A. E. Housman, Thomas

Hardy—a kind of modern day Epicureanism in their determination to strike a philosophical attitude toward the pains and sufferings of social struggle and their withdrawal into positions of artistic passivity. It accounts for Gissing's attraction to the work of Arthur Schopenhauer, whom he invokes in an essay "The Hope of Pessimism," written in 1882. The essay marked his intellectual rejection of positivism, which he called "agnostic optimism," and its faith in the power of the social sciences to ameliorate the human condition. Such optimistic faith, embodied as well in modern Protestantism, encourages "the spirit of egotism," whose "latest outcome is the predominance of commercial competition." Instead, "there is, in truth," he argues, "only one kind of worldly optimism which justifies itself in the light of reason, and that is the optimism of the artist. The artistic mind, as Schopenhauer demonstrates, is . . . the subject contemplating the object without disturbing consciousness of self. In the mood of artistic contemplation the will is destroyed, self is eliminated, the world of phenomena resolves itself into pictures of absolute significance, and the heart rejoices itself before images of pure beauty" (*George Gissing* 96, 95).

John Goode warns us that Gissing is not a systematic thinker, and that it is unwise to attach too much importance to expressions of this sort, that Gissing was guided as much by material concerns as by ideational ones. "Instead we have a series of attitudes derivative from and in defence against other possibilities. The stress on calmness is not simply a bit of eclectic philosophy. It is seen to rely on circumstances which have to be exploited and to be enjoyed, and . . . it depends on the recognition of privilege." Goode argues, nonetheless, that "Gissing's particular culturalism, his slightly *arriviste* snobbery . . . that shallow structure of desire . . . supplies a specific focus" to his perception of society (*George Gissing* 44, 47–48). While this may be so, it provides a focus that in a work like *The Nether World* obscures the social and economic dynamics of the urban condition he is attempting to analyze, and baffles the reader. And it relegates Gissing—and Butler et al.—to a position in which high culture stands in their lives for retreatism, Epicureanism, a kind of aestheticized passivity. The pessimism that Gissing takes on as almost a philosophical stance, and that, as David Daiches and John Lester have pointed out, permeates the mood of the last decades of the century among certain artists and intellectuals, is an expression of a sterile culturalism.[12] As we had charted in the previous chapter, the new social mastertext of the last decades of the nineteenth century in England is culturalism—both in the sense of the effort to appropriate the middle and lower classes into a continuum of culture, but also in the newly popular anthropological meaning to the term: the lower classes as primitive or underdeveloped or alien. Although Gissing held out little hope for the inclusion of the lower working class in culture, his own culturalism of hellenistic studies, gentrified country retreats, and muted passions reflected his curiously conservative notions of that discourse.

Fredric Jameson suggests that what we have here is a sign or trace of the ideologeme of Nietzschean ressentiment, where, among victimized groups (and those who think themselves victimized), the only way of reaction—that of deeds—is unavailable to them, so it is replaced by an imaginary vengeance. The primary effect is the revolutionary activity of the underclasses, but a secondary effect is seen in those dissatisfied intellectuals who foment imaginary violence as well, but now against the putative revolutionaries, rather than against established power (Jameson 201–2). Gissing thus appreciates the antagonism of the lower classes toward their social conditions—even shares at some level their resentment of the arrogance and indifference of privilege—and yet believes that the poor and lower working classes must keep in their place. While an "exile" from the comforts and assurances of upper class society, Gissing nonetheless disavows any sympathetic identification with the underclasses. We can now supplement Jameson's insight by factoring in the specific social configuration in which this all takes place: the culturalism of the late century, and Gissing's own particular relation to it.[13]

Indeed, just as Gissing could not comfortably be a part of the acculturation process of his time and class, he also presents (as does Morrison) an image of the nether world that seems to remove it from the discourse of the cultural altogether. To understand this image, we need to examine the affect of a novel such as *The Nether World,* and also focus for a moment on the other major female character, Clara Hewett. The affective responses generated by the novel are particularly vexing because they consist both of a deadening, despondent fatalism and of surges of intense melodrama. Sidney Kirkwood epitomizes the former, for at every stage he seems to repress both his desire and his anger. We are told that he originally aspired to be an artist, and showed some talent at it, but unfortunately his father suffered severe economic reverses, and, troubled by Sidney's lack of direction, apprenticed him to a jeweler. The narrator ironically remarks that this saved Sidney from sowing his wild oats, and as the novel progresses, we watch him ossify into a kind of stoic, acting out of a severe personal morality, a man "reckless of the pain he gave to others so long as his own self-torture was made sufficiently acute" (235). Circumstances, but also something in his own nature, make Kirkwood into a figure of deflected desire, whose passion for Clara, and then for Jane, is kept in check—the presence of the male body always obscured.

Clara Hewett, on the other hand, unleashes desire with melodramatic force. Born into poverty, but born stunningly beautiful and quick of mind, "many a time had she sobbed out to herself, 'I wish I could neither read nor write! I wish I had never been told that there is anything better than to work with one's hands and earn daily bread!'" (82). She has no friends, except for Sidney, whose love she disdains, largely from her determination to spite herself and others in every way. She burns—and, as we shall see, the feverish language carries special connotations—with desire to rise above the nether world, and she risks everything to do so by becoming an actress: one of the least honorable of careers for a woman but the one that fits creatures who can be no better than imposters in the world above their own. "Self-assertion; to be no longer an unregarded atom in the mass of those who are born only to labour for others; to find play for the strength and the passion which, by no choice of her own, distinguished her from the tame slave. Sometimes in the silence of night she suffered from a dreadful need of crying aloud, of uttering her anguish in a scream like that of insanity" (86).

Clara Hewett constitutes, then, for Gissing, a site of class desire, of *political* resistance to the injustices of society. As often as the narrator describes Clara's self-ruinous, haughty, spiteful nature—her essential selfishness—in melodramatic expositions, he attempts to lay the blame for it upon the "social forces" that have condemned her to poverty. "Suppose she'd been the daughter of a rich man, then everything we now call a fault in her would either have been of no account or actually a virtue" (102). Her rejection of Sidney's apparently disinterested love is described as a "fierce, unscrupulous rebellion" (86). "The access of self-pity" in her "was followed, as always by a persistent sense of intolerable wrong, and that again by a fierce desire to plunge herself into ruin, as though by such an act she could satiate her instincts of defiance. It is a phase of exasperated egotism common enough in original natures frustrated by circumstance—never so pronounced as in those who suffer from the social disease" (94).

The correlation between "social disease" and the passionate destructive urges of Clara has to be taken on faith. Withheld from the story of Clara Hewett is the description of the process through which she became so alienated—the indignities and sufferings of growing up poor and of being intelligent and sensitive enough to perceive them—and absent, also, are accounts of the workings of the larger social order (the economic and political conditions) that create such circumstances. For Gissing the causes of Clara's misery almost have to be extrapolated:

> Natures such as hers are as little to be judged by that which is conventionally the highest standard as by that which is the lowest. The tendencies which we agree to call good and bad became in her merely directions of a native force which was at all times in revolt against circumstance. Character thus moulded may go far in achievement, but can never pass beyond the bounds of suffering.... As often as our conventions give us the opportunity, we crush them out of being; they are noxious, they threaten the frame of society. Oftenest the crushing is done in such a way that the hapless creatures seem to have brought about their own destruction. (295)

Such ruminations expose as much as they seem to dissemble, for such a passage reveals some of the uneasiness with which the observing consciousness confronts this site of rebellion—a site so melodramatically cast as female sexuality. Once again in the Victorian period the sexually vital woman has been cross-coded with class desire; not, as in Dickens, with the middle class male's ambivalence toward competitiveness, but now with the bitterness and potential dangerousness of the underclasses.

Neil Hertz has analyzed this as "male hysteria," a moment in texts when political dangers are represented as sexual dangers, deriving, in the Freudian economy, from the fear of castration that arises upon viewing the female, the castrated other. All the psychic energies that are being employed to hold the male self together (and correspondingly to hold the patriarchal social order together) are concentrated on the moment when the threat of the woman manifests itself as a threat to the political order as well (Hertz 27). Hertz argues that the specter of the dangerous woman is evoked only to be overcome, symbolically through the suppression or the destruction of the woman. Thus a site of subjective meaning is raised and then canceled, obliterated before our eyes. In Gissing's novel, Clara joins a traveling acting troupe as an understudy, and when the female star walks out on the show, she is invited to fill in as the lead in a melodrama. The episode is sexually charged, for it is clear that the manager of the company wants Clara as a mistress. On the night when Clara is to act in her first great part, however, a jealous fellow actress dashes vitriol into her face, scarring her horribly. What follows is one of the most melodramatic meetings in all of literature, when Sidney visits Clara after the incident. She wears a veil to prevent him from seeing her. Not only is she faceless—and thus unrepresentable—but she has almost lost the power of speech: "yet it was with difficulty that she commanded utterance . . . her voice failed again . . . her faltering voice sank lower and lower . . ." (283–84). Almost at the point of erasure, Clara makes a final effort to assert herself, in an uncanny scene:

> There came a marvellous change—a change such as it needed either exquisite feeling or the genius of simulation to express by means so simple. Unable to show him by a smile, by a light in her eyes, what mood had come upon her . . . by her mere movement as she stepped lightly towards him, by the carriage of her head . . . she prepared him for what she was about to say. . . . He knew that she smiled, though nothing of her face was visible; he knew that her look was one of diffident, half-blushing pleasure. (287)

At one level, this attempts to reassert the primacy of the male observer, for Clara can be read and articulated only by Sidney. The dangers that Clara represents—of sexuality, resentment, and social resistance—are subordinated to the interpretive male gaze. Yet the passage tells of Clara's ability to communicate through the movements of her body. Later, in fact, the text will insist on the continued allure of her graceful, willowy frame, and the felt presence of this faceless, almost inarticulate body. In addition, the narrative persistently refers to the feverish state in which she is often gripped: "the fever that then sustained her was much the same as she used to know before she had thoroughly accustomed herself to appearing in front of an audience. . . . With burning temples, with feverish lips, she moved about her little room like an animal in a cage" (291–92, 293). A similarly febrile quality characterizes Gissing's prose and plotting. The melodrama of the novel, its bursts of anger (as in the description of the lower classes in the Crystal Palace); its absence of exposition and its impatience with the development of character or situation; its continual, agitated domination over its material; its confused critical and philosophical position—all lend it a feverish character.

Fever, of course, is a symptom of real bodily illness. It is more than an impression; it is a pathological characteristic. Some quality beyond the representation of emotion thus intrudes itself into Gissing's text; the body makes its presence felt. On the symbolic level, Gissing negates the rebellion of the lower orders—signified in Clara's female sexuality—by making its face unrecognizable, unrepresentable, and yet allows it to manifest itself, as the body is manifested by fever. Lower class resentment acquires palpability and intensity.

The condition of the nether world in Gissing (and in Morrison) is represented as pathology: not a cultural phenomenon but a condition represented through symptoms of the body. As *The Nether World* says, there is something called "a social disease." This is less a medicalization of the social vision (although the disease metaphor of the 1840s has a persisting attraction) than an effort to convey, in a physiological metaphor, a particular sensation of social experience. It is ironic that the effort is made in *The Nether World* to read those symptoms through the female body (as you recall, Jane, too, was at the mercy of the almost autonomous rebellions of her body), for the male body cannot be made the register. It is still able to suppress the fever; it is still inviolate in some way, as rigorous as Sidney Kirkwood is in self-repression. Yet the slums and the world of the underclasses had entered the Victorian discourse as a sphere for the registering of male energies and fantasies. And it is clear from a reading of Morrison's slum novel that it is male experience that has gone awry. The intensification of misogynistic brutality illustrates an inability to establish any coherence to masculine desires and rebellions. The frustration and anger manifests itself, in its clinically repressed form, all the way up from the Jago through Sidney Kirkwood to George Gissing and those who think like him—frustration and anger over social inequality, the futility of revolution, the diminution of passion, the sterility of cultural experience. And it is all the more tightly bound because the male body cannot be allowed to register the symptoms. Having become, through the pathology of the representation of the lower orders in the 1880s and 1890s, the emblem of this malaise, the body, and especially the male body, must seek new forms in which it is able to express that ill.

- CHAPTER 4 -

Hell Hath Its Flâneurs:
The Discourse of the Abyss

Abyssal Discourse and the *Flâneur*/Prophet

Gissing's response to East End poverty was, like Hardy's to rural poverty, to associate energy with antisocial behavior and enervation with the requirements of goodness. There was a type of active energy that writers could deploy, however: the energy required by social investigation and reporting. The combination of culturalist critique, moral judgment, and risk-taking that these activities required and called forth signifies a change in the conceptualization of working and lower class life among male intellectuals in the 1890s, especially among those we associate with what we are calling the "discourse of the abyss." If the model of the earnest social investigator offered a possible male (and female) role for middle class writers, the dangers posed by life in the East End, dangers underlined by the writing of naturalists like Morrison, made the role of the reporter implicitly a risk-taking adventure: those who harrowed hell did so presumably because the news they had to report was of immediate, if not apocalyptic, importance to their middle class readers, and it was purchased at the price of an adventure which the investigator must narrate, an adventure which stages his own heroic persistence in the face of unbelievable degradation and danger.

The 1890s is also the great decade of the aesthetic *flâneur*. Inspired by an earlier generation of dandies such as Disraeli and Count D'Orsay and invigorated by the example of Baudelaire and the Goncourt brothers in France, a generation of aesthetes, of whom Oscar Wilde became the most infamous, took to the streets of London and Paris, intent upon a form of costumed self-display that paradoxically centralized the male gaze. As the case of Huysmans' fictional Des Esseintes reveals, a paradox underwrites the dandiacal self-fashioning of the late nineteenth-century aesthete: to take the stage and become the object of others' gazes serves to justify the rigorously judgmental and invariably tasteful exercise of one's own critical gaze. Baudelaire notes the paradox when he writes in the 1860s that, for the aesthetic *flâneur*, "to see the world, to be at the very centre of the world, and yet to be unseen of the world, such are some of the minor pleasures of those independent, intense and impartial spirits, who do not lend themselves easily to linguistic definitions. The observer is a prince enjoying his incognito wherever he goes" (Baudelaire 400). For the dandy, it was the visibility of his costumed self that allowed him the freedom to be unknown and unobserved. That duality—the cynosure of all eyes, yet unknown to the world—gave him a special perspective and a special relationship to knowledge. As critics such as Jonathan Freedman have noted, the late-Victorian aesthete is yet one more manifestation of the advancing professionalization of English society: "For what is the aesthete but the consummate professional: the possessor of a 'monopoly of knowledge' about the provenance and extent of this mysterious entity, 'the aesthetic'" (Freedman xix).[1]

The *flâneur's* duality—seen yet unseen—manifests itself as a dual relationship with the object of one's gaze. To become an aesthetic "boulevardier" was to adopt a posture that seemed to offer an uneasy compromise between passionate engagement with a variety of experiences and detachment from experience, which unfolds before one at something of an emotional distance, like a scientific experiment. However paradoxical the stance, there is no question that it is precisely this practice which Pater is urging "a few young men" to adopt in his justly famous—and later suppressed—"Conclusion" to *The Renaissance: A Study*, and which Wilde would later represent through the split dandy figure of Lord Henry Wotton, the leisured, insouciant, but rigorously detached experimenter, and Dorian Gray, the initially innocent Faustian character, who gives himself over to direct involvement with a variety of experiences too delightful/shameful to be detailed in any direct way in the novel.

In a recent article in *Victorian Studies*, George Levine argues that Walter Pater was engaged in a rigorously ascetic epistemological project that bears a great deal of resemblance to the stance of Karl Pearson. What both figures share is a dedication to grasping the object of knowledge through understanding the role of the subject in constructing the world. Neither fits, of course, the "dandyesque" model because neither was interested in the public visibility for which Wilde was noted. Nevertheless, Levine underlines the point that a rigorous epistemological project with at least scientific pretensions lay at the heart of Aestheticism. The voracious appetite for knowledge which Pater celebrates is, one might argue, what makes both Huysmans' Des Esseintes and Wells' Dr. Moreau parallel figures despite their many obvious differences.

In the case of Wilde and others, East London held more than the promise of spectacularized criminality and deplorable poverty. It offered the prospect of pleasure, precisely because it was populated by boys willing to offer sex for money. In his interesting and wide-ranging book *The Wilde Century*, Alan Sinfield argues that "the queer" was constructed, or rather made visible, through a process that required the Wilde trial of 1895 to stamp its meaning on "the queer." While Wilde himself marked the public transition from "aesthete" to "dandy" when he postured in bright green pantaloons and lace in his 1882 journey across America while lecturing boorish Americans about art, it was the revelations of the 1895 trial—in particular the dramatic testimony of the three East End rent boys, Alfred Wood, Charles Parker and Fred Atkins, about how they performed sexual services for Oscar, reinforced by the testimony of a hotel chambermaid about certain "stains" she found on Oscar's bedsheets—that clinched the case against him. As Sinfield puts it: "The image of the queer cohered at the moment when the leisured, effeminate, aesthetic dandy was discovered in same-sex practices, underwritten by money, with lower-class boys" (Sinfield 121). Trevor Fishers has recently concluded that Wilde was most likely covering for his lover, Lord Alfred Douglas, who was the one who had actually engaged the boys for sex (Fishers). Douglas took advantage of upper class immunity and was never called to testify about who stained the sheets, although he did make an eleventh hour offer, telegraphed from Paris and rejected by Wilde's lawyer, to offer new testimony in the libel trial. What he offered to testify to has never been revealed publicly. Whatever he had to offer, it was Wilde finally who took the punishment and Wilde who came to stand in the public mind thereafter for the combination of leisured "effeminacy," aesthetic religiosity, and same-sex passion that conditioned the popular image of "the homosexual" for generations. Building on the reputation it had already acquired in the "Maiden Tribute" scandal for being a treasure trove of available lower-class female prostitutes, East London, thereafter, represented a rich quarry of sexually available males as well. Anything and anyone in the East End could be had—for money—and the masculine gazer stands as both spectacle and spectator in relationship to this scene.

The notion that East London's own disadvantages could afford opportunities for the middle class subject intrepid enough to risk exploring its possibilities was of course implicit already in the more socially respectable goals of the missionaries and philanthropists. The East London we discussed in chapter 2 is a particular kind of nether world, a place in need of economic redemption, and because of that, a place of philanthropic enterprise for earnest middle class crusaders such as Samuel Barnett's young university men, or the COS and Salvation Army. As we saw, in Walter Besant's view East London is a city unto itself, but one which lacks precisely what the investigator can bring to it, and thus, East London creates opportunities for middle class philanthropy of all sorts including such "culturalist" projects as the People's Palace. While we have already discussed (in chapter 3) the attempts by Gissing and Morrison to reject this image in favor of a thoroughly exteriorized East End, a city of hopelessness that lies outside of, and indeed resists, middle class resituation of it within a narrative of redemption, we want to focus here on a particular strategy for recuperation that implicitly concedes this exteriority near the turn of the century but nonetheless resituates East London within a rich fantasy discourse: the discourse of the "abyss." What this discourse offers is a particular mode of engagement for the middle class "reporter," an opportunity for middle class subject construction that will feature a combination of engagement and self-display and detachment. In other words, in this discourse, the experience of descent yields a type of *frisson*, however attenuated, that is largely absent from the work of Gissing and Morrison.

Indeed, a moralistic repudiation of exactly the type of sexual pleasure this hell invites one to witness was what W. T. Stead's "Maiden Tribute" series in the 1880s was ostensibly about. Sensationalist discourse of the "Maiden Tribute" sort, however, typically invites its audience to participate vicariously in the same thrills that adhere to the vices it is ostensibly preaching against. Whether it be Wilde's real (or imagined) use of East London youth for sexual pleasure, or Richard Jefferies' and H. G. Wells' construction of East London as an alien space of barbarism, or Charles Masterman's, Jack London's, and Sherlock Holmes' use of the East End as an opportunity for self-liberating disguise, the East End comes to occupy a particular fantasy niche: a hell that is not without its pleasures, one of which is the opportunity it opens for the middle class male observer to manage it through the twin activities of self-display/disguise and knowledge construction.

We associate this particular male subject position with the boulevardier in order to differentiate it from the more earnestly self-effacing explorations of Charles Booth and his army of investigators (including his cousin-in-law Beatrice Webb). What Booth and the Webbs shared, above all, with the missionaries, the University men of Toynbee Hall, and the Salvation Army, was an earnest dedication to the amelioration of the worst aspects of poverty in the midst of plenty.[2] The "explorers of the abyss"—both fictional and historical—that we will discuss in this chapter, however, do not quite share that ameliorative faith (with the possible exception of Charles Masterman, who was committed to amelioration as a political project, although, as we shall see, his 1902 work *From the Abyss* is anything but hopeful). Engaged in a process of professional class subject construction they, like the aesthetes who were their contemporaries, have substituted for that faith a rigorously detached critical consciousness that necessarily entails a great deal of skepticism about certain well-accepted narratives of social progress. Moreover, the subject which they construct for themselves is one that would become increasingly visible as a "male" type in the late Victorian period: professional, detached, but also adventurous (in a childish way, perhaps) in the risking of his identity. We have referred to this stance as a "male" stance both because it involves emotional distancing and because it often involves embracing a play of identities such as that associated with the actual adventures of Richard Burton and the fictional adventures of writers such as Stevenson and Kipling in the Victorian age. Moreover, it entails, for the most part, a self-conscious rejection of the "melodramatic" or "sentimental" conventions discussed in chapter 1. Its stance of antagonism to sentimental convention and a coldly distanced attitude toward suffering is part of what leads us to associate it particularly with a certain construction of male subjectivity in the late nineteenth century.[3]

The differential relation of men and women to these issues is even more pronounced in the 1890s than before. As Judith Walkowitz has argued in her analysis of the Men and Women's Club of the 1880s (a group which included Maria Sharpe, Olive Schreiner, and Karl Pearson), Stead's "Maiden Tribute of Modern Babylon" provided women intellectuals with a "melodramatic voice" to be used in discussing heretofore forbidden topics of sexual danger in ways that often put these women at odds with males. These gendered differences often came to the surface in club debates in the 1880s:

> "Maiden Tribute" set the scene for the club's inauguration and gave women in particular the courage and incentive to undertake such a daring venture. "Maiden Tribute" and the feminist politics of prostitution had made public discussion of sexual danger possible for women, and brought into the open the ominous "shadows," "spectres," and "haunting fears" that darkened their views of heterosexual relations. In the club and elsewhere, melodrama provided women with a cultural resource, a language of emotion, in stark contrast to the disembodied voice of reason and science that presumably set the tone of the club. Melodrama was also a politicized language that drove women "by fear into [public] speech." The women of the club brought to their discussions and debates a pervasive sense of sexual vulnerability, organized around a specific melodramatic script of sexual danger. (Walkowitz 144)

This meant that discussions in the Men and Women's Club tended to cast males and females into separate groups, with males, like Pearson, articulating the detached, "scientific" view while women such as Olive Schreiner found themselves speaking melodramatically about sexual danger for the first time. The detached tone had become a signifier of a certain male professional posture of objectivity. Not surprisingly it was the male members of the club who were comfortable seeing themselves as daring critics of conventional views about birth control and sexual conventions, while the women, more often than not, found themselves pressed to defend conventional moral codes because they contained built-in protections for otherwise vulnerable women.

Of course, the "social purity" campaign of Josephine Butler against the Contagious Diseases Act had set the stage for this measured form of female frankness. It was Butler who risked—and, indeed, encountered—public opprobrium for attempting to hold men, at least rhetorically, to the same standard of sexual morality to which women of the middle class had always been held in the Victorian age, and it was Butler who was accused of immorality for daring to speak publicly against sexual immorality. When Stead's "Maiden Tribute" series publicly announced the fact that it was possible for men to buy young working class girls for purposes of sexual exploitation, it seemed to authorize respectable women to speak about even more acute sexual horrors than the double standard that so preoccupied Butler—the sexual slavery of young working class girls—and it gave middle class women an authorized rhetorical mode in which to speak about it. The language of melodrama had never been a language of measured rationality and distanced objectivity, but it did pay lip service to conventional moralism by working as much through allusion and indirection as through direct representation. As we have already discussed in relation to *The Bitter Cry of Outcast London,* the unmistakable markers of the Stead style are the eliciting of powerful emotional reactions from his readers by asserting boldly but somewhat evasively and generally and then leaving many of the details to the imagination of his readers—to create the impression that boldness of mind goes along with the ability to imagine details that must be withheld from public expression in the interest of good taste.

A good example of typical Steadian overstatement occurs in the first letter on the topic in the *Pall Mall Gazette* of July 6, 1885: "It is a veritable slave trade that is going on around us; but as it takes place in the heart of London, it is a scandal—an outrage on public morality—even to allude to it" ("Maiden Tribute" 1). The metaphor of the "slave trade" provokes a canned reaction of moral outrage from the reader while the notice of the geographic location—"in the heart of London"—locates that outrage "at home," indeed, almost in the domestic space itself. Like Josephine Butler, Stead is targeting male lust, the lust responsible for the prostitution industry to begin with, and thus his language insinuates that his implied reader—whether male or female—already has an intimate familiarity with this domestic devil.[4] The *Pall Mall Gazette's* reporting on a seemingly distant phenomenon—the forced enlistment of working class girls from East London in the ranks of prostitutes—is thus immediately resituated close to home, in the heart of the bourgeois family whose members presumably know something about that domestic devil whether or not they allow themselves to discuss it publicly. The second clause ("it is a scandal—an outrage on public morality—even to allude to it") performs the characteristic rhetorical gesture of sensationalism: insinuating at once that he will tell and that he won't, that he will speak in a language of indirection that is the tribute virtue pays to the middle class reader's sense of delicacy. Moreover, that last clause implicitly concedes that telling is itself transgressive—even in the interest of the greater public good—and thus constructs his subject position as a Butleresque heroic figure, willing to risk public opprobrium for introducing a distasteful subject, but solely in the interest of a higher moral duty to the public. After all, Stead himself did face trial in the Eliza Armstrong case in September of 1885 after the *Pall Mall Gazette* had published its account of the success of his attempt to "purchase" her. The reader is implicitly invited to participate in the guilty pleasures of such a stunted disclosure, his or her curiosity awakened by the promise of horrors too indelicate to be revealed, yet too pressingly real to be avoided. Like much melodramatic discourse throughout the century, this is radically conservative: producing a scandalous titillation effect that ultimately works to reinforce conventional moral codes.[5]

Three of the writers we will examine in this chapter visit an East London that has already been constructed as "hell" in the imagination of their middle class readers by generations of social investigators who have gone before: a place of godlessness, acute suffering, disease, and sexual depredations, not only those associated with prostitution, but those reinforced in 1888 and 1889 by the *Times'* (and other newspapers') lurid coverage of the so-called "Whitechapel Horrors."[6] However, the male writers we will discuss here by and large eschew the conventions of melodrama in favor of a spare discourse that substitutes a more coldly distanced form of subject construction that we have identified as a "male professional" perspective on poverty. This writing does not eschew sensuality, by any means. Indeed, a central appeal of the "descent" literature is its careful delineation of abject phenomena, a careful detailing of the middle class subject's own sensual reaction to that abjection. The pull of the popular image of the East End imposed certain constraints on the writers we will discuss in this chapter, constraints that pull Jack London toward Dantesque clichés and H. G. Wells toward ethnographic conventionality. However, the dominant tone is a distanced tone and the style a spare one. The explorer who boldly descends into the abyss and returns shaken but intact, returns also to place that experience in a political perspective that, not surprisingly, is given purchase by the intrepid explorer's willingness to run personal risks to bring his readers the truth.

Darwinism and the Residuum

The increasing cultural separateness of the East End, its place as a home to a "de-moralized" working class, an embruted residuum, was at least partly a result of social changes created by London's unique role in Britain's growing industrial economy. We have already noted Gareth Steadman Jones' argument that the process of spatial division between social classes was exacerbated, both by suburbanization and by London's economic niche as a small manufacturing city. The former accelerated the spatial withdrawal of the middle class from the precincts of the poor, leaving the poor to live in increasingly overcrowded slums by the 1880s, in effect concentrating them in an area which increasingly was seen as the abode of crime, degradation, and sin by many middle class people. These social changes had much to do with the traditionally "casual" nature of much London labor and consequently with many of the social problems created by the impermanence of employment. As Jones argues, "The effect of the industrial revolution on London was to accentuate its pre-industrial characteristics" (Jones, *Out of London*, 26). Even the great Dock Strike of 1889, an important moment in British labor history, ironically reminded Londoners that, however important London remained as a world port, it was no longer the shipbuilding capital of Britain, having surrendered that title to smaller cities decades earlier.

At the same time, the Darwinian revolution had given birth to new biologistic explanations for social problems, the most popular of which, the theory of urban degeneration, seemed to offer the hope of explaining the pathological effects of poverty within the city. Those who subscribed to this theory believed that city life led to the hereditary weakening of the working classes, and that this process was stemmed only temporarily by periodic infusions of "better blood" in the form of immigrants from the countryside. The term "degenerate" had been introduced into evolutionary discourse in 1857 by the Frenchman Morel, but it was given new life by the investigations of "the criminal mind" of the Italian Darwinist Cesare Lombroso, who influenced a variety of English thinkers and writers in the 1880s including Robert Louis Stevenson, whose Mr. Hyde has become the classic literary example of the "criminal degenerate" (and who is notably a member of the professional class, not the working class). However, few at the time could ignore the close correlation between poverty and crime, and thus "degeneracy" was rather easily seen as, alternately, cause and effect of the physical depredations of life in the "abyss." As J-P Freeman-Williams argued in "The Effect of Town-Life on the General Health," an essay he published in 1890:

> The child of the townsman, . . . is bred too fine, it is too great an exaggeration of himself, excitable and painfully precocious in its childhood, neurotic, dyspeptic, pale and undersized in its adult state, if it ever reaches it . . . If it be not crossed with fresh blood, this town type, in the third and fourth generations becomes more and more exaggerated . . . it has been maintained with considerable show of probability that a pure Londoner of the fourth generation is not capable of existing. (Quoted in Jones, *Outcast London*, 127)

This is one formulation of a theory embraced by a number of intellectuals at the end of the century including Charles Booth, Alfred Marshall, and Llewelyn Smith (who was one of Booth's investigators). Although the argument was usually cast in terms of fears that the London working class was growing physically weaker with every generation, as Jones reminds us, what actually troubled employers most about the London workingman was a more "active" trait: his truculence. Immigrants from the countryside were welcomed precisely because they were believed to be more pliable than the sullen town-bred type (Jones, *Outcast London*, 130).

The debate that raged over the hypothesis of urban degeneration often relied on statistics emerging from Army and Navy recruiting offices. This became especially pronounced in the years leading up to and following the Boer War of 1899–1902. In an essay called "The Cult of Infirmity" which he published in the *National Review* in October of 1899, Arnold White, a Liberal imperialist, cited the statistic that 403 out of every 1,000 recruits in Manchester were rejected as unfit by army recruiters. Most estimates of the degree of urban working class debility cited figures in the range between 30–40 percent, although White himself later raised his estimate, eventually claiming that three in five urban working class males were unfit to meet the minimal physical requirements set by the army and navy (Soloway 140). Karl Pearson complained about the lack of scientific rigor of people like White, although he himself remained deeply troubled by the neo-Malthusian prospect that the more productive middle and upper classes, whose falling birthrates he documented, were on their way to being demographically engulfed by unfit lower class people—"race suicide" was the term usually used for this unwelcome social trend.

In 1905 at the end of the Balfour administration, a report called the Interdepartmental Committee Report was issued. It was a summary of views of the subject current at that time. While not explicitly endorsing the biologistic argument that the poor were "degenerate" (that remained an important minority view on the committee), it nonetheless managed to orchestrate many of these contentious voices into one anxious chorus:

> Nearly everyone agreed that while there was indisputable evidence of deplorable ill health and physical inadequacy, it was unsatisfactory for resolving the conflicting diagnoses and prognoses responsible and learned people offered to the public. Nevertheless, a minority of witnesses ranging from physicians to factory inspectors were sure that city

life had altered the course of evolution and created a smaller, weaker labouring class whose diminished physical and mental capacity was being transmitted to an ever-expanding number of unfit people. While some authorities took comfort in the thought that these degenerates would eventually die off in accordance with the laws of natural selection, others were fearful that their proliferation would actually be facilitated by the more humane values and institutions of modern civilization. (Soloway 149)

To its credit, the report did endorse some "environmental" explanations for the deplorable physical condition of the working class, and thus inspired some of the first steps toward welfare state amelioration. For example, prompted by the report's conclusions, the new Liberal administration, in 1906 and 1907, decided to provide for the feeding and medical inspection of school children for the first time in British history. However, the hopeful call for government action after decades of inaction sat uneasily on the same pages with ruminations about inevitable hereditary "weakening," for government attempts at amelioration would presumably only exacerbate that problem by helping to preserve more "degenerates" who would then presumably reproduce themselves.

Arnold White was perhaps the most vociferous exponent of this Darwinist Malthusianism at the turn of the century. Attracted to Francis Galton's science of eugenics, White came to public attention in the 1880s with a book that offers a eugenic explanation of London's social problem. His 1886 book, *The Problems of a Great City,* joins the discussion of the plight of the urban poor inaugurated by Mearns's contemporary *Bitter Cry of Outcast London,* but offers, in place of that pamphlet's tone of hystericized melodrama, a brutally rational eugenic solution to the problem of the poor: forced sterilization. Addressing the issue of high birthrates among the pauperized classes, White writes:

> Criminal and pauperized classes with low cerebral development renew their race more rapidly than those of higher nervous natures. Statesmen idly stand by, watching in such moments as they can spare from the strife of party the victory of battalions destined to misery and crime over the struggling army of the prudent and the self-controlled. Birth into certain quarters of London is birth into an environment from which there is no escape. At three years old baby lips lisp oaths so bestial as to be coarse in the betel-stained mouths of the crew of a Coromandel *dhoney*. At six, little girls are initiated by their mothers

> into practices so loathsome the gorge rises at the thought. At ten, girls and boys alike are unclean spirits limited in their power for evil only by their abilities. Dynasties of criminals and paupers hand down from generation to generation hereditary unfitness for the arts of progress and all that brings greatness to a nation, and engage themselves in warring against all forms of physical and moral order. Where a man is criminal himself, the cause of crime in others, and the begetter of criminal posterity, it seems to be an act of mere self-protection on the part of this generation to segregate him. (White 49)

The rhetoric here, of course, has its own hystericized edge, and the vision of the future in this paragraph seems to be structured almost as a "eugenic melodrama." Blurring the distinction between Darwinian natural selection and Lamarckian inheritance of acquired traits in its use of the term "hereditary," this passage gradually builds a sinister vision of the future, reinforced by military metaphors (the "battalions destined to misery and crime" successfully overcoming the "struggling army of the prudent and the self-controlled"), and aided by the swift and steady march of the unfit, from one three-year-old spewing oaths to many ten-year-old boys and girls already actively at war with civilized values. The threat of engulfment of the "prudent" middle class reader by the uncivilized spawn of the degenerate classes is reinforced here in the way White evokes growing poor children of grotesque vitality. In White's vision, poor children are not weak, stunted gutter-snipes, likely to drop in the streets at any moment from inanition. Rather they are very vital degenerates, brimming with antisocial energy, mass-produced in the slums of London, and sent out to prey on the neurasthenic middle classes whose own civilized qualms, expressive of their "higher nervous natures," presumably cause them to hesitate about taking actions to protect themselves as bold as those recommended by White. In short, the lesson of his book seems to be that civilization has no choice but to protect itself through a systematic form of eugenic barbarism, even if "barbaric" behavior is precisely what civilization claims to eschew.

Despite the faith in social engineering displayed by eugenicists like White, the theory of urban degeneration would help to underwrite a particular attitude of hopelessness toward the East London residuum, an attitude which emerges in a variety of discursive forms at the end of the century, ranging from the proto–science fiction fantasies of Richard Jefferies and H. G. Wells, to the urban exploration narratives of Jack London and Charles Masterman, to the work of Llewelyn Smith in

Booth's great study.[7] The work of these figures is steeped in the assumptions of this late-century degeneration hypothesis, and that is precisely what makes them different in significant ways from the work of Gissing and Morrison. Despite the abundant sympathy of some of these writers—London and Masterman most notably—for the plight of the poor, they nonetheless find themselves harrowing a "hell" which can only absorb but never disgorge lost souls. Whatever their differences, most of these writers shared the belief that the pathologies of the East London poor are far greater and far more intractable than can be accounted for by "de-moralization" and the culture of criminality. The "abyss" into which the urban poor have fallen puts its seal upon their foreheads, marking them as its own forever. At the same time, these writers inevitably are led to celebrate, indirectly usually, the brave reporter who, like Dante without his Virgil, descends into the depths to illustrate the depravities of East End life (in London's case this is done literally with a number of photographs). In other words, their writings foreground the experience of poverty as an opportunity for the male reporter/hero to register his disgust as the reader's disgust with the spectacle before him, a disgust which the embruted locals seem largely unable to register themselves, to detail (to a greater or lesser extent) his own self-fashioning to make the descent, and to offer a summary account of the reasons why reform is impossible and redemption ultimately unthinkable.

Science Fiction, the Abyss, and the Male Imagination

The theme of urban degeneration and the centrality of the detached scientific observer, one might say, were both present at the birth of science fiction. They inform the work of two writers—Richard Jefferies and H. G. Wells—most responsible for developing the dystopic novel in the direction of what would come to be known as "science fiction." Set in imagined futures which have seen a significant degradation of the conditions of life in Britain, Jefferies' *After London* (1885) and Wells' *The Time Machine* (1893) offer visions of an urban industrial society fallen into desuetude largely because of the failure of industrial culture to solve the problem of class. Moreover, both novels underline the idea that economic specialization is implicated in this process. The very specialization that is so central a feature of advanced industrial society cuts people off from a more comprehensive knowledge of the material conditions of life, and that ignorance is rendered in stark terms in both novels: in Jefferies, for instance, British society has reverted to an anarchic Dark Age, its countryside menaced by dangerous "bushmen" descended from the urban poor who fled London as it collapsed into a viscous ooze, the remnants of its "civilized" citizens huddled behind palisades made of tree trunks, living in gross ignorance of the state of technological sophistication once possessed by the ancients. In Wells' novel, Britain has degenerated into "two nations," populated by the parasitical and inebriated "Eloi" and the foundational but resentfully dangerous "Morlocks," who are pitted against one another in a deadly, but curiously listless, war. Both novels feature heroes who have triumphed somehow over the limitations of a highly specialized division of labor, and *The Time Machine*, at any rate, deliberately figures the main character, the Time-Traveler, as a professional—a scientist—comfortably ensconced in a social circle of other male professionals (including an editor and what the text calls a "new journalist") who eagerly await his reports on conditions in Britain many centuries in the future.

Richard Jefferies was best known in his day as a chronicler of the virtues of rural life. Born in rural Wiltshire in 1848, he produced a series of novels, newspaper articles, and nonfiction essays which vaunted the superiority of rural to town life. Such novels as *Hodge and His Masters* (1880) reveal an obvious political preference for farmers and a hostility to the values he associated with the city (this sympathy for the plight of freeholding and tenant farmers makes him less than sympathetic to the rural working class as well). His novels *Wood Magic* and *Bevis* established his reputation as a notable writer of children's tales. In 1885 just two years before his early death, he published *After London; or, Wild England*. It is a novel which extends the plot of his earlier boys' adventure tale *Bevis* but supplies the kind of dystopic detail that could hardly have had much appeal to children.

The state of cultural and political degeneracy into which England has lapsed in the novel is implicitly traced to the collapse of London. As the narrator tells us, one day the eastward flow of the Thames became blocked, causing London to revert to a greasy swamp and creating the vast inland lake which covers much of what was once England at the time the novel opens. No image of fecund possibility to Jefferies, the city is rather nothing more than a "dead" swamp sitting on top of buried cloacae, and, in some mysterious way the novel is not very clear about, the source of Britain's historic reversion to barbarism (Jefferies 69).

The narrative traces the adventures of young Felix, the son of a local baron, who builds a canoe one day and sails off across the inland sea in search of adventure. What he discovers along the way comes in a series of revelations that register as a story of British cultural degeneration. He finds, for instance, that Britain has declined into a neomedieval state of baronial rivalry with no centralized kingly authority. He also discovers that much of the countryside is haunted by people known as the "bushmen," the evolutionary "survivals" of what once were the urban poor and working class. These "bushmen" are a menacing bunch who attempt to set upon anyone who leaves the protected confines of the wooden palisades that surround Felix's father's baronial estate. Interestingly, they carry what are called "spuds": tools which are themselves implicit signs of cultural and technological degeneration because of the fact that they serve multiple, rather than singular, functions (killing enemies, killing animals for food, cutting up food, and so on). Even Morrison's "cosh," the weapon of choice of the Jago thug, serves a more specialized function than the spud. Indeed, differentiation of function—different tools for different purposes—is implicitly treated in *After London* as a lost art associated with a more civilized past. Only the main character, Felix, is somehow able to surmount the technical and social ignorance which seems to enclose all the other characters in the book, and to do so in a way that joins the utopian technical experimentalism of Crusoe, the heroic middle class figure who surmounts all divisions of labor, with the journalistic social adaptability of Mayhew: alone, Felix is able to explore the shores of the vast inland sea by teaching himself to build a canoe and improvising, à la Henry M. Stanley or Winwood Reade, ways of ingratiating himself with the savages he finds himself thrown among.

This theme of "overspecialization" is one of the more peculiar notes of complaint in the middle class discourse on urban poverty. Like much else we examine in this book, it seems to reveal less about working class conditions of life in East London than it does about middle class nostalgia—in this case, for a preindustrial way of life, a nostalgia which accounts on some level for the popularity of the Robinson Crusoe story in the nineteenth century. As Martin Green has demonstrated, the Robinson Crusoe story was an extremely popular motif in nineteenth century adventure literature, inspiring hordes of imitators. It was often recycled either directly (as in domesticated knock-offs such as Wyss's *Swiss Family Robinson*) or indirectly (in such popular fictional updatings as R. M. Ballantyne's *Coral Island*).[8] Green locates the appeal of these stories in the compelling fantasies they nurture of preindustrial life charged with the values of adventure, of life lived before the alienating effects of modern production had separated the workman from his handicraft and narrowed both his skills and his knowledge to a very small part of the production process, before the scope of middle class worklife had been narrowed to a desk in a dimly lit office. The Crusoe figure seems to surmount this narrowing of vision, and the Crusoe story offers an expanded and exciting narrative of world-scale economic endeavor infused with breathtaking adventure. Moreover, Defoe's hero implicitly recapitulates the history of the development of Western technology on his island by himself, achieving self-sufficiency all by hand. Indeed, the very notion that readers might find Crusoe's story of his—ultimately futile—struggle to carve a canoe out of a tree trunk enjoyable says much about the changing nature of the economic world in which the eighteenth- and nineteenth-century reader was embedded. It testifies to the phantasmic appeal of a hard-working subject who must overcome the narrowness that is a condition of life in an urbanized capitalist economy—the condition of life of the middle class reader—in order to survive. Crusoe's painstaking detailing of the pains he took to procure food and protect himself on the island presumably would not appeal to people who still bake their own bread, weave their own cloth, and build their own houses. Such activities lack the requisite novelty. Not only do such people lack the leisure time that middle class people of the eighteenth and nineteenth centuries were able to devote to reading novels, but the representations of everyday work in the first two-thirds of the novel would seem banal to such a reader: a recapitulation of his everyday reality rather than a very "tellable" tale of novel experience. For the presentation of "novel" experience by the novel had been central to its cultural mission since the end of the seventeenth century. As Lennard Davis points out, eighteenth century fiction emerges out of what he calls an originally undifferentiated "news/novels" discourse, and the reading pleasure it afforded was very much tied to its ability to impart "novelty" to its readers, the etymological kinship between the term "novel" and the word "news" testifying to a kinship that was only later sundered under pressure from the legalistic invention of "fictionality" (through the passage of the Stamp Acts) (Davis 131–36).

While the tendency of nineteenth-century middle class history was toward a greater and greater specialization which fostered the development of the modern professional with his own claims to unique expertise, the nightmarish mirror image of middle class professional specialization is "proletarianization" within the working class: the "de-skilling" process, central to the initial success of the steam-powered textile industry and then later adapted to the needs of other manufacturing industries, that reduced workers' skills to a narrower base of abilities appropriate to only one job and consequently left them less adaptable to the demands of new types of work. A classic instance of this complaint occurs in Walter Besant's book *East London,* a work to which we referred in chapter 2. While noticing that East London is a city of many crafts (22–23), Besant argues that these can only be practiced by a specialized labor force. However, it is overspecialization that ultimately—and ironically, we might add—debilitates East Londoners, making them inflexible and unable to learn new skills and adapt them to new jobs, ultimately leaving them vulnerable to the vagaries of seasonal unemployment, which was the distinguishing feature of London's working class life. Thus, in inventorying the types of casual labor associated with different areas of East London, Besant says,

> In watchmaking, which belongs to Clerkenwell, a man will go through life in comfort knowing but one infinitesimal piece of work—how to make one small bit of a watch; so in these East End trades a man or a woman generally knows how to do one thing and one thing only, and if that one piece of work cannot be obtained the man is lost, for he can do nothing else. (*East London* 23)

The irony here is that "expert" discourse on the causes of poverty will increasingly identify "expertise" itself among the working class and the "residuum" as one of the root causes of poverty. The middle class professional, we might say, establishes his own claim to expertise by diagnosing the "problem" of expertise among the poor. As we shall see, this paradoxical discourse on "expertise," which vaunts the specialized knowledge of the middle class observer while denigrating that of his working class subject, is ultimately related to an emerging anxiety in the 1890s, as the hopes once entertained for culturalist philanthropy give way to fears that "mass" culture can only produce a parody of high culture.

Thus, what we see in Jefferies is the same issue turned around: the sign of degeneration in the bushman is the inability to specialize, to use tools for specialized purposes. Yet, ironically, that is precisely what the Crusoe figure, Felix, does not do either. His more "comprehensive" vision of the social order represented in *After London* is achieved precisely through his ability to surmount the narrow vision that overspecialization imposes, and this involves his having to learn a variety of new handicrafts—sometimes with a great deal of initial awkwardness. To deconstruct for one moment: lack of specialization is associated here both with the comprehensive vision of the Crusoe character and with the "savagery" of the degenerate bushman. This paradox was of course the paradox of Besant's own career. While he waxes nostalgic in *East London* about the days when one man made an entire shoe from scratch, we would do well to remember that Besant was the man more responsible than any other for establishing authorship as a specialized profession when he served as the influential president of the Society of Authors in the late nineteenth century.[9]

Lest we forget, it is important to note that the complaint that the division of labor in modern societies is inherently stultifying goes back at least to the Age of Reason, and that a vigorous criticism of "proletarianization" emerges from the work of the man who is most identified with the founding of political economy and with the celebration of comparative advantage. In Book 1 of the *Wealth of Nations*, Adam Smith tells us why the specialization which is so useful to the economy in general is so stultifying to the worker who becomes overspecialized:

> The man whose whole life is spent in performing a few simple operations generally becomes as stupid and ignorant as it is possible for a human creature to become . . . His dexterity at his own particular trade seems, in this manner, to be acquired at the expence of his intellectual, social, and martial virtues. But in every improved and civilized society this is the state in to which . . . the great body of the people, must necessarily fall, unless government takes some pains to prevent it. It is otherwise in barbarous societies . . . [here] invention is kept alive, and the mind is not suffered to fall into that drowsy stupidity, which, in a civilized society, seems to benumb the understanding of almost all the inferior ranks of people. (Quoted in Gagnier, *Insatiability* 23)

What would emerge in the nineteenth century as the critique of "proletarianization" is itself already adumbrated in the "primitivist" theme in Smith, whose most important work nonetheless provided the most compelling arguments for encouraging worldwide economic specialization.[10] As Regenia Gagnier reminds us, however, Smith's vision of industrial society is a profoundly ironic one: what "proletarianization" brings is a vast increase in productive power, and consequently, wealth, that compensates for the social ills of overspecialization ("Law of Progress" 316).

Underwriting the ideological incoherence that afflicts Jefferies' novel is a reactionary "republicanism" akin to Cobbett's: a belief that ultimately virtue resides in the countryside, in a more "simple" way of life that enables civilized virtue, one that dampens ressentiment by assigning each individual an important place in a traditional hierarchical order, and that puts a brake on growing social discord by assigning the landlord responsibility for caring for his lesser charges. While the landscape depicted in the novel hardly resembles the ordered and civilized way of life evoked in the moment of its loss in Goldsmith's "Deserted Village," there is little doubt that the same nostalgic values inform Jefferies' anti-urbanism in the novel.[11] Felix's own abilities have little to do with his education and everything to do with a kind of native risk-taking empiricism: a willingness to go out and learn by experiencing first-hand the strange world beyond his father's palisades. Felix's own technical knowledge, which springs from that same native empiricism, is far in advance of the people he moves among, and his innate skill in improvising solutions to military and economic problems only he completely grasps make him ultimately victorious over the savages he finds himself facing. Yet the contradiction remains. Incapable of offering a consistently reactionary vision of the social order because of its implicit but undisguised commitment to the ideology of progress, this book nonetheless attempts to paper over its ideological contradictions with a purely imaginary resolution: the success of the heroic main character.

Wells's *The Time Machine*, a more complex and interesting "dystopic" novel, was published in 1893, and it relates the issue of class division to the theme of division of labor in a more trenchant, if just as unsatisfying, way. Its main character, the Time-Traveler, is presented as a courageous scientist/journalist venturing forth into an unknown and frightening future from the comfort of his own drawing room where stands that remarkable testament to his technological prowess—the time machine. The novel was written by a man with a strong scientific background (he studied with none other than T. H. Huxley) and strong socialist credentials (an early member of the Fabian Society, he later alienated many of the other members and went off on his own). Like the other writers discussed here, Wells tends to foreground the values that underwrite his main character's "professional class" heroism: his scientific detachment, his demystifying fearlessness, his energy, and his ability to bridge worlds and to register as a regrettable absence what none of the other characters in the main narrative are capable of considering: peace between hostile social classes. As with Jefferies, the world of the future which he explores is presented as one in which a dramatic gulf has opened up between social classes analogous to that separating distinct species. The gentle people he meets at first, the Eloi, are presented as physically delicate and sexually undifferentiated. Indeed, the Time-Traveler at first celebrates this lack of sexual differentiation as a sign that these people have achieved a utopian triumph over the need for reproduction of the species, and consequently, freed themselves from the yoke of the sexual division of labor which, in the Time-Traveler's own day, largely confines "respectable" women to the home and men to the workplace:

> Seeing the ease and security in which these people were living, I felt that this close resemblance of the sexes was after all what one would expect; for the strength of a man and the softness of a woman, the institution of the family, and the differentiation of occupations are mere militant necessities of an age of physical force; where population is balanced and abundant, much childbearing becomes an evil rather than a blessing to the State; where violence comes but rarely and off-spring are secure, there is less necessity—indeed there is no necessity—for an efficient family, and the specialization of the sexes with reference to their children's needs disappears. We see some beginnings of this even in our own time, and in this future age it was complete. This, I must remind you, was my speculation at the time. Later, I was to appreciate how far it fell short of the reality. (74)

The gender-based division of labor that marks patriarchal societies such as Victorian Britain's seems to have significantly eroded in the future society of the Eloi. He sees no evidence that the Eloi treat each other with violence, and, indeed, no evidence that they are governed by strong passions at all, whether sexual or fiercely maternal and protective. No one, male or female, works. The land seems conventionally "edenic" in many ways, with no signs of insects, no evidence of disease, no signs even of commerce:

> Social triumphs, too, had been effected. I saw mankind housed in splendid shelters, gloriously clothed, and as yet I had found them engaged in no toil. There were no signs of struggle, neither social nor economical struggle. The shop, the advertisement, traffic, all that com-

merce which constitutes the body of our world, was gone. It was natural on that golden evening that I should jump at the idea of a social paradise. The difficulty of increasing population had been met, I guessed, and population had ceased to increase. (79)

Indeed, the entire population has a childlike quality—they possess a peculiar innocence without childish curiosity—and the truth of that observation is reinforced when the Time-Traveler saves one of the Eloi, Weena, from drowning as the nearby Eloi stand idly by, incurious and unwilling to help. Weena's subsequent docile attachment to the Time-Traveler is finally more disturbing than gratifying. In her parasitical attachment to him and in her physically "immature" body, which clearly lacks secondary sexual characteristics, she seems to function as a satirical vehicle for Wells to use in lambasting both the conventional Victorian notion of the ornamental female and the Victorian notion of innocent childhood on which she is modeled.[12]

What the Time-Traveler gradually comes to understand, though, is that the future state of social organization represented by the Eloi is finally undesirable and demoralizing, precisely because the triumph over "pain" and "natural necessity" takes the "keen" edge off human intelligence:

> What, unless biological science is a mass of errors, is the cause of human intelligence and vigour? Hardship and freedom: conditions under which the active, strong, and subtle survive and the weaker go to the wall; conditions that put a premium upon the loyal alliance of capable men, upon self-restraint, patience, and decision. And the institution of the family, and the emotions that arise therein, the fierce jealousy, the tenderness for offspring, parental self-devotion, all found their justification and support in the imminent dangers of the young. Now, where are these imminent dangers? There is a sentiment arising, and it will grow, against connubial jealousy, against fierce maternity, against passion of all sorts; unnecessary things now, and things that make us uncomfortable, savage survivals, discords in a refined and pleasant life. (79)

Although Wells's narrator does not pause long here to consider the implications of this paragraph, they go to the heart of the project of social amelioration (and even of the nastier projects associated with Social Darwinists like Arnold White). To seek to relieve pain and suffering, to attempt to make the human lot more bearable, is to seek to eliminate the very conditions—"hardship and freedom"—that prompt human beings to develop their best qualities. As the Time-Traveler puts it: "We are kept keen on the grindstone of pain and necessity, and, it seemed to me, that here was that hateful grindstone broken at last!" (Wells 81). The novel is dystopic precisely because it presents what seems like a conventionally utopian achievement—the seeming conquest by the Eloi of the "animal" conditions of life—as a social outcome to be deplored. The "We" of that quote, however, is not the "We" of the whole herd. Rather, it is the "We" of the "evolutionarily fit": the small number of "keen-edged" who are able to pass on their qualities to subsequent generations.

The Time-Traveler later infers, though, that the seeming ease of the Eloi is somehow enabled only by the underground work of the loathsome, apelike, Morlocks who inhabit the nether regions and make a habit of surfacing at night to dine on stray Eloi. The brutal nature of this future world, inhabited not only by Carlyle's "dandies" but also by his "drudges," is exemplified in the Eloi's loss of technical knowledge which the professional class of Victorian Britain still possesses in abundance. The Time-Traveler's escape in the end is made possible only when he starts a massive fire which neither the Morlocks nor Eloi seem to understand how to put out. Unlike the Victorian professional middle class, the Eloi seem not only to inhabit a lotus-land which requires no work of them, but to have lost the capacity for suppressing the very underclass which is slowly preying on them. The nightmarish nature of Wells's imagined world seems to lie not in the fact that life in this society of the future is rendered awful by a brutally binary class structure, but rather in the fact that the ruling class has lost the will and the technical means to efficiently suppress the lower classes (the Eloi are, among other things here, Wells's parody of Victorian Aesthetes). The Eloi have lost their "keen edge" in all metaphorical senses of that term: an "edge" which the novel hints ought to be used for the suppression of the lower classes and the preservation of class privilege for the genteel elite (a strangely elitist position for a man who claimed to be a socialist, although that particular paradox of professionalism runs through much of this literature and was of course constitutive of Fabian socialism). The epilogue finds Wells confusedly celebrating Weena's gift of flowers as a sign of the gratitude and "mutual tenderness" between her and the Time-Traveler: the genteel aspirations of Victorian professionalism, represented above all by the Time-Traveler's own social group, find their dim echo in the etiolated, reduced affect of the Eloi, condemned to wither rather than to rule efficiently and effectively.

So far so good. The novel then can be read as a proto-fascist call to reinvigorate the ruling classes and to celebrate danger and conflict as the elements which keep the human "edge" keen. However, one can also press this reading of the book one step further in a deconstructive direction. As the book he wrote the next year, *The Island of Dr. Moreau*, reveals, Wells was quite capable of taking a conventional cultural opposition and turning it on its head to reposition his critique. Prendick, you may recall, in that novel initially thinks that Dr. Moreau is a vivisectionist, experimenting, as Moreau himself puts it, with "lower animals" in order to move them "up" the evolutionary continuum—to "humanize" them. Yet, Prendick's initial disgust with Moreau stems not from hearing the latter's crimes detailed but from hearing the cries of pain of the pumas on which he is experimenting. It is the feral cry of pain that humanizes the animal for Prendick and produces a sympathetic reaction that suspends category distinctions—if only temporarily. Moreau himself assumes that he is doing good for these creatures by giving them the opportunity to "rise" up the evolutionary ladder. However, that motive is shown to be monstrous rather than philanthropic. Not only do the creatures inevitably revert to type, especially after tasting blood, but the process of humanization itself is revealed as so inhumane—it involves nightly torture of innocent creatures in the "House of Pain"—it induces Prendick to flee the company of Montgomery and Moreau out of disgust in order to join the much more welcome society of his fellow creatures, his fellow animals. The novel inverts the conventional hierarchy of the human and the animal and convicts Moreau of inhumanity precisely for suppressing his animality—his ability to imagine the other's pain. That this imaginative ability has two antithetical sides to it—the "blood lust" of the predator and the "sympathetic suffering" of one who can imagine himself as potential prey—means that it is a more complex phenomenon than human binary categories—and most models of unitary subjectivity—can easily account for.[13]

In a strangely similar way, *The Time Machine* initially foregrounds the Time-Traveler's rather too-confident assumption that the Eloi constitute a ruling class who have achieved a utopian triumph of sorts over what used to be the controlling condition of human life: the need to work. Believing that the viciously binary class structure of Victorian society—"capital" and "labour": the West End and the East End—has reached its logical conclusion in this land, he naturally assumes that the Eloi are the ruling class and the Morlocks the descendants of the long-oppressed working class, having worked underground so long their eyes have grown lidless and their flesh pallid. He sums up this tentative hypothesis midway through the book:

> So, in the end, above ground you must have the Haves, pursuing pleasure and comfort and beauty, and below ground the Have-nots, the Workers getting continually adapted to the conditions of their labour. Once they were there, they would no doubt have to pay rent, and not a little of it, for the ventilation of their caverns; and if they refused, they would starve or be suffocated for arrears. Such of them as were so constituted as to be miserable and rebellious would die; and, in the end, the balance being permanent, the survivors would become as well adapted to the conditions of underground life, and as happy in their way, as the Upper-world people were to theirs. As it seemed to me, the refined beauty and the etiolated pallor followed naturally enough. (104)

What he discovers, though, when he descends to the land of the Morlocks disturbs this rather too-tidy binary vision of "dandies" and "drudges" somewhat. As he submits briefly and with rapidly increasing unease to being inspected by the curious Morlocks, the Time-Traveler speaks of feeling an "instinctive" loathing for these beings with chinless faces and lidless eyes (113). In fact, this episode makes him feel "like a beast." When he then discovers that the white meat the Morlocks had been eating was actually Eloi flesh, he reacts with revulsion, realizing now that the Morlocks are surely human, for apes are much more "discriminating" than humans in their tastes and would presumably not dine on their own kind (129):

> And suddenly there came into my head the memory of the meat I had seen in the Under-world. It seemed odd how it floated into my mind: not stirred up as it were by the current of my meditations, but coming in almost like a question from outside. I tried to recall the form of it. I had a vague sense of something familiar, but I could not tell what it was at the time. (chapter 7)

The Time-Traveler's reaction here can no longer be read as a simple recoil from contact with creatures of a different species in their difference, a recoil that is easily understood within the terms of a logic that preserves the subject in its own sense of separateness from the too-easily vilified object. Rather a more profound transvaluation of experience is going on here, as the Time-Traveler suddenly awakens to the possibility of kinship, not with the Eloi, but with the Morlocks. A transmutation of basic categories is occurring, precipitated by an experience governed by the logic of abjection, of the Time-Traveler's "vague sense of something familiar" that "float[s]" in as if from outside. As Kristeva argues, true abjection is not caused by lack of cleanliness or health. Rather it is caused by "what disturbs identity, system, order" (Kristeva 4). The Time-Traveler is having exactly that experience here: an experience of revulsion that precedes differentiation, an experience that is complexly tied up with his own realization of his own desires—i.e., any desire:

> There is nothing like the abjection of self to show that all abjection is in fact recognition of the *want* on which any being, meaning, language, or desire is founded. (Kristeva 5)

What disturbs order here is precisely the inability to differentiate his own desire for "meat" from the Morlocks' desires for his "meat." The momentary suspension of the boundary between self and other, man and ape, Eloi and Morlock, he who desires meat and he who fears being meat, places him momentarily in an indefinable space, oscillating between antithetical categories of being, subject and object, predator and prey. His revulsion cannot be explained any longer as the revulsion of a human from an anthropophagous ape, for that "other," that anthropophagous ape, is also himself. Rather, revulsion is bound to desire, a binding that inevitably means that the subject is no longer one. Revulsion here is a complex marker of identity, really of identification. I am one with those who make me sick. As we have discussed earlier, the *flâneur's* simultaneous occupation of antithetical categories—subject and object at one and the same time—characterizes many attempts to report on the abyss while descending into it, and Wells's Time-Traveler, although earnest rather than insouciant, runs a similar risk of identity.

His decision, then, that the Morlocks are malign is, odd as it may sound, his way of marking his identity with them. It is the Morlocks who, after all, have hidden away his time machine in hope of learning how it works. It is the Morlocks who are enterprising and energetic in response, no doubt, to the fearful conditions of their lives. It is the Morlocks who fit the Time-Traveler's definition of a people who have not lost their vigor and intelligence because their lives are governed by hardship. Not surprisingly, then, it is the Eloi who now strike the Time-Traveler as leading merely a bovine existence (156). In fact, he decides, finally, that they are the Morlocks' cattle: a decision that implies a complete inversion of his initial assumptions about the relationship between the two classes, and which retrospectively revalues his edenic ideal by investing it with the meaning of a childish wish to put an end to desire. What but human vanity could have led him to assume that a herd of pacific cattle comprise the dominant class in this strange world, that those who dwell above ground in a state of moral and aesthetic anesthesia should be taken to be the rulers? This leads Wells's Time-Traveler to a final biological sermon about adaptation:

> It is a law of nature we overlook, that intellectual versatility is the compensation for change, danger, and trouble. An animal perfectly in harmony with its environment is a perfect mechanism. Nature never appeals to intelligence until habit and instinct are useless. There is no intelligence where there is no change and no need of change. Only those animals partake of intelligence that have to meet a huge variety of needs and dangers. (149)

While he leaves the land ablaze, the trail behind him littered with lifeless Morlocks, brained by his iron bar in his escape, the novel ends with this tragic implication: the scientist returns to his circle of professional colleagues bearing the implicit message that social amelioration is the wrong road, that class warfare is what preserves the keen edge of human curiosity, and that struggle rather than social peace is necessary to human progress. It is a strangely bleak vision inspired by the "naturalistic" (and perhaps very "Victorian") idea that the class conflict we carry on is always a conflict with ourselves, although it does break with conventional "othering" to some extent by dramatizing the main character's uneasy identification with the downtrodden but vigorous.

Insofar as it acts as a warning to the present, the novel is also, by virtue of that fact, a complex apology for the Mandarin class and for the perpetuation of class distinctions which, ostensibly, it is the sworn purpose of professionals to attempt to alleviate (although it should go without saying that this professional ideal justifies class privilege on the new grounds of merit, not inheritance). It unfolds all the central contradictions in the ideology of the late-Victorian professional class, contradictions evident in the Fabian plan for "permeation," which required the installation of prominent socialists in positions of social power and influence so that they can then allow their ideas to "permeate" the ruling class; and in the settlement movement, which was based on the modeling of upper class tastes to a working class presumed to be in need of such education because unaware of what it ought to desire. In what follows we will discuss two writers who usher the Victorian age to a close at least partly by embodying these unresolved contradictions in their writing.

People of the Abyss and Reporting as Adventuring

Queen Victoria died in 1901 after 64 years as reigning monarch—the longest reign in British history. When she assumed the throne in 1837, London was the largest city in the world with almost 2 million inhabitants. When she died in 1901, it was still the largest city in the world, having grown to accommodate 4.5 million inhabitants (Porter 186).

The first two volumes of the first modern statistically based study of the nature of class in London, Charles Booth's *Life and Labour of the People of London*, appeared in 1889 and 1892. As we mentioned in chapter 2, Booth's inventory of the state of London at the end of Victoria's reign carefully divided the population into eight social classes, four above and four below the line that Booth was the first social investigator to draw: the poverty line. Booth's famous map of London also color-coded every neighborhood according to which of the social classes predominated there. It is safe to say that by 1902, as Edward VII officially assumed the throne that had been his mother's possession for so many years, both the extent of London poverty and its geographic distribution had been measured and mapped. No social investigator who descended into "the abyss" of East London could convincingly portray himself as entering terra incognita—although more than a few continued to do just that. The landscape of London poverty was no longer virginal territory, and thus twentieth-century social investigators begin with a set of assumptions that are far different from those governing Mayhew's journey 50 years earlier. The "descent" is now something of a "return," a "return" in which the investigator must pay tribute, implicitly or explicitly, to those who have harrowed this hell before him, those who have left their footprints. Hell now has a relatively long history and a readily recognizable imagistic tradition, and part of that history is a history of investigation: more than half a century of poking and prodding at the body of the urban poor in search of solutions to the vexing question of how abject poverty persists—perhaps grows—in the face of the evident prosperity that industrialism has brought to the middle and upper classes. While Charles Booth himself seems to have been convinced that poverty had actually decreased since Mayhew began his interviews for the *Morning Chronicle*, in this opinion he was in the minority among social investigators of the day. His map indeed shows many pockets of "respectability" on many of the blocks of East London. As Himmelfarb has argued, "the English became more conscious of poverty and more distressed by it precisely as the material, political, and educational conditions of the poor improved" (*Poverty and Compassion* 32). The carefully detailed statistical measures Booth featured in his magnum opus are, to some extent, meant to lower the emotional tone in discussions of poverty, to stick a statistical pin in melodramatic windbags such as Rev. Andrews Mearns, allowing readers to step away from close focusing on the individual tragedy of poverty to attain a more "comprehensive," if inevitably abstracted, vision of a complex whole through statistical measures.

When the American writer Jack London visits East London in 1902 with his Kodak camera, he is deliberately treading a path already worn smooth by the footsteps of such social explorers as Mayhew, Greenwood, Sims, Mearns, and William Booth—not to mention the investigators organized by Charles Booth.[14] Moreover, London is self-consciously aware that he is traversing a landscape already overwritten by these other writers. He makes a point of visiting the site of Arthur Morrison's Jago, at one point, in order to comment on its transformation, he unashamedly draws liberally from Charles Booth's statistics, and he even spends a night in a workhouse in imitation of Greenwood's adventure of 1866.[15] He likewise casts himself unapologetically in the role of Dante harrowing hell, his chapter headings larded with allusions to an heroic "descent" (indeed, London himself many years later credited Wells's Time-Traveler's descent to the underground world of the Morlocks as the inspiration for his own "descent" into East London). While this work is unusual in its time for its spare, economical prose and its attempt—not always successful—to break with the conventions of melodramatic representation, it cannot claim the freedom from prestructuration that Mayhew was able to achieve to a limited extent.[16] Indeed, the overall movement of the narrative is from individuation to abstraction, as the story of how he disguised himself and then penetrated the rookeries of East London gradually yields to chapters which lay out statistical breakdowns of the daily diets of those who live in the abyss.

Like Wells's Time-Traveler, London encounters a "race of people" in East London whose difference from middle class norms marks them as irretrievably other: "short of stature and of wretched beer-sodden appearance," they appear even more physically alien as he descends further. A typical description occurs when he visits Christ's Church, Spitalfields Garden: "On the benches on either side was arrayed a mass of miserable and distorted humanity, the sight of which would have impelled Doré to more diabolical flights of fancy than he ever succeeded in achieving. It was a welter of rags and filth, of all manner of loathsome skin diseases, open sores, bruises, grossness, indecency, leering monstrosities, and bestial faces" (London 62). While descriptions of the poor as bestial and disease-ridden had become commonplace in the Darwinian atmosphere of 1890s Britain, what makes London's adventures readable is the way he stages his own self-preservation in an atmosphere seemingly so conducive to demoralization, disease, and death at the hands of criminal toughs. Rather than staging himself as a transcendental subject, London devotes pages to describing a careful girding of the loins in preparation for his descent: he dilates at length on the details of how he arranged to find a room in the East End for a few months, on how he managed to dress himself as a fair imitation of a local, and, above all, on how he managed to survive confrontations with the diseased and the criminal that would have done in a lesser man. The story of the harrowing of hell is also a story of the professional heroism of the journalist. In the grand tradition of other nineteenth-century reporter/actor/ethnographers (Sir Richard Burton's pilgrimage to El-Medinah and Mecca comes to mind), London's "descent" comes with all the requisite ethnographic trappings that clearly establish the otherness of the other if only because of the fact that the reporter must take such pains to convince the other that he is not reporting on him.

The reasons for this are not hard to discern. The requirements of disguise impose certain conditions. London is addressing in his work a middle class reading public that largely refuses to recognize the poor as individuated subjects. In the guise of one of these "others," he cannot address this audience. Members of the mob lack individual voices, but reporters are valued precisely for their individual voices. As a reporter defined by his individuality but disguised as one of the faceless crowd, London occupies the same uneasy subject-object status that we described above in relation to Wells's Time-Traveler. Something like the same complicity with the imagined middle class reader that we saw in Greenwood and others is established in this book, although London takes advantage of that presumed intimacy to administer a hyperbolic tongue-lashing to his reader on more than one occasion. He does not enjoy the same easy cosmopolitan relationship with that fictional entity, the inscribed reader, that Greenwood usually affects. Rather the relationship is constructed as a more deliberately contentious one.

Nevertheless, Jack London does not readily blend in to the scenery in East London either. He does not much resemble the mainly older, disease-ridden workhouse inmates with whom he spends much of his time. He is young, comparatively healthy, and cursed with an inexpungable American accent. When he addresses his imagined audience, he is given to reminding his middle class readers of his more abstract but also comprehensive vision of the economic and geographic dynamism of the city, of the perpetual outward expansion of degradation and despair that, although condensed in the form of the history of this particular city, is part of a larger economic process occurring throughout the world:

> Far, far out on the fringe of the city, live the small businessmen, little managers, and successful clerks. They dwell in cottages and semidetached villas, with bits of flower garden, and elbow room, and breathing space. They inflate themselves with pride and throw chests when they contemplate the Abyss from which they have escaped, and they thank God that they are not as other men. And lo! down upon them comes Johnny Upright and the monster city at his heels. Tenements spring up like magic, gardens are built upon, villas are divided and subdivided into many dwellings, and the black night of London settles down in a greasy pall. (*People* 29)

Interestingly, this vision of the city's dynamism is cast in terms of threat to a carefully earned class status, as the city's very growth threatens to engulf the petty bourgeois clerks on its outer fringes. The city is a growing empire of degradation marching inexorably outward. The slumming holiday that Jack London takes in order to write the book, his carefully managed and temporary descent down the ladder of class, is implicitly presented here as the unwelcome permanent fate awaiting all the self-satisfied lower middle class clerks of East London. The geographic metaphor maps neatly onto the metaphor of class[17] and the city's dynamism is presented as a threat to the well-being of all who think they have escaped. And the mention of "elbow room" Americanizes the fear of falling by conjuring up the ghost of a suburbanization—the desire for greener spaces "out there" in the distant land where the dream of upward mobility necessitates leaving the "monster" city behind—that reinvents the psychological escape from poverty and working class status as a process of moving toward gentility and its associated countryside, a movement always doomed to be ultimately self-defeating (hence the preoccupation with an always already lost "natural world" toward which the subject drives himself). Beatrice Webb's "consciousness of sin" drove her into the East End as an act of expiation, as we have discussed in chapter 2. Jack London, though, who came from humble roots in California, lacks the sense of *noblesse oblige* of the wealthy railroad heiress, courted by would-be prime ministers and well-known intellectuals. Consequently, while Webb's diary is ruminative, we see the style as appropriate for one who writes to justify her life as an act of contrition for social guilt she inherited but did not earn. London, by contrast, uses a much-celebrated spare style unsuited to the kind of staging of self-meditation that we see in Webb and in so much of the middle class fiction of the Victorian period. Rather, London casts himself as something of an impassioned—indeed, impatient—intellectual caught in an adventure tale.

London is also drawn toward greater and greater abstraction as he struggles to find "typifying" examples to illustrate his larger thesis. The following passage, a typification of the respectable working class, is an example:

> In the evenings the men can be seen at the doors, pipes in their mouths and children on their knees, wives gossiping, and laughter and fun going on. The content of these people is manifestly great, for, relative to the wretchedness that encompasses them, they are well off.
>
> But at the best it is a dull, animal happiness, the content of the full belly. The dominant note of their lives is materialistic. They are stupid and heavy, without imagination. The Abyss seems to exude a stypefying atmosphere of torpor, which wraps about them and deadens them. The Unseen holds for them neither terror nor delight. They are unaware of the Unseen; and the full belly and the evening pipe, with their regular 'art an' arf,' is all they demand, or dream of demanding, from existence. (43)

What galls him is the "content" of these people. The emergence of a contemptible abstraction—"mass man," "the crowd," really "the norm"—is being registered here, as it is even more so in Masterman's book published the same year.

Yet "mass man" can only emerge in response to a new form of reification, of abstraction, that allows generalization. And central to this process was the evolution of statistics and the encouragement it gave to "normalization" throughout the century. Ian Hacking traces its emergence back to the 1820s and 1830s, and locates its birth in a fascination with deviance and criminality: "If one wanted to give frequency statistics a bad name, one might contend that nearly all the early frequencies were frequencies of immorality and 'degeneracy,' and that the enthusiasm for statistics was part of an operation of information and control intended to eliminate deviance. Fascination with deviance from the norm, and even the use of 'normal' to mean what usually happens, also began in the 1820s" (Hacking, "Comment" 452). So powerful was this new tool, that it promised to transform people's understanding of social life. With the proclamation of Poisson's "law of large numbers" in 1835, the possibility of a completely determined social order was on the horizon, celebrated by those, like Henry Buckle, who believed that history was governed by laws as fixed as those governing the natural world. Thus, Quetelet, in studying statistical regularities in criminality, proclaims that one can know in advance "how many men will bloody their hands with violent murders, how many will be counterfeiters, how many poisoners, just as one can enumerate in advance the births and deaths that will occur in a given year" (Hacking, "Cracks" 469). Statistical thinking made possible a new type of Victorian determinism, as the "law of large numbers" dictates deterministic patterns sometimes belied by individual stories. That approach is quite clear especially in London's chapter called "The Hunger Wail," which presents a depressing statistical inventory of an underfed residuum.

As a good novelist, London is certainly not unaware of the importance of the individual to put flesh on the general. However, these instances are narrated in the interest of establishing a figurative pattern—so that the individual instance takes on symbolic import, so that it "argues" synecdochically a more general point about the condition of England. Nowhere is this clearer than in the passage where London, staying overnight in the Whitechapel workhouse, meets two men fresh from the smallpox hospital:

> Conversation was slack at first, standing there, till the man on one side of me and the man on the other side of me discovered that they had been in the smallpox hospital at the same time, though a full house of sixteen hundred patients had prevented their becoming acquainted. But they made up for it, discussing and comparing the more loathsome features of their disease in the most cold-blooded, matter-of-fact way. I learned that the average mortality was one in six, that one of them had

been in three months and the other three months and a half, and that they had been 'rotten wi' it.' Whereat my flesh began to creep and crawl, and I asked them how long they had been out. One had been out two weeks, and the other three weeks. Their faces were badly pitted (though each assured the other that this was not so), and further, they showed me in their hands and under the nails the smallpox 'seeds' still working out. Nay, one of them worked a seed out for my edification, and pop it went, right out of his flesh into the air. I tried to shrink up smaller inside my clothes, and I registered a fervent though silent hope that it had not popped on me. (London 92)

Insinuating both the common mortality of journalist and poor subjects alike, this passage manages to particularize both the ravages of disease to which the poor are prey, the reified consciousness of the victims of disease themselves (the men here are said to report the "average mortality" in the smallpox hospital, as if they were Jack Londons themselves), and the risks to life that the journalist undertakes to represent them in print. Indeed, the act of writing itself becomes heroic, as the journalist demonstrates unusual self-restraint in detailing how he subjected himself to the same workhouse fare as the other inmates:

> At eight o'clock we went down into a cellar under the Infirmary, where tea was brought to us, and the hospital scraps. These were heaped high on a huge platter in an indescribably mess—pieces of bread, chunks of grease and fat pork, the burnt skin from the outside of roasted joints, bones, in short, all the leavings from the fingers and mouths of the sick ones suffering from all manner of diseases. Into this mess the men plunged their hands, digging, pawing, turning over, examining, rejecting, and scrambling for. It wasn't pretty. Pigs couldn't have done worse. But the poor devils were hungry, and they ate ravenously of the swill and when they could eat no more they bundled what was left into their handkerchiefs and thrust it inside their shirts. (London 110)

And if the everyday act of eating isn't heroic enough, London goes on to describe the delight of one of his companions, Ginger, on discovering some pork bones with meat still on them in a pile of medical waste that had been sprayed with disinfectant (London 111–12). These passages serve an important symbolic function that goes beyond simply dramatizing the risks run by London himself, one which transcends the individuality of the scene. We see that when we connect, as readers, the episode of Ginger hungrily gathering up pork bones sprayed with disinfectant with the tragically ironic theme that runs throughout: the theme of sustenance for the poor as *pharmakon*. Insofar as it prolongs life, it protracts the suffering of the downtrodden. Tina Young Choi has recently argued that disease becomes, especially in the writings of Chadwick and Gavin, "a trope for a new urban epistemology, for describing the connective social relations, both troubling and productive, made possible and even probable by urban living conditions" (Choi 270). The function of statistics then is to impose a rational control on such risk through the notions of "percentage" and "probability," investing even middle class existence in the city with a *frisson*, however attenuated, associated with running risk. Of course, disease functions to tie the middle class reader to the lower class subject, as we see in *Bleak House*, where Esther Summerson's pock-marked face materializes her connection—metonymical and metaphorical—with Jo, Charley, and finally, her own father, Nemo, who dies in Krook's boarding house. In *People of the Abyss*, the episode in which Jack London discusses smallpox with the two denizens of the Whitechapel workhouse suggests yet another way in which disease ties the slumming middle class subject to the lower class victims among whom he moves: by risking infection but escaping it, he not only establishes his heroic credentials but he associates the running of those risks with a larger ideological project to which his book is dedicated. The book becomes a dramatization of what we might call the successful management of disgust in the interest of a certain kind of cross-class solidarity, a public act of very political slumming.

The book is also symptomatic in some respects of the irruption of nationalist ideology in the discourse on poverty at the end of the century, an event that helps construct a certain middle class anxiety about the health of what Mary Poovey has identified as the "body politic." The so-called Age of National Efficiency saw many efforts to tie anxiety about an unhealthy British working class to efforts to improve the health of the entire British nation: efforts ranging from the Social Darwinist nightmares of eugenicists like Arnold White to the ameliorative projects of "municipal socialism" and "imperial federation" that marked the political career of Joseph Chamberlain. Informing the whole of Jack London's critique of London poverty is a nationalistic thesis about history that posits that Britain is rapidly losing out in a contest for world economic supremacy with the United States and Germany.[18] Generations of poverty have, in his view, produced an irreversible physical and moral decline in the British population:

As I say, the young are high-strung, nervous, excitable; the middle-aged are empty-headed, stolid, and stupid. It is absurd to think for an instant that they can compete with the workers of the New World. Brutalized, degraded, and dull, the Ghetto folk will be unable to render efficient service to England in the world struggle for industrial supremacy which economists declare has already begun. (London 231)

The one small hope of reversing this, in London's view, lies in what he refers to as "better management." Typical of the Age of National Efficiency in many respects, London's book ends with a call not for democratic redistribution of wealth but rather for efficient and farsighted management—a new ruling class of farseeing rulers. Like Wells, whose socialism was sharpened on a decidedly authoritarian whetstone, London finds himself calling for a better-managed social order. The democratic implications of his own hobnobbing with the poor of East London are eventually lost sight of as London reverts to an authoritarian vision of a rightly ordered social order, presided over by a far-seeing Mandarin class of managers.

The implications of that move are profoundly antidemocratic, as London painfully demonstrates the impossibility of the London working class rising above itself to see the social order in a broader, and more detached, view. London's meeting with the labor leader, Dan Cullen, one of the principal figures in the Great Dock Strike of 1889, initially seems to offer hope that at least some members of the London working class are capable of a more comprehensive view of social conditions. However, those hopes are soon disappointed. London apostrophizes Cullen, whom he meets while the latter is dying in a hospital, in terms that suggest that even Cullen is incapable of the more comprehensive vision necessary to success because he was denied the means, that comprehensive "wisdom" itself may be a prerogative of a more comfortable class status:

> Poor Dan Cullen! A Jude the Obscure, who reached out after knowledge; who toiled with his body in the day and studied in the watches of the night; who dreamed his dream and struck valiantly for the Cause; a patriot, a lover of human freedom, and a fighter unafraid; and in the end, not gigantic enough to beat down the conditions which baffled and stifled him, a cynic and a pessimist, gasping his final agony on a pauper's couch in a charity ward.—'For a man to have died who might have been wise and was not, this I call a tragedy.'" (*People of the Abyss* 164)

A project which begins in the psychological democracy of the age of sentiment ends with a reinstantiation of rigid psychological divisions between those who have and those who have not, and the process is aided by the very representational strategies that, in Dickens' work, constitute invitations to share in a common humanity. The great irony of London's writing on East London is that the humanizing strategies employed to draw the working class back into humanity's fold, end up reifying, dehumanizing, and alienating them even further.

To be sure, London is in sufficient control of his tone to be able to use dehumanization as a deliberate, and effectively passionate, rhetorical strategy. He converts it into political anger:

> And day by day I became convinced that not only is it unwise, but it is criminal for the people of the Abyss to marry. They are the stones by the builder rejected. There is no place for them in the social fabric, while all the forces of society drive them downward till they perish. At the bottom of the Abyss they are feeble, besotted, and imbecile. If they reproduce, the life is so cheap that perforce it perishes of itself. The work of the world goes on above them, and they do not care to take part in it, nor are they able. Moreover, the work of the world does not need them. There are plenty, far fitter than they, clinging to the steep slope above, and struggling frantically to slide no more. (40)

However, the question this passage raises—to what extent is this a genuine eugenic argument and to what extent mock eugenic argument?—is part of a larger question about the conflicting elements in London's own political views (is he a committed socialist? a Social Darwinist? a Nietzschean elitist? an American nationalist?) that remain unreconciled to this day. The Malthusian argument of the text generates strange paradoxes. Because a grim Malthusian might applaud the spectacle of the starving poor pawing greedily at a pile of waste food from a hospital sprayed with disinfectant, all the better to accelerate the only known "cure" for poverty, he might be tempted to cite the evidence of London's book as proof that the workhouse system seems to be working just fine. Eating, for the poor of London's book, is finally governed by the logic of the *pharmakon:* food is both remedy and poison at one and the same time. And, the darkly tragic implications of such a position inevitably infect all judgments of value when it comes to the poor, as charity is grimly conceptualized as murder and murder a form of charity.

To some extent, London's account displays the powerfully influential imprint of Gustav LeBon, whose influence on social commentators at the end of the nineteenth century can often seem ubiquitous. Indeed, an emerging critique of "mass culture," influenced by LeBon's analysis of the powerfully coercive force of "the crowd," gradually comes to be conflated with the critique of the "de-moralizing" effects of abject poverty. However, it is in Masterman's *From the Abyss*, published only a few months before London's study, that one sees a more systematic application of the analysis of the crowd to the analysis of poverty. The result is an even more effective exteriorization of the poor in the face of the manifest evidence of the author's sympathy for them, for Masterman adapts LeBon's contention that the individual and the crowd are psychologically incommensurable.[19] What makes Masterman's work unusual is its insistence on explicitly bringing together a critique of the way Britain treats its poor with condemnation of an emerging mass culture and the economic system which gave it birth. The "poor" and the "masses" are effectively conflated, and thus Masterman's tone inflects the tone of the sympathetic social investigator with the worldly irony typical of the late-Victorian critic of mass culture. Indeed, in Masterman's somewhat abstract if impassioned analysis, the sins of the poor are the sins of the "masses," and the "abyss" an ever-expanding zone of abjection complexly tied to the cyclical nature of investment and disinvestment which is the central feature of capitalism in action locally:

> So in a kind of an irresistible muddy wave the Abyss rolls sullenly onward. Behind us the city is depopulated, our houses are torn down and stamped out, great warehouses and business premises huddle us forward. In front is the land of plenty, upon which we are falling as the chosen people on the nations of Canaan. (47)

Less a determinate and confined space than a place of disinvestment in an economic order which structurally requires disinvestment to complement investment, the poor of East London do not threaten the middle classes from afar but rather threaten to become them as they expand their empire geographically.

The equating of the poor with the masses begins right away: "Whence did they all come, these creatures with strange antics and manners, these denizens of another universe of being?" (3). Informed by the same rhetoric of alarm that informed Matthew Arnold's discussion of the rude unenfranchised "Populace" trampling Hyde Park flower beds thirty years earlier, Masterman's alarm causes him to suggest rather than state, "But within there is a cloud on men's minds, and a half-stifled recognition of the presence of a new force hitherto unreckoned; the creeping into conscious existence of the quaint and innumerable populations bred in the Abyss" (3). The ambiguous meaning of the word "conscious" here is symptomatic. Does it refer to "the crowd" becoming "conscious"—and therefore more deliberately threatening—for the first time, or does it refer to the crowd's first becoming an object of "conscious" attention of the middle classes? We don't know. But the context in which Masterman was writing suggests it may be both. Not only had the threat of lower class criminality and disease been increasingly impressed upon the consciousness of the middle class public over the closing decades of the nineteenth century, but the contemporaneous celebrations of the relief of Mafeking had impressed upon many of Masterman's contemporaries (Hobson most famously in his work *The Psychology of Jingoism*) a growing realization that the lower class "crowd" was capable of mass action, of dangerous because "directed" effort.[20] Indeed, this is one of the features of the "crowd" that most troubled the readers of LeBon: the tendency of the "crowd" to directed action, to the exercise of organized but usually malign mass will independent of the will of the individual, does not necessarily require all the individual members of the "crowd" to be physically contiguous to one another, especially in the age of the penny press: "The disappearance of conscious personality and the turning of feelings and thoughts in a definite direction, which are the primary characteristics of a crowd about to become organised, do not always involve the simultaneous presence of a number of individuals on one spot" (LeBon 15). Whipped to a frenzy of indignation by the penny press, the "just-conscious" lower class crowd is capable of almost any action that those who surrender their individual will to the general will are capable of.

Less concerned than Jack London with sensationalized reporting of the physical details of East End poverty, Masterman is much more interested, like Matthew Arnold, in a disciplinary project, in calling for the construction of a viable form of mass education that is informed by an ideal close to Arnold's "Culture." A graduate of Christ College, Cambridge, Masterman based his book on observations made while he was living in Camberwell to which he moved in 1890. However, the very bitterness which makes him such an acute observer and writer about the East End takes some of the sting out of his criticism as well.

Hence, Masterman dilates on the life of the fictional "John Smith," a deliberate abstraction, a member of the "respectable working class" not yet fallen into "the abyss," a creature invented by Masterman to embody what the settlement movement conceives as the "educable" working class man whose taste is in need of being formed by his betters. In Masterman's view, this settlement movement "ideal" is suspect because it can never be realized:

> He [John Smith] appears to regard 'Our English Poets' and 'The Duties of Citizenship' with equal disfavour: neither Beethoven nor Wagner are able to drag him from his den. So the Settlements are now pausing: somewhat perplexed, somewhat saddened, acknowledging that the first frontal attack has failed, but doubtful in what direction to initiate a flanking movement: still resolute, however, to pursue the solution of the problem, 'to strive, to seek, to find, and not to yield.' (58)

As with Greenwood earlier, the irony here is a worldly irony that establishes the speaker as not "of the Abyss" despite his repeated use of the pronoun "we." To raise the abyss-dweller to the level of "John Smith" seems to him a goal of dubious social worth, and throws into question the wisdom of philanthropic exercises. The "we" suggests a factitious communal construct denied by Masterman's rhetoric.

Despite his role as social ideal of a sort, "John Smith" is enervated, finally, a figure incapable of reaching after something higher and more worthwhile, unable to be "dragged from his den" by anyone. His opposite number here is the "hooligan," a more interesting figure to Masterman, although, as Masterman concedes, as much an abstraction as "John Smith" because created to serve the self-interested propaganda interests of the settlement movement, in particular, its need to conjure up a social menace: "The 'hooligan' is bred in the Abyss, yet in the Abyss we never hear of the hooligan. He is a product created for the world beyond" (64). The "hooligan," if he actually existed, would at least seem to aspire to a better life, seem to possess the energy that would make him capable of it, unlike "John Smith." However, as a member of "the crowd," he can only do so in a menacing collective way:

> Despite this, it is, perhaps, the most welcome feature of Abysmal life. It exhibits, at least, a refusal placidly to acquiesce; a reaching out of the human spirit towards a life larger and less confined: a protest, however vague and uncontrolled, against a purely material satisfaction: a

movement resistant to that stagnation which is the precursor of
inevitable death. (70–71)

Interestingly, Masterman both concedes the ideological hegemony of middle class constructions of the East End—despite the fact that he was modeled originally on Patrick Hooligan of South London, the "hooligan" is actually a production of philanthropic discourse; he doesn't "exist" in the East End—and then seeks to unsettle that hegemony, if only in a small way, by finding subversive potential in the construct.

The essays close with an ironic celebration of a man "raised to fame" by virtue of his spectacular and grisly death—by carbolic acid. The function of the spectacle of poverty here is to moralistically embody a threat which potentially could infect the entire body politic: the threat of a debased "mass" culture which is represented here in its two opposite forms: the earnestly "private" one of "John Smith" and the spectacularly, and very publicly, threatening one of "the hooligan." Yet, as Masterman concedes, his representations have little relationship to the Real, based as they are on bogeymen constructed by philanthropic discourse to serve its own ends. Masterman's book is itself a "second-order" study, not so much of poverty, as of the middle class need to represent it in these antithetical reified ways. The sophisticated reader of Masterman thus becomes a participant in implicitly affirming that the poor are unknowable because all attempts to grasp them as particularized objects of knowledge end up returning us to always already conventionalized constructs, "types" which serve mainly to embody the professional desires of those who make a living claiming to help alleviate poverty (here principally the settlement movement and the COS). Yet, despite the self-enclosure of this discourse, Masterman hollows out a signifying space for the poor, who cannot exist independently of the middle class reader's imagination of them but who can signify within that imagination possibilities of being that are ultimately not recuperable—certainly not recuperable within the terms of philanthropic categories of meaning.

The almost "Conradian" language of Masterman's rendering thus serves to foreground his meta-awareness of the middle class consciousness of poverty as a conflicted, self-undermining discourse, much as Conrad's description of the landscape of the Congo in *Heart of Darkness* (published the same year) serves to reinforce the point that, in attempting to grasp the Other, one is invariably plunged into a nightmarish, solipsistic world complexly underscored by the desires and fears of the subject attempting to find his way. Thus, Masterman, in discussing how East London poverty saps the "vitality" of its residents, leaving them unable and unwilling to struggle manfully against overwhelming odds, converts that loss of nerve and will into a Conradian metaphorical landscape of organic enervation in which the distinction between subject and object worlds, between the desire to live and the desire to pass out of existence, have collapsed into one another:

> Until at length all the glory and life and struggle of the tropical forest has passed away for ever; and in its place stretch the wide spaces of sullen swamp, and dull, gnarled, fruitless trees, and the silence of stagnant, scum-coated pools, and the salt, interminable, tideless sea. (17)

The use of organic metaphors here seems to foretell a literal "dehumanization" of the urban landscape at the very moment that the landscape itself is being complexly overwritten by the psychology of the middle class subject. The distinction between self and other, between middle class investigator and lower class subject, between the conceptual tool and the social reality it is meant to symbolize, no longer seems worth delineating, and he instead reverts to a very abstract prophetic voice, promising a Schopenhauerean nightmare resolution in which Darwinian struggle gives way to enervation and loss of energy, the gradual triumph of the law of entropy over the promise and energy liberated by class struggle.

Masterman went on to serve ably as an M.P. in the House of Commons between 1906 and 1918. In his later work called *The Condition of England* (1909), he adopts an even more stridently "Carlylean" tone, castigating "mediocrity" in a tone of rising despair over what his contemporary, the American social critic Thorstein Veblen, called "conspicuous consumption" of the idle classes in the face of the persistent poverty of the poorer classes and the persistent mediocrity of the middle class:

> The present extravagance of England is associated with a strange mediocrity, a strange sterility of characters with supreme power in Church and State. It is accompanied, as all ages of security and luxury are accompanied, by a waning of the power of inspiration, a multiplying of the power of criticism. The more comfortable and opulent society becomes, the more cynicism proclaims the futility of it all, and the mind turns in despair from a vision of vanities. (*Condition* 32)

In light of the above, it is probably not so surprising that, like too many of his generation, he would welcome World War I as an event that would call forth the best in men rather than the worst, an opportunity to call upon one's energies in defense of ideals that transcend economic self-interest. Early in the war, Masterman himself was appointed by Lloyd George to head the War Propaganda Bureau, and in that role organized an array of writers including Kipling, Galsworthy, Bennett, Hardy, Buchan, and Conan Doyle to produce pamphlets which cast Britain's role in a positive light. Only two Army officers were allowed to take pictures of the Western Front. The penalty for anyone else doing so was death by firing squad. Instead, Masterman commissioned a number of well-known artists to draw and paint wartime scenes. Not a few of these complained about the tight governmental controls over their work, including severe restrictions on including depictions of English bodies in the final product. In effect, Masterman's own gifts as a social critic and Parliamentary orator would lead him into work which essentially distorted the truth about the Western Front, where working class men died by the hundreds of thousands for a cause that was difficult to defend and even more difficult to explain in the postwar period, a hell that he helped to make appear less hellish than it was.

- CONCLUSION -

Representing the Poor and Forestalling Abjection

This book is about the intersection of gender and class. More specifically, our contention in this book has been that the interests of a predominately male professional class, which was in the process of formation throughout the nineteenth century, strongly influenced, indeed determined, the ways in which the Victorians represented poverty in the city of London. London was in the process of unprecedentedly rapid growth in the nineteenth century, and this rapid growth entailed many painful social adjustments. Although London was not the center of the First Industrial Revolution (the northern cities were), it was the center of British trade, the hub of its new transportation infrastructure, the focus of its banking activities, the center of its political life: in many respects, a large stage on which the developing middle classes could play out their relationship with the rest of British society while seeking a new and expanded role within that social order. The puzzling growth of abject poverty, which seemed to accompany the growing prosperity and political power of the Victorian middle class, could be noted in London, its social effects observed and discussed, and solutions proposed and carried out. Indeed, as we have argued, the seeming growth of abject poverty stimulated the process of middle class self-definition, as middle class professionals rose to answer the ethical challenge of poverty in the midst of plenty, offering solutions which drew on scientific expertise, which required the mediating role of the reporter, and which charged middle class life with a an enlarged ethical mission to alleviate suffering, whether it took the form of philanthropic efforts in the slums or heart-rending novelistic exhortation over which any good soul could cry.

While most of the writers we examine here are male, the issue of gender is more complicated than a simple biological model would seem to suggest. Indeed, it is our contention that a broader notion of gender is essential to understanding how this discourse on urban poverty operated. We discern, in this writing, the operation of certain class- and gender-based anxieties which derive as much from middle class male experience as from the observed reality of urban poverty. Fear about competition, to take one example, a fear that is constitutive of the Victorian male professional imaginary, inflects the representations of the poor from the early Victorian period, encouraging the construction of an "East End" which takes on the metaphorical clothing of a threatening labyrinth, in which the identity of the middle class subject is under constant threat by a feminine abject. The "threat" here is to the integrity of the middle class male self, and it is forestalled in a variety of ways which we have discussed. Although they took many different and complicated forms, we contend that attempts to forestall the collapse of defining boundaries served to shore up a middle class male subjectivity coming under threat by a variety of social phenomena. Moreover, that "threat" also opened up new possibilities for the professional class, as the discovery of poverty in the midst of plenty created opportunities to exercise ethical impulses in the public sphere, as the representation of the poor created new material for reporters to feed to a hungry public, as the descent into the abyss served the purpose of heroicizing the act of representation itself.

The discourse of the "abyss" which we have examined in chapter 4 marks a final change in the Victorian middle class's assertion of its right to interpret the reality of life for the urban lower classes. It would be wrong, of course, for us to suggest that this discourse constitutes anything like the "final word" on the subject in the Victorian age. Writers like Wells, London, and Masterman were themselves involved in a very fraught relationship with contending discourses on poverty at the time: the "sentimental" tradition, the "culturalist" or the settlement movement, the COS, Booth's emergent "sociological" tradition. These discourses overlap in their interests even if they construct their object—the urban poor—often in rather different ways, as we have already seen. Moreover, one could argue that the latter were more politically "effective" in the long run, as Britain, especially in the aftermath of World War I, took tentative steps in the long process of building a modern welfare state dedicated to diminishing class antagonism and raising the poor up to a minimal standard of humane life. Surely, the latter movement, however one measures its success or failure, was influenced and shaped more directly by the political achievements of Fabian "permeation," the success of the unionization movements, and—perhaps most importantly—the experience of social solidarity enforced during two punishing world wars in the twentieth century than by the arguments of impassioned intellectuals with a bleak view of the prospects for interclass understanding.

What is striking, though, about what we are calling the discourse of the "abyss" is, finally, its awareness of its own self-enclosure: to follow Masterman in pursuit of "the hooligan" and "John Smith" does not even require a trip to East London. We have been, to some extent, pursuing a tale of the gradual imposition of ideological hegemony, achieved finally at the end of the century, and symptomatized by the self-enclosure of this discourse. The "otherness" of the urban poor passes, in Masterman's writing, into a kind of sameness, as writing about the East End devolves into a critical complaint about the limited structures of value and significance available to the middle class writer who wishes to awaken his readers to the reality of social problems in their midst. In that sense, some of this writing becomes a kind of second-order writing on urban poverty in relation to the need for self-assertion of the middle class male writer. While we have attended throughout this study to the self-consciousness of these discourses, their writers' winking awareness that they are addressing a middle class audience in the terms familiar to the middle class, a tendency evident in Dickens and Greenwood no less than in Gissing, London, and Masterman, we must nonetheless acknowledge, at the end, the ability of some of this writing to register an alien sensibility and alien possibilities that signify beyond what they seem to. There is a sense in which the achievement of hegemony marks the moment of its contestation: the possibilities glimpsed beyond the veil of conventionalized representation strategies are themselves signs opening into a different universe of understanding, as yet, in the pre-War era, still powerless to be born.

- NOTES -

Notes to Introduction

1. See Lauren Goodlad's recent, and persuasive, argument that the new nineteenth-century "professional" ethos involved as much competitiveness as its opposite number—the "entrepreneurial" ethos ("A Middle Class Cut in Two" 154). It is, of course, Harold Perkin, in *The Rise of Professional Society* (1989), who is most responsible for differentiating a developing "professional" ethos from what he calls the "entrepreneurial ethos" of Victorian middle class society.

2. Simon Joyce argues in *Capital Offenses*, "the dominant trend of urban social observation during the nineteenth century . . . [was one] which sought to maintain an absolute distinction between the spectating subject and the contemplated object" (*Capital Offenses* 22).

3. Louis James chronicles the working class editions and variations on this literature in *Fiction of the Working Man*.

4. The empire provides another such theatre for the acting out of elements of this male fantasy. As the various images of the London underworld as "darkest Africa on our own doorstep" indicate, the slums are often depicted as objects of the imperialistic imagination, whose domestic implications have been documented by Patrick Brantlinger in his *Rule of Darkness*, Dan Bivona in *Desire and Contradiction: Imperial Visions and Domestic Debates in Victorian Literature*, and Anne McClintock in *Imperial Leather*.

5. Although we do not have space to develop the theme fully here, it should be noted how much emphasis work in Victorian Studies over the past ten years has given to challenging the traditional "separate spheres" model of Victorian middle class life. The recent work of John Tosh, Amanda Anderson, Elizabeth Langland, and Karen Chase and Michael Levenson, to name just a few, has registered this theme over and over again. That the so-called "domestic sphere" was hardly a haven from intense competitive pressures is familiar to readers of Victorian domestic fiction, even if it is sensation novels such as *East Lynne* that highlight the intensity of female-to-female competitiveness within that sphere most melodramatically. Moreover, as Tosh has argued, the traditional "separate spheres" notion has

obscured the fact that Victorian middle class males enjoyed the "distinctively masculine privilege" of relatively unrestricted access to both "domestic" and "public" spheres (Tosh 77).

6. It is important to note that the term "East End" in the discourses we examine here is used as often in a cultural as in a geographic sense throughout the nineteenth century, gradually evolving a geographical specificity only in the 1880s and 1890s while retaining, nonetheless, its cultural meaning as that which opposes a hegemonic "West End." As Simon Joyce points out in *Capital Offenses*, "the hegemonic culture represented by London's West End . . . requires a correspondingly demonized East End, against which it is able to validate and consolidate its generalizable, normative, and (supposedly) classless values" (*Capital Offenses* 37). Dickens' "East End," for example, was more often than not, St. Giles in the West End. Jack London's, by contrast, was East London, although even he stretches the term to embrace a broader geographic conception of poor London.

7. Originally published in the *Pall Mall Gazette*, the sketch is reprinted in Keating, *Into Unknown England* 33–34.

8. For a more sustained treatment of this issue, see Debra Epstein Nord's *Walking the Victorian Streets*.

9. Gagnier 90–91. Mayhew, IV, 2–22.

Notes to Chapter One

1. See Seth Koven's *Slumming* for an interesting discussion of Greenwood's "A Night in a Workhouse." Koven argues that the story insinuates that the workhouses enabled the sexual exploitation of younger boys and men by older men, although given the conventions of the day, the story can do no more than hint at this theme. Koven 25–87.

2. The professional becomes, as Harold Perkin observes, one prominent formulation for the middle class male's role in the mid- to late-nineteenth century. *Origins*, chapters VIII–IX. For an overview of how the "professional" comes to differentiate himself from the "bourgeois" male, see Perkin's *The Rise of Professional Society*. As mentioned in the Introduction, identification with the aims of the "professional" class did not exempt one from competitiveness. This is certainly clear in the case of Dickens. For an account of how male writers began signing their essays in the periodical press and how this connected with the emergence of a new category of "literature" that came increasingly to be distinguished from "book chat" and, indeed, to acquire cultural prestige in the era of mass literacy, see Laurel Brake, *Subjugated Knowledges*.

3. For a discussion of the wide range of Bohemian male life in nineteenth-century London and the fraught issue of "respectability," see Huggins.

4. Brake's *Subjugated Knowledges* is particularly good on the subject of how from the mid-nineteenth century onward, certain honorific cultural categories are erected to differentiate the valuable work of the professional from the putatively less valuable work of the hack. Whether it is William Michael Rossetti opining that the only art criticism likely to be of any use in the future is that by "professional men" who can speak "ex cathedra [about] what attempts in art are desirable to be made"

(19) or Matthew Arnold, coining the term "New Journalism" in 1887 in order to differentiate what he considered the demotic brand of Stead-inspired popular sensationalism from the trustworthy and informed "old journalism" that he presumably had been practicing for thirty years (83), the late nineteenth century saw many instances of middle class male professional intellectuals attempting to vaunt their own expertise, devalue that of nonprofessionals, and construct the outlines of new objects which it becomes their social duty to discuss publicly: "literature," "art," "cultural criticism," rather than the penny dreadful, "sensation" fiction, and sensational journalism which kowtows to popular taste for stimulation at all costs. This is by no means an exclusively male phenomenon, as anyone who has read Margaret Oliphant's intemperate attack on sensation fiction can see, but it was particularly associated with middle class male professionals who had the ready access to influential organs of opinion that many women lacked.

5. It is worth noting here that there is some evidence that actual working class reading habits were not that different from the habits of many middle class people. Jonathan Rose has recently argued that it was the great literary "classics" which formed the most important and influential reading material for most working class people in the nineteenth and twentieth centuries—at least for most of those working class people who wrote the memoirs which formed the basis for his study. See his *The Intellectual Life of the British Working Classes*.

6. For a particularly lucid explanation of suture, its conceptualization in the work of Emile Benveniste and others, and of the ideological interpellation of the subject, see Kaja Silverman, "Suture" and *The Subject of Semiotics* 194–236.

7. For an interesting discussion of the politics of working class literacy, see Brantlinger's *The Reading Lesson* 93–120. Among other things, Brantlinger argues that only Tory writers like Disraeli, among the early generation of Victorians responding to Chartism, were able to allow the working class to represent itself in discourse. Middle class writers (such as Kingsley and Eliot) tended to work hard (and anxiously) to de-legitimize working class radical discourse.

8. Quoted in "Opinions in the Weekly Reviews: Workhouse Management," *Pall Mall Gazette*, 20 (January 1866): 3.

9. Mearns was assisted in the preparation of the article by James Munro and W. C. Preston.

10. See Chase and Levenson on the "unwalled poor": "the definition of a family was architectural as well as biological" (Chase and Levenson 47–48).

11. Beatrice Webb's (née "Potter's") allegation that incest is common among the urban poor appeared in her 1888 report in Booth's *Life and Labour of the People of London*. Cited in Himmelfarb, *De-Moralization*: 118.

12. The closest anyone has come is Deborah Wynne in her recent book *The Sensation Novel and the Victorian Family Magazine*.

13. *Quarterly*, 113 (April 1863): 501.

14. Quoted in Hughes, p. 7.

15. Interestingly, Hadley argues that early nineteenth-century melodrama appears to be doing the same thing but is actually rooted in an earlier, nonperformative, patriarchal mode of social identity formation in which performance and being are not separate (Hadley 21). Edmund Burke harkens back to that mode in his *Reflections*, when he argues that in tearing off the "drapery" of social authority,

the French revolutionaries were not simply laying bare some shameful "truth" but were rather destroying civilization itself: the accoutrements of "civilization"—its "staging"—are its essence.

16. This is clearest in the case of Gladstone, the "People's William," although Bright was also a precursor of this new "populist" style which was made necessary when the three great Parliamentary reforms of 1832, 1867, and 1884 broadened the franchise significantly. See Jenkins's description of the launch of Gladstone's "Midlothian" campaign against Disraeli's pro-Turkish foreign policy—the first truly modern, populist political campaign in Britain (Jenkins 399–434).

17. Since pundits are still today constantly complaining about this process, one must assume that it is a defining feature of middle class culture since the late nineteenth century: a culture in which a discursive nostalgia for a pure "private sphere" marks its always already contaminated state, much as nostalgia for a lost "haven in a heartless world" becomes the index of the always already fallen state of our social order.

18. Quoted in Schultz, p. 29.

19. Quoted in Schultz, p. 62.

20. "The 'parades of Pain' that Tennyson rehearses in *In Memoriam* and the martyrdom of Sydney Carton in Dickens' *Tale of Two Cities* are just two instances in which masculine identity is realized through a regimen of solitary but emphatically visible suffering, which claims the authority of manhood while estranging the hero from all forms of collective identity" (Adams 16).

21. It is interesting and more than a little alarming to see the return of the "moralization" of poverty and its effects in the contemporary work of an historian as astute as Gertrude Himmelfarb. In *De-moralization*, she offers what sounds like a moral defense of the New Poor Law, suggesting that a society that punishes poverty is inevitably expressing the high value it places on work and self-respect: "Today the very word 'stigma' has become odious, whether applied to dependency, illegitimacy, addiction, or anything else. Yet stigmas are the corollaries of values. If work, independence, responsibility, respectability are valued, then their converse must be devalued, seen as disreputable. The Victorians, taking values seriously, also took seriously the need for social sanctions that would stigmatize and censure violations of those values" (*De-Moralization* 142).

22. Needless to say, "purity" is a constructed category, usually set in opposition to defilement, but capable of taking a wide range of forms. The classic statement of purity's relationship to the culturally determined schemas that construct it can be found in Mary Douglas, *Purity and Danger*.

23. We are thinking particularly of his famous description of the Podsnap plate in Book I, chapter 11 of *Our Mutual Friend*.

24. See Terry Lovell, *Consuming Fiction* and N. N. Feltes, *Modes of Production of Victorian Novels*.

Notes to Chapter Two

1. *My Apprenticeship* 173–74. Those interested in Webb should consult Deborah Epstein Nord's study, *The Apprenticeship of Beatrice Webb*.

2. Webb was hardly alone in the Victorian age in attempting to subdue egoism

through a commitment to the ascetic rigors of scientific pursuits. George Levine has recently written about two others—Karl Pearson and Walter Pater—in a similar light.

3. As Lauren Goodlad reminds us, "Foucauldian" theorists, of whom Donzelot is a prime example, have too often relied too heavily on French models from which they have generalized to all of Europe. Britain was notably the "least bureaucratized" of the major European states during this period (*Victorian State* 8). That said, it is nonetheless demonstrably true that surveillance of the Victorian working class in Britain was accelerating throughout the century. The passage of the Education Act of 1870 gave new impetus to the process as school inspectors such as George R. Sims fanned out across London charged with the duty of assessing whether working class children were attending the board schools.

4. Although Philip Abrams argues that British sociology defined itself only when it graduated beyond empiricism into a discipline that could develop theories about the nature of the social process (p. 85).

5. This is registered in a number of working class autobiographies which tell the story of how the Education Act required attendance at the Board Schools. See, for instance, P. A. Heard's *An Octogenarian's Memoirs* or Thomas Bell, *Pioneering Days*.

6. See Jeffrey Minson for a discussion of the theories of the "prehistory" of the nineteenth century family, pp. 194–202.

7. Donzelot, "Preface to the English Edition."

8. Child custody laws favored fathers throughout the century, although the late century saw some changes. See Chase and Levenson on the case of Lady Caroline Norton (Chase and Levenson 21–45). The Matrimonial Causes Act of 1878 first granted custody of children under 10 years of age to a mother upon proof that the father was abusive or neglectful (Stone 140).

9. See Nord, *Apprenticeship,* esp. chapter 5.

10. Debra Epstein Nord argues that in choosing an "analytic" posture toward poverty that drew her to work with her cousin Charles Booth, Webb was choosing a "masculine" rather than a "feminine" vocation. *Walking* 190.

11. For analysis of that debate, see Goode, "The Art of Fiction: Walter Besant and Henry James," Mark Spilka, and N. N. Feltes.

12. We have more to say about Besant's analysis of lower class work in chapter 4.

13. Meacham 12. See also Briggs and Macartney.

14. Quoted in Meacham 38.

15. For an excellent analysis of *All Sorts* in the context of political reform, see Neetens.

16. See Bowlby.

17. Besant stresses in his other writings that East London is primarily a crafts and industrial area (*East London*). But it is vastly different from Mayhew's vital scene; gone essentially is the varied costermonger society, and Besant observes that most workers now do piece work in which they can have little identification with the finished product (27). And in these writings as well, the theme is the need for more cultivation among the lower classes.

18. See Birkin and Bowlby.

19. Baudrillard, especially chapter 5.

20. Simon Joyce argues, "middle-class philanthropy and reform movements worked upon the needs of the East End poor to promote a revised version of

working-class culture which was no longer articulated within a traditional model of class conflict. Such a model was instead consistently demonized by the discourses of urban reform as regressive and exhausted, out of step with new projections of class cooperation." ("Castles in the Air" 2)

21. See Bailey.
22. Cottam chapter 2.
23. Gallagher chapter 9.
24. Wim Neetens shrewdly argues that Besant's strategy was to demarcate the respectable working class from "the unfit, the degraded classes." Neetens 257.

Notes to Chapter Three

1. We are indebted for the biographical material to Peter Keating's "Biographical Study," in *A Child of the Jago*. Suffolk: The Boydell Press, 1969: 11–36, and to Michel Krzak's "Preface" to *Tales of Mean Streets*. Suffolk: The Boydell Press, 1983: 7–10.

2. While we recognize that *Mean Streets* is a collection of short stories, and shares with the late nineteenth century short story in general its Chekhovian and Maupassantian restraint and relative absence of dramatic modulation, nonetheless, we would argue that the subject matter of many of the late nineteenth century English short stories affects the form. For another instance in which the refusal to treat the heroine as an auratic object of commodity desire dictates the style, we would point to Dorothy Richardson's *Pilgrimage*.

3. For a particularly lurid critique of naturalism, see Arthur Symons' essay, "A Note on Zola's Method," pp. 154–64. See also Henry James, "Nana," 1880, pp. 84–96.

4. See Bowlby for an account of the fascination of the naturalist writers with the department store.

5. *New Review*, 16, no. 94 (March 1897), 329.

6. For accounts of Morrison's influence, see Ted Morgan, *Maugham*, and Edward Garnett's reader's report on "A Lambeth Idyll" (its first title) for T. Fisher Unwin, reprinted in *W. Somerset Maugham: The Critical Heritage*: 22.

7. Gertrude Himmelfarb takes this one step further in the late twentieth century when she argues that contemporary historians are victims of the illusion that the Victorian middle and working classes lived by different values. See *DeMoralization*.

8. *Subjectivities* 124. See Gagnier's wonderful description of Henry Nevinson's short stories, pp. 124–31.

9. See "The Culture Industry: Enlightenment as Mass Deception," in Max Horkheimer and Theodor W. Adorno, *Dialectic of Enlightenment*.

10. See Bowlby chapters 6 and 7.

11. It is ironic to read of the failure of Jane's education in light of Jonathan Rose's contention that such a course of reading was seen by many working class people as a liberating way out of the small-minded, quotidian concerns that grinding poverty imposed. Gissing's view is clearly darker, and closer to that of Charles Masterman, as we shall see in Chapter 5.

12. See John Lester, *Journey Through Despair 1880–1914*, and David Daiches, *Some Late Victorian Attitudes*.

13. This helps account for the particular style, the dead classicism, that Jameson says characterizes Gissing's writing, for it is in itself a symptom of the particular culturalism of the alienated late nineteenth century intellectual. By contrast, classicism has a very different role—more vital—in the emergence of Aestheticism and the construction of homosexual identity among the middle and upper middle classes at the end of the century. See Linda Dowling's *Hellenism and Homosexuality in Victorian Oxford*.

Notes to Chapter Four

1. We are taking a somewhat different view of this issue from that argued by Debra Epstein Nord in *Walking the Victorian Streets*. While Nord makes the valuable point that the streetwalking woman often came to represent the "experience of the masculine spectator" (Nord 6), she also views the *flâneur* as essentially retreating into invisibility à la Baudelaire. As we will argue below, the pose of disinterested observation does not make one invisible, but rather makes one's costumed self the visible center of a scene ordered by one's own active assumption of a role on the urban stage. See also Walkowitz's classic discussion of urban spectatorship (Walkowitz 15–39) and James Eli Adams's argument that a number of male roles—Victorian gentleman, Carlylean hero, Tractarian priest, and Tennysonian poet—are implicated in a dandyesque theatricality they profess to disdain (Adams 10).

2. This assertion needs to be qualified as well, because Toynbee Hall was given the mission of reshaping of working class lives through the public staging of middle class tastes.

3. Amanda Anderson offers the broadest definition of Victorian "detachment" in *The Powers of Distance*: "*Detachment* is meant to encompass not only science, critical reason, disinterestedness, and realism, but also a set of practices of the self, ranging from stoicism to cosmopolitanism to dandyism" (*Powers* 7).

4. See Butler, "Social Purity."

5. "If, as John Bender and D. A. Miller variously contend, the novel became that 'cultural institution,' to borrow Miller's words, that upheld privacy and the existence of an 'autonomous "secret" self,' then early melodrama—as it was written, adapted and performed before English men and women—was the mode that, by exposing the secrets of the self and other private sites, insisted on the primacy of an older ethic" (Hadley 71).

6. On East London's "godlessness," see Roy Porter: "Three surveys (1851, 1886 and 1903) documented this popular paganism. East and South London had the nation's lowest church attendance. In working-class inner areas fewer than one in five attended a place of worship. London was no city of God: on Sunday 30 March 1851 only 874,339 of London's population of 2,362,236 attended any form of public worship" (Porter 298). On the press and the "Whitechapel Horrors," see L. P. Curtis. It is worth noting the irony that the closing of 200 East London brothels by the Metropolitan police in early 1888 as a direct response to the 1886 repeal of the Contagious Diseases Act forced many prostitutes to prowl the streets late at night, exposing more East London women to the risk of evisceration by "Jack the Ripper" than would have been the case had the brothels continued to be tolerated by the police.

7. Llewelyn Smith was committed to the Lamarckian view that acquired bad traits would inevitably be inherited by subsequent generations of the poor (Walkowitz 35).

8. Martin Green, *Seven Types of Adventure Tale* 47–68. We would argue that much Victorian travel literature served a similar fantasy function for middle class readers, especially such works as Henry M. Stanley's narratives of his African explorations, which were major bestsellers in the Victorian age.

9. See Feltes, *Literary Capital*, 65–102.

10. On "proletarianization" see Harry Braverman. For a discussion of Kipling's treatment of the natural world in *The Jungle Books* as governed by a complex division of labor that fosters the interdependency necessary to social order, see Bivona, *British Imperial Literature*, pp. 69–98.

11. See Raymond Williams' discussion of Goldsmith in *The Country and the City* 74–78.

12. James Kincaid's *Child-Loving* offers a now-classic statement of how the Victorian insistence on childish sexual "innocence" worked to eroticize children by providing just the repressive cover such fantasy needs.

13. Nietzsche will, of course, refer to this dichotomy as "master" and "slave" moralities" and distinguish the controlling virtue of the former as contempt for weakness and the controlling virtue of the latter as mercy. See *Beyond Good and Evil*: 199–237.

14. That does not keep him from continually insisting that he is exploring "unknown" territory. See Peluso 64.

15. Victorian travel literature was often given to retraversing an already written landscape. Pratt's *Imperial Eyes* discusses this from an angle different from Said's *Orientalism*.

16. We certainly do not mean to suggest that the book is free of hyperbole, for even the few passages quoted here supply notable examples of that rhetorical device.

17. Notably, this "neat" mapping of class and geography was something Charles Booth's map of London had already challenged by showing that many members of the "respectable" classes continued to live in East London in the last two decades of the nineteenth century, especially along some of its main avenues.

18. See Robert Peluso's discussion of how London's discussion of "efficient management" repositions the United States as an efficient bureaucratic-industrial state poised to replace a decaying British imperial metropole: 70–74.

19. There are too many examples of this to be worth citing all, but here is just one: "Moreover, by the mere fact that he forms part of an organised crowd, a man descends several rungs in the ladder of civilisation. Isolated, he may be a cultivated individual; in a crowd, he is a barbarian—that is, a creature acting by instinct." Widener 62.

20. In her recent book, Paula M. Krebs claims that at the time of the Boer War, the British press tended to cast the Boers as an "entire country of the lower class" (Krebs 108). This tendency emerges with great clarity from Millicent Fawcett's report on conditions in the British concentration camps for Boer women and children: "Fawcett's nationalism and the class privilege that allowed her to see the Boer mothers in camps as ignorant, lower-class women who, like slum-dwelling English, needed housekeeping lessons from the middle class, prevent her from letting her feminism challenge British imperialism" (Krebs 78).

- WORKS CITED -

Abrams, Philip. *The Origins of British Sociology 1834–1914*. Chicago: University of Chicago Press, 1968.
Adams, James Eli. *Dandies and Desert Saints: Styles of Victorian Masculinity*. Ithaca, NY: Cornell University Press, 1995.
Althusser, Louis. *Lenin and Philosophy*. Trans. Ben Brewster. London: New Left Books, 1971.
Altick, Richard. *The English Common Reader: A Social History of the Mass Reading Public 1800–1900*. Chicago and London: University of Chicago Press, 1957.
Anderson, Amanda. *Tainted Souls and Painted Faces: The Rhetoric of Fallenness in Victorian Culture*. Ithaca: Cornell University Press, 1993.
———. *The Powers of Distance: Cosmopolitanism and the Cultivation of Detachment*. Princeton and Oxford: Princeton University Press, 2001.
Anderson, Benedict. *Imagined Communities: Reflections on the Origin and Spread of Nationalism*. London: Verso, 1983.
Anonymous. *Quarterly* 113 (April 1863): 501.
Armstrong, Nancy. *Desire and Domestic Fiction: A Political History of the Novel*. New York & Oxford: Oxford University Press, 1987.
Bailey, Peter. *Leisure and Class in Victorian England: Rational Recreation and the Contest for Control, 1830–1885*. London: Routledge & Kegan Paul, 1978.
Baudelaire, Charles. "The Painter of Modern Life." *Selected Writings on Art and Artists*. Trans. P. E. Charvet. Harmondsworth, Middlesex, U.K.: Penguin, 1972: 390–435.
Baudrillard, Jean. *For a Critique of the Political Economy of the Sign*. Trans. by Charles Levin. St. Louis: Telos Press, 1981.
Bell, Thomas. *Pioneering Days*. London: Lawrence and Wishart Ltd., 1941.
Berridge, Virginia. "Popular Sunday Papers and Mid-Victorian Society." *Newspaper History from the Seventeenth-Century to the Present Day*. George Boyce, James Curran, and Pauline Wingate, eds. London: Constable, 1978.
Besant, Walter. *All Sorts and Conditions of Men: An Impossible Story*. New York and London: Harper & Brothers Publishers, 1902.

———. *The Autobiography of Sir Walter Besant*. New York: Dodd, Mead and Company, 1902.

———. *East London*. New York: The Century Co., 1899.

Birkin, Lawrence. *Consuming Desire: Sexual Science and the Emergence of a Culture of Abundance 1871–1914*. Ithaca: Cornell University Press. 1988.

Bivona, Daniel. *Desire and Contradiction: Imperial Visions and Domestic Debates in Victorian Literature*. Manchester: Manchester University Press, 1990.

———. *British Imperial Literature, 1870–1940: Writing and the Administration of Empire*. Cambridge: Cambridge University Press, 1998.

Booth, William. *In Darkest England and the Way Out*. New York: Funk & Wagnalls, 1890.

Bowlby, Rachel. *Just Looking: Consumer Culture in Dreiser, Gissing and Zola*. New York and London: Methuen, 1985.

Brake, Laurel. *Subjugated Knowledges: Journalism, Gender, and Literature in the Nineteenth Century*. Hampshire and London: Macmillan, 1994.

Brantlinger, Patrick. *The Reading Lesson: The Threat of Mass Literacy in Nineteenth-Century British Fiction*. Bloomington and Indianapolis: Indiana University Press, 1998.

———. *Rule of Darkness: British Literature and Imperialism, 1830–1914*. Ithaca and London: Cornell University Press, 1988.

———. *The Spirit of Reform: British Literature and Politics 1832–1867*. Cambridge: Harvard University Press, 1977.

Braverman, Harry. "Capitalism and the Division of Labor." *Classes, Power, and Conflict*. Eds. Anthony Giddens and David Held. Berkeley: University of California Press, 1982: 148–56.

Briggs, Asa and Anne Macartney. *Toynbee Hall: The First Hundred Years*. London: Routledge & Kegan Paul, 1984.

Brooks, Peter. *The Melodramatic Imagination: Balzac, Henry James, Melodrama and the Mode of Excess*. New York: Columbia University Press, 1985.

———. *Reading for the Plot: Design and Intention in Narrative*. New York: Vintage Books, 1988.

Brown, Lucy. *Victorian News and Newspapers*. Oxford: The Clarendon Press, 1985.

Burke, Edmund. *A Philosophical Enquiry into our Ideas of the Sublime and the Beautiful*. Edited and with an introduction by James. T. Bolton. Oxford: Basil Blackwell, 1967.

———. *Reflections on the Revolution in France*. London: Penguin, 1979.

Burke, Thomas. *The Real East End*. Illus. Pearl Binder. London: Constable and Co. Ltd., 1932.

———. *The Wind and the Rain*. London: Thornton Butterworth Ltd., 1925.

Butler, Josephine E. *Social Purity*. London: Morgan and Scott, 1879.

Chadwick, Edmund. *Report on the Sanitary Condition of the Labouring Population of Gt. Britain*. Introduction by M. W. Flinn. Edinburgh: Edinburgh University Press, 1965.

Chase, Karen and Michael Levenson. The Spectacle of Intimacy: A Public Life for the Victorian Family. Princeton and Oxford: Princeton University Press, 2000.

Childers, Joseph. *Novel Possibilities: Fiction and the Formation of Early Victorian Culture*. Philadelphia: University of Pennsylvania Press, 1995.

Choi, Tina Young. "Writing the Victorian City: Discourses of Risk, Connection, and Inevitability." *Victorian Studies* 43.4 (2001): 561–85.

Clark, G. Kitson. *The Making of Victorian England.* Cambridge: Harvard University Press, 1962.

Cottam, Daniel. *Social Figures: George Eliot, Social History, and Literary Representation.* Minneapolis: University of Minnesota Press, 1987.

Cross, Nigel. *The Common Writer: Life in Nineteenth-Century Grub Street.* Cambridge and New York: Cambridge University Press, 1985.

Curtis, L. Perry. *Jack the Ripper and the London Press.* New Haven and London: Yale University Press, 2001.

Cvetkovitch, Ann. *Mixed Feelings: Feminism, Mass Culture, and Victorian Sensationalism.* New Brunswick, NJ: Rutgers University Press, 1992.

Daiches, David. *Some Late Victorian Attitudes.* New York: Norton, 1969.

Davis, Lennard J. "A Social History of Fact and Fiction: Authorial Disavowal in the Early English Novel." *Literature and Society: Selected Papers from the English Institute, 1978.* Ed. Edward W. Said. Baltimore and London: The Johns Hopkins University Press, 1980: 120–48.

Diamond, B. L. "A Precursor of the New Journalism: Frederick Greenwood of the *Pall Mall Gazette.*" Ed. Joel H. Wiener. *Papers for the Millions: The New Journalism in Britain, 1850's to 1914.* New York: Greenwood Press, 1988: 25–46.

Dickens, Charles. *Bleak House.* New York: W. W. Norton & Company, 1977.

———. *Oliver Twist.* New York: Dodd, Mead and Co., 1941.

Disraeli, Benjamin. *Sybil, Or the Two Nations.* London: Oxford, 1934.

Donzelot, Jacques. *The Policing of Families.* Trans. Robert Hurley. New York: Pantheon Books, 1979.

Dowling, Linda. *Hellenism and Homosexuality in Victorian Oxford.* Ithaca: Cornell University Press, 1994.

Dyos, H. J. *Exploring the Urban Past: Essays in Urban History.* Eds. David Cannadine and D. A. Reeder. Cambridge: Cambridge University Press, 1982.

——— and D. A. Reeder. "Slums and Suburbs." H. J. Dyos and Michael Wolff, eds. *The Victorian City: Images and Realities.* London: Routledge & Kegan Paul, 1973. II, 360.

Egan, Pierce. *Life in London.* London: Sherwood, Jones & Co., 1823.

Engels, Frederick. *The Condition of the Working Class in England.* London: Granada Publishing, 1969.

Feltes, N. N. *Literary Capital and the Late Victorian Novel.* Madison: University of Wisconsin Press, 1993.

———. *Modes of Production of Victorian Novels.* Chicago: University of Chicago Press, 1986.

Fishers, Trevor. "The Mysteries of Oscar Wilde." *History Today* 50.12 (Dec. 2000) [online: http://www.historytoday.com/dt_front.asp?gid=19963&aid=&tgid=19963&amid=&g19963=x].

Fox Bourne, H. R. *English Newspapers: Chapters in the History of Journalism.* 2 vols., London, 1887: II. Reprint New York: Russell & Russell, 1966. v. 2.

Freedman, Jonathan. *Professions of Taste: Henry James, British Aestheticism, and Commodity Culture.* Stanford: Stanford University Press, 1990.

Freud, Sigmund. *Totem and Taboo.* Trans. A. A. Brill. New York: Random House, 1918.

Gagnier, Regenia. *The Insatiability of Human Wants: Economics and Aesthetics in Market Society.* Chicago and London: University of Chicago Press, 2000.

———. "The Law of Progress and the Ironies of Individualism in the Nineteenth Century." *NLH* 31 (2000): 315–36.

———. *Subjectivities: A History of Self-Representation in Britain, 1832–1920.* New York and Oxford: Oxford University Press, 1991.

Gallagher, Catherine. *The Industrial Reformation of English Fiction 1832–1867.* Chicago: University of Chicago Press, 1985.

Garnett, Edward. Reader's report on "A Lambeth Idyll" for T. Fisher Unwin. Reprinted in *W. Somerset Maugham: The Critical Heritage.* Eds. Anthony Curtis and John Whitehead, eds. London: Routledge & Kegan Paul, 1987: 22.

Gavin, Hector. *Sanitary Ramblings: Being Sketches and Illustrations of Bethnal Green.* London: Frank Cass and Company Limited, 1971.

George Gissing: Essays and Fiction. Ed. Pierre Coustillas. Baltimore: The Johns Hopkins University Press, 1970.

———. *The Nether World.* London: The Harvester Press, 1974.

———. *Thyrza: A Tale.* Brighton: Harvester Press, 1974.

Goode, John. *George Gissing: Ideology and Fiction.* New York: Barnes and Noble, 1979.

———. "Margaret Harkness and the Socialist Novel." *The Socialist Novel in Britain: Towards the Recovery of a Tradition.* Ed. H. Gustav Klaus. New York: St. Martin's Press, 1982: 45–66.

———. "The Art of Fiction: Walter Besant and Henry James." *Tradition and Tolerance in Nineteenth Century Fiction.* Eds. David Howard, John Lucas, and John Goode. London: Routledge & Kegan Paul, 1966: 1243–81.

Goodlad, Lauren. "'A Middle Class Cut in Two': Historiography and Victorian National Character." *ELH* 67 (2000): 143–78.

———. *Victorian Literature and the Victorian State: Character and Governance in a Liberal Society.* Baltimore and London: Johns Hopkins University Press, 2003.

Green, Martin Burgess. *Seven Types of Adventure Tale: An Etiology of a Major Genre.* University Park: Pennsylvania State University Press, 1991.

Greenwood, James. *Low-Life Deeps: An Account of the Strange Fish to be Found There.* London: Chatto & Windus, 1881 [1875].

———. *The Seven Curses of London.* London: Basil Blackwell, 1981 [1869].

Hacking, Ian. "Comment: In Praise of the Diversity of Probabilities." *Statistical Science* 5.4 (November 1990): 450–54.

———. "Nineteenth-Century Cracks in the Concept of Determinism." *Journal of the History of Ideas* 44.3 (July–September 1983): 455–75.

Hadley, Elaine. *Melodramatic Tactics: Theatricalized Dissent in the English Marketplace, 1800–1885.* Stanford: Stanford University Press, 1995.

Harding, Arthur. *East End Underworld: Chapters in the Life of Arthur Harding.* Ed. Raphael Samuel. London: Routledge & Kegan Paul, 1981.

Heard, P. A. *An Octogenarian's Memoirs.* Devon: Arthur H. Stockwell, Ltd., 1974.

Hegel, G. M. W. *Hegel's Philosophy of Right.* Trans. T. M. Knox. Oxford: Clarendon, 1953.

Henkle, Roger B. *Comedy and Culture: England 1820–1900.* Princeton: Princeton University Press, 1980.

Hertz, Neil. "Medusa's Head: Male Hysteria under Political Pressure." *Represen-*

tations 4 (Autumn, 1983): 27–54.

Himmelfarb, Gertrude. *The De-Moralization of Society: From Victorian Virtues to Modern Values*. New York: Knopf, 1995.

———. *The Idea of Poverty: England in the Early Industrial Age*. New York: Vintage Books, 1985.

———. *Poverty and Compassion: The Moral Imagination of the Late Victorians*. New York: Knopf, 1991.

Hoggart, Richard. *The Uses of Literacy*. London: Penguin Books, 1984.

Hollingshead, John. *Ragged London in 1861*. New York: Garland, 1985 [rpt.].

Horkheimer, Max and Theodor W. Adorno. *Dialectic of Enlightenment*. Trans. John Cumming, 1944 [New York: Continuum, 1990].

Huggins, Mike J. "More Sinful Pleasures? Leisure, Respectability and the Male Middle Classes in Victorian England." *Journal of Social History* 33.3 (Spring 2000): 585–601.

Hughes, Winifred. *The Maniac in the Cellar: Sensation Novels of the 1860s*. Princeton: Princeton University Press, 1980.

Humphreys, Anne. *Henry Mayhew*. Boston: Twayne, 1984.

———. *Travels into the Poor Man's Country: The Work of Henry Mayhew*. Athens: University of Georgia Press, 1977.

James, Henry. "Nana." *The Future of the Novel: Essays on the Art of Fiction*. New York: Vintage Books, 1956: 84–96.

James, Louis. *Fiction of the Working. Man, 1830–1850*. London: Oxford University Press, 1963.

Jameson, Fredric. *The Political Unconscious: Narrative as a Socially Symbolic Act*. Ithaca: Cornell University Press, 1981.

Jay, A. Osborne. *A Story of Shoreditch: Being a Sequel to 'Life in Darkest London.'* London: Simpkin, Marshall, Hamilton, Kent & Co., 1896.

Jefferies, Richard. *After London: Or, Wild England*. London: Cassell & Co., 1885.

Jenkins, Roy. *Gladstone*. London, Basingstoke, and Oxford: Macmillan, 1996.

Jones, Gareth Stedman. *Languages of Class: Studies in English Working Class History, 1823–1982*. Cambridge: Cambridge University Press, 1983.

———. *Outcast London: A Study in the Relationship Between Classes in Victorian Society*. Oxford: Clarendon Press, 1971.

Joyce, Patrick. *Visions of the People: Industrial England and the Question of Class 1848–1914*. Cambridge: Cambridge University Press, 1991.

Joyce, Simon. *Capital Offenses: Geographies of Class and Crime in Victorian London*. Charlottesville and London: University of Virginia Press, 2004.

———. "Castles in the Air: The People's Palace, Cultural Reformation, and the East End Working Class." *Victorian Studies* 39.4 (1996): 513–38.

Kaplan, Amy. *The Social Construction of American Realism*. Chicago: University of Chicago Press, 1988.

Kaplan, Fred. *Sacred Tears: Sentimentality in Victorian Literature*. Princeton: Princeton University Press, 1987.

Katz, Jonathan Ned. *The Invention of Heterosexuality*. New York: Dutton, 1995.

Keating, Peter. "Biographical Study." Arthur Morrison. *A Child of the Jago*. Suffolk: The Boydell Press, 1969: 11–36.

———. *The Haunted Study: A Social History of the English Novel, 1875–1914*. London: Secker & Warburg, 1989.

———. *Into Unknown England: Selections from the Social Explorers.* London: Fontana/Collins 1981.

———. *The Working Classes in Victorian Fiction.* London: Routledge & Kegan Paul: 1971.

Kincaid, James. *Child-Loving: The Erotic Child and Victorian Culture.* New York: Routledge, 1992.

Kipling, Rudyard. "The Record of Badalia Herodsfoot." *Many Inventions,* 1893. New York: Doubleday, Doran & Company, Inc., 1941: 355–85.

Koven, Seth. *Slumming: Sexual and Social Politics in Victorian London.* Princeton and London: Princeton University Press, 2004.

Krebs, Paula M. *Gender, Race, and the Writing of Empire: Public Discourse and the Boer War.* Cambridge: Cambridge University Press, 1999.

Kristeva, Julia. *Powers of Horror.* Trans. Leon Roudiez. London: Columbia University Press, 1999.

Krzak, Michael. "Preface." Arthur Morrison. *Tales of Mean Streets.* Suffolk: The Boydell Press, 1983: 7–10.

Lane, Christopher. *The Burdens of Intimacy: Psychoanalysis and Victorian Masculinity.* Chicago: University of Chicago Press, 1999.

Law, John (Margaret Harkness). *A City Girl.* New York: Garland, 1984 [London: Vizetelly, 1887].

———. *Out of Work.* London: Swan Sonnenschein & Co., 1888.

Laws, Kim. *Paternalism and Politics: The Revival of Paternalism in Early Nineteenth-Century Britain.* London: Macmillan, 2000.

Lees, Lynn Hollen. *The Solidarities of Strangers: The English Poor Laws and the People, 1700–1948.* New York and Cambridge: Cambridge University Press, 1998.

Le Bon, Gustave. *The Crowd: A Study of the Popular Mind.* London: T. F. Unwin, 1916.

Lester, John. *Journey Through Despair 1880–1914: Transformation in British Literary Culture.* Princeton: Princeton University Press, 1968.

Levine, George. "Two Ways Not to be a Solipsist: Art and Science, Pater and Pearson." *Victorian Studies* 43.1 (Autumn 2000): 7–41.

London, Jack. *The People of the Abyss.* London: Macmillan, 1903.

Lovell, Terry. *Consuming Fiction.* London: Verso, 1987.

Maine, Sir Henry. *Ancient Law.* London: J. M. Dent and Sons, 1936 [original printing: 1857].

Marcus, Steven. *Engels, Manchester and the Working Class.* New York: Vintage Books, 1975.

Marshall, David. *The Surprising Effects of Sympathy.* Chicago and London: University of Chicago Press, 1988.

Masterman, C. F. G. *The Condition of England.* London: Methuen, 1911.

———. *From the Abyss.* New York and London: Garland reprint, 1980.

Maugham, W. Somerset. *Liza of Lambeth.* London: Heinemann, 1966.

Maxwell, Richard C. "Henry Mayhew and the Life of the Streets." *Journal of British Studies* 17 (1977–78): 87–105.

Mayhew, Henry. *London Labour and the London Poor.* London: Griffin, Bohn and Company, 1861. Vols. I and II.

McClintock, Anne. *Imperial Leather: Race, Gender, and Sexuality in the Colonial Conquest.* New York: Routledge, 1995.

Meacham, Standish. *Toynbee Hall and Social Reform, 1880–1914: The Search for*

Community. New Haven: Yale University Press, 1987.
Mearns, Andrew. *The Bitter Cry of Outcast London.* Ed. Anthony S. Wohl. New York: Humanities Press, 1970.
Minson, Jeffrey. *Genealogies of Morals: Nietzsche, Foucault, Donzelot and the Eccentricity of Ethics.* New York: St. Martin's Press, 1985.
Moretti, Franco. *Signs Taken for Wonders: Essays in the Sociology of Literary Forms.* Trans. by Susan Fisher, David Forgacs, and David Miller. London: Verso, 1983.
Morgan, Ted. *Maugham.* New York: Simon and Schuster, 1980.
Morrison, Arthur. *A Child of the Jago.* Suffolk: The Boydell Press, 1969.
———. "The Children of the Jago." *Daily News* (Saturday, December 12, 1896): 6.
———. "What is a Realist?" *New Review* 16.94 (March 1897): 326–36.
———. *Tales of Mean Streets.* Suffolk: The Boydell Press, 1983.
Neetens, Wim. "Problems of a 'Democratic Tent': Walter Besant's Impossible Story." *Novel* 23 (1990): 247–64.
Nietzsche, Friedrich. *Beyond Good and Evil.* Trans. Walter Kauffmann. New York: Random House, 1966.
Nord, Deborah Epstein. *The Apprenticeship of Beatrice Webb.* Amherst: University of Massachusetts Press, 1985.
———. *Walking the Victorian Streets: Women, Representation, and the City.* Ithaca and London: Cornell University Press, 1995.
Olson, Donald J. "Victorian London: Specialization, Segregation, and Privacy." *Victorian Studies* 17 (1974): 265–78.
"Opinions in the Weekly Reviews: Workhouse Management," *Pall Mall Gazette,* 20 (January 1866): 3.
Paine, Thomas. "Rights of Man: Being an Answer to Mr. Burke's Attack on the French Revolution." *The Writings of Tom Paine.* Volume II: 1779–1792. Ed. Moncure Daniel Conway. New York: AMS Press, 1967.
Peluso, Robert. "Gazing at Royalty: Jack London's *The People of the Abyss* and the Emergence of American Imperialism." *Rereading Jack London.* Ed. Leonard Cassutto and Jean Campbell Reesman. Stanford: Stanford University Press, 1996: 55–74.
Perkin, Harold. *The Origins of Modern English Society, 1780–1880.* London: Routledge & Kegan Paul, 1969.
———. *The Rise of Professional Society: England Since 1880.* London: Routledge, 1989.
Poovey, Mary. *Making a Social Body: British Cultural Formation, 1830–1864.* Chicago and London: University of Chicago Press, 1995.
———. *A History of the Modern Fact: Problems of Knowledge in the Sciences of Wealth and Society.* Chicago and London: University of Chicago Press, 1998.
Porter, Roy. *London: A Social History.* London: Hamish Hamilton, 1994.
Richards, Jeffrey. "Introduction." James Greenwood. *The Seven Curses of London.* London: Basil Blackwell, 1981 [1869].
Richardson, Dorothy. *Pilgrimage.* New York: Knopf, 1938.
Ricoeur, Paul. *The Symbolism of Evil.* Trans. by Emerson Buchanon. New York: Harper & Row, 1967.
Riley, Denise. *"Am I That Name?" Feminism and the Category of 'Women' in History.* Minneapolis: University of Minnesota Press, 1988.
Ritchie, J. Ewing. *The Night Side of London.* 3rd ed. London: Tinsley Bros., 1861.
Roberts, Robert. *The Classic Slum.* Manchester: Manchester University Press, 1971.

Rook, Clarence. *The Hooligan Nights: Being the Life and Opinions of a Young and Unrepentant Criminal.* New York: Holt, 1899.
Rose, Jonathan. *The Edwardian Temperament: 1895–1919.* Athens: Ohio University Press, 1986.
———. *The Intellectual Life of the British Working Classes.* New Haven: Yale University Press, 2001.
Said, Edward. *Orientalism.* New York: Pantheon Books, 1978.
Samuel, Raphael. *East End Underworld: Chapters in the Life of Arthur Harding.* London and Boston: Routledge & Kegan Paul, 1981.
Sartre, Jean-Paul. *What is Literature?* Trans. by Bernard Frechtman. Gloucester: Peter Smith, 1978.
Schultz, Raymond. L. *Crusader in Babylon: W. T. Stead and the* Pall Mall Gazette. Lincoln: University of Nebraska Press, 1972.
Silverman, Kaja. *The Subject of Semiotics.* New York: Oxford University Press, 1983.
———. "On Suture." *Film Theory and Criticism: Introductory Readings.* Eds. Leo Braudy and Marshall Cohen. 5th ed. New York: Oxford University Press, 1999: 137–47.
Sims, George R. *How the Poor Live* and *Horrible London.* New York and London: Garland, 1984. Reprint of 1889 edition. London: Chatto & Windus, 1889.
Sinfield, Alan. *The Wilde Century: Effeminacy, Oscar Wilde, and the Queer Moment.* London: Columbia University Press, 1994.
Smith, Adam. *The Theory of Moral Sentiments.* Facsimile of Yale University Library 1759 copy. New York: Garland, 1971.
Soffer, Reba N. *Ethics and Society in England: The Revolution in the Social Sciences 1870–1914.* Berkeley: University of California Press, 1978.
Soloway, Richard. "Counting the Degenerates: the Statistics of Race Degeneration in Edwardian England." *Journal of Contemporary History* 17.1 (January 1982): 137–64.
Spilka, Mark. "Henry James and Walter Besant: 'The Art of Fiction Controversy.'" *Novel* 6 (1973): 101–19.
Stallybrass, Peter and Allon White. *The Politics and Poetics of Transgression.* London: Methuen, 1986.
Stead, W. T. "The Maiden Tribute of Modern Babylon, I." *The Pall Mall Gazette.* Monday, July 6, 1885.
Stone, Lawrence. *The Road to Divorce: England 1580–1987.* New York and Oxford: Oxford University Press, 1990.
Symons, Arthur. "A Note on Zola's Method." *The Symbolist Movement in Literature.* New York: E. P. Dutton and Co., Inc. 1919: 154–64.
Taylor, Charles. *Modern Social Imaginaries.* Durham and London: Duke University Press, 2004.
Thompson, F. M. L. *The Rise of Respectable Society: A Social History of Victorian Britain, 1830–1900.* London: Fontana Press, 1988.
Tillotson, Kathleen. *Novels of the Eighteen-Forties.* Oxford: Oxford University Press, 1954.
Tosh, John. *A Man's Place: Masculinity and the Middle-Class Home in Victorian England.* New Haven and London: Yale University Press, 1999.
Traill, H. D. "The New Fiction." *The New Fiction and Other Essays on Literary Subjects.* London: Hurst and Blackett, Ltd., 1897: 1–26.

The Unknown Mayhew. Eds. Eileen Yeo and E. P. Thompson. New York: Pantheon Books, 1971.
The Victorian City: Images and Realities. Eds. H. J. Dyos and Michael Wolff. Vols. 1–4. London: Routledge & Kegan Paul, 1977.
Walkowitz, Judith. *City of Dreadful Delight: Narratives of Sexual Danger in Late Victorian London.* London: Virago, 1992.
———. *Prostitution and Victorian Society: Women, Class, and the State.* Cambridge: Cambridge University Press, 1980.
Webb, Beatrice. *The Diary of Beatrice Webb.* Ed. by Norman and Jeanne Mackenzie. Cambridge: Harvard University Press, 1982–84.
———. *My Apprenticeship.* London: Longmans, Green and Co., 1926.
Weeks, Jeffrey. *Sex, Politics, and Society: The Regulation of Sexuality since 1800.* London and New York: Longman, 1989.
Wells, H. G. *The Island of Dr. Moreau.* New York: Dover, 1996.
———. *The Time Machine: An Invention.* Ed. Leon Stover. Jefferson, NC and London: McFarland & Co., 1996.
White, Arnold. *The Problems of a Great City.* London: Remington and Co. Publishers, 1886.
Widener, Alice. *Gustave Le Bon, the Man and his Works: a Presentation with Introduction, First Translations into English, and Edited Extracts.* Indianapolis: Liberty, 1979.
Wiener, Martin J. *English Culture and the Decline of the Industrial Spirit, 1850–1980.* Cambridge: Cambridge University Press, 1981.
Williams, Raymond. *The Country and the City.* Oxford: Oxford University Press, 1973.
———. *Keywords: A Vocabulary of Culture and Society.* New York: Oxford University Press, 1976.
Wohl, Anthony S. *The Eternal Slum: Housing and Social Policy in Victorian London.* London: Edward Arnold, 1977.
Wright, Patrick. *On Living in an Old Country: The National Past in Contemporary Britain.* London: Verso, 1985.
Wynne, Deborah. *The Sensation Novel and the Victorian Family Magazine.* New York: Palgrave, 2001.
Yeo, Eileen and E. P. Thompson. *The Unknown Mayhew.* New York: Pantheon, 1971.
Zola, Émile. "The Experimental Novel." *The Experimental Novel and Other Essays.* Trans. Belle M. Sherman. New York: Haskell, 1964: 1–54.

INDEX

abjection and the abject, 23, 25, 55–59, 64, 67, 77, 90, 105, 144, 161, 173, 179
Abrams, Philip, 80
abyss, 6, 24, 80, 101, 126, 137, 140–41, 149, 163, 173–74, 180
Adams, James Eli, 5
adventure and adventure literature, 20, 26, 109–10, 137, 151–52, 163, 166
aesthetes and aestheticism, 137–39, 141, 158
affect, 23, 36, 45–46, 52, 67, 90–91, 132. *See also* female affect; enervation
Africa, 86
aggression, 7
Althusser, Louis, 31
Altick, Richard, 33
Anderson, Amanda, 4, 73
Anderson, Benedict, 4–5
Arnold, Matthew, 48, 73, 102, 130, 173–74
Arnold, Thomas, 92
ascetic, 138
Austen, Jane, 82

Balfour, Arthur, 146
Ballantyne, R. M., 151; *Coral Island*, 151
Barnett, Samuel, 69, 93, 140

Baudelaire, Charles, 137–38
Beaudrillard, Jean, 99
Bennett, Arnold, 178
Berridge, Virginia, 43
Besant, Walter, 89–103, 112, 116, 140, 153–54; *All Sorts and Conditions of Men*, 95; *Autobiography*, 91; *East London*, 153–54
Bildungsroman, 110
Birkin, Lawrence, 98
Boer War, 124, 146
"Bohemians," 28–29, 41
Booth, Charles, 23, 71, 79–81, 91, 103, 141, 146, 163–64, 180; *Life and Labour of the People of London*, 79–81, 103, 163
Booth, William, 86–87, 103, 164; *In Darkest England and the Way Out*, 86–87
bourgeois. *See* middle class
Braddon, Mary Elizabeth, 41–42; *Lady Audley's Secret*, 41–42
Brooks, Peter, 52–54, 64
Brown, Lucy, 26
Browning, Elizabeth Barrett, 85; *Aurora Leigh*, 85
Buchan, John, 178
Buckle, Henry, 168
Bulwer Lytton, Edward, 7
bureaucrats, 7

Index

Burke, Edmund, 32; *A Philosophical Enquiry into our Ideas of the Sublime and the Beautiful*, 32
Burke, Thomas, 74, 94–95; *The Wind and the Rain*, 74; *The Real East End*, 74
Burton, Richard F., 141, 165
Butler, Josephine, 65, 142–43
Butler, Samuel, 130–31

capitalism and the marketplace, 13–15, 26, 36–37, 47, 50, 68–73, 75–80, 92, 96, 99, 108, 173
Carlyle, Thomas, 68–69, 158, 177
Chadwick, Edwin, 68, 170
Chamberlain, Joseph, 82–83, 87, 170
character, 7, 70, 81, 93, 127
charity, 50, 68, 76, 126, 172
Chase, Karen, and Michael Levenson, 42, 44
Choi, Tina Young, 170
cholera, 2
class conflict, 24, 43, 92, 101, 149, 155, 162, 180
class consciousness, 1, 18–19, 48, 68, 72, 112
class differences, 20, 42, 92, 99
class relations, 27, 80, 86, 92
class(es), lower, 6, 29, 35, 42, 72–74, 93, 97, 100, 107, 109–10, 116–19, 123, 128–29, 132, 136–37, 158, 166, 174
class(es), upper, aristocracy, and gentry, 42–43, 89, 94–95, 99, 101, 107–9, 112–13, 118, 126, 130 163
class(es), upper middle, 70, 78, 83, 88, 91–92, 130
class(es), working, 13, 16–17, 22, 28, 37, 72, 91, 95–98, 100, 103, 120–25, 129, 137, 142–43, 145–47, 150, 152, 160, 163, 166, 170–72, 175, 178
classification, 16–18, 80
Clifford, Paul, 7
Cobbett, William, 155
cockney school, cockney, and the Cockney Novel, 123–24, 129
Collins, Wilkie, 41–42, 45; *The Moonstone*, 41–42; *The Woman in White*, 41, 45

colonies and colonialism, 22
commodity and commodification, 18, 63, 108, 128
competition and competitive ethos, 11, 13–15, 18, 27, 47, 54, 72, 97, 109, 131, 180. *See also* male competitiveness
Conan Doyle, Arthur, 178
Conrad, Joseph, 176
consumption and consumerism, 33, 63, 71, 73, 75–76, 97, 99, 103, 115, 118, 127, 129–30, 177
Contagious Disease Acts, 65
C.O.S., 23, 76–77, 93, 140, 176
Cottam, Daniel, 101
Crimean War, 69
criminal(s) and crime, 11, 40–42, 49, 111–12, 123, 139, 144, 148–49, 168, 174
Cross, Nigel, 28, 41
Crystal Palace, 129, 135
Cullen, Dan, 171
culturalism, 23–24, 30, 35, 37, 67, 87, 91–94, 96–97, 101–3, 116, 124, 130–32, 137, 140, 153, 174, 180
culture, 20, 23–24, 30, 35, 37, 91–3, 99–103, 113, 123–25, 130, 144, 174
culture, high, 153
Cvetkovich, Ann, 45–46

Daiches, David, 131
The Daily News, 111, 119
dandy, 138–39. *See also* aesthete and *flâneur*
Darwin, Charles, 56, 75, 101, 144–45, 147–48, 177. *See also* Social Darwinism
Davis, Lennard, 152
death, 2–3, 38, 55, 62, 105
Defoe, Daniel, 151; *Robinson Crusoe*, 151–52
degeneration and degeneracy, 54, 56–57, 89, 94, 101–2, 145–51, 153, 168, 170
de Goncourt, Edmond and Jules, 109, 137; *Germinie Lacerteux*, 109
dehumanization, 44, 91, 109, 177
de-moralization, 40, 56–57, 83, 144,

149, 156, 165, 173
deserving poor, 76
desire, 3, 10, 16, 29, 45, 52, 67, 61, 82–83, 89, 91, 97–98, 107, 118, 133, 161–62, 176; repressed, 59
detachment, 3, 23, 25–28, 66, 73, 82, 140–42, 149, 155, 171
Dickens, Charles, 6, 10–11, 13–17, 28–29, 39, 50, 57–66, 68, 73, 101, 104, 118–20, 172, 181; *Bleak House*, 41, 58–66, 80, 170; competitiveness, 14–16; *Dombey and Son*, 16, 57; *Great Expectations*, 15; *Household Words*, 28; *Little Dorrit*, 15; *The Old Curiosity Shop*, 15; *Oliver Twist*, 110; *Our Mutual Friend*, 16, 63; *Pickwick Papers*, 14; voyeurism, 15
discourse, 4, 9, 20, 24, 72, 137, 140, 151, 170, 176
disease, 2–3, 38–39, 59, 86, 117, 133, 135, 144, 165–66, 168, 170, 174
Disraeli, Benjamin, 137
dissolution, 55
division of labor or economic specialization, 77, 149–58. *See also* gendered division of labor
Dock Workers' Strike of 1889, 88, 145, 171
domesticity and the domestic, 7–8, 11, 21, 37, 40, 42, 44–46, 50, 53, 60–61, 65–66, 78, 143. *See also* masculine domesticity and private sphere
Donzelot, Jacques, 23, 72–76; "the social," 23, 72–76
D'Orsay, Alfred Count, 137
Dyos, H. J., 56

East End or East London, 9, 23–24, 40, 55, 68, 73, 78–80, 83, 86, 88–91, 95–96, 99, 101, 103–8, 110, 116, 119–21, 124–26, 137, 139–40, 143–44, 149, 151, 153, 159, 164–67, 171–73, 176–77, 180
economics and economy, 75, 96–98, 108–10, 115–17, 122, 125, 131–32, 140, 144, 149, 152, 154, 156, 166, 173, 178
Education Act of 1870, 74

Egan, Pierce, 6, 18; *Life in London*, 6, 18
egoism and egotism, 70, 131, 133
Eliot, George, 43, 101–2; *Middlemarch*, 43
enervation, 67, 85–87, 89, 95, 101, 103–4, 137, 177
Engels, Friedrich, 30, 88; *The Condition of the English Working Class*, 30
engulfment, fear of, 40, 67–70, 148
ethics, 14, 24, 32, 35, 67, 73, 75, 77–79, 82–83, 85–87, 89, 91–92, 98, 107, 110, 116–17, 123
eugenics and eugenicists, 147–48, 170, 172

Fabian socialism and Fabian Society, 68, 70, 155, 158, 180
family, nuclear, 77
female, 23–24, 50, 57, 59, 77, 104, 106, 110, 137, 156; abject, 23–24, 45, 57, 77; affect, 46, 57, 67, 132; body, 135–36, 157; desire, 83, 89; as ethical force, 108–10; as social mediator, 78; as object of social intervention, 77–81, 96; sexuality, 59, 89; subjectivity and identity, 60, 69, 83–84, 86–88, 107; victim, 25, 62–66
female desire, 24, 62–67
feminine, the, 45, 83
feminist, 88
feminized and feminization, 23, 25, 67
feminized lower classes, 96
Fielding, Henry, 7; *Jonathon Wilde*, 7
filth, 2–3, 37, 53, 55
Fishers, Trevor, 139
flâneur, 137–38, 161
Foucault, Michel, 45, 47, 72
Fox Bourne, H. R., 28
Freedman, Jonathan, 138
Freeman-Williams, J-P, 145
Freud, Sigmund, 134

Gagnier, Regenia, 124, 154
Gallagher, Catherine, 102
Galsworthy, John, 178
Galton, Francis, 147
Gavin, Hector, 2–4, 170

Gay, John, 7; *The Beggar's Opera*, 7
gendered division of labor, 77, 156–58
gentleman, 5, 25, 28–29, 32, 76, 95
gentry, 43, 132, 158. See also classes, upper
Gissing, George, 24, 94, 104, 124–37, 140, 149, 181; "The Hope of Pessimism," 131; *The Nether World*, 24, 124–36; *New Grub Street*, 127; *Thyrza*, 127
Gladstone, William Ewart, 82
Goldsmith, Oliver, 155; "The Deserted Village," 155
Goode, John, 88, 127, 131
Gordon, General Charles "Chinese," 49
Green, Martin, 151
Green, T. H., 91–92
Greenwood, Frederick, 28
Greenwood, James, 6–10, 23, 25–35, 50, 93, 164, 166, 181; The "Amateur Casual," 9–10, 25–26; *Low-Life Deeps*, 9, 25, 27–29; "A Night in the Workhouse," 9–10, 25, 35; *The Seven Curses of London*, 25, 29–35; *The True History of a Little Ragamuffin*, 25
Gross, John, 48

Hacking, Ian, 168
Hadley, Elaine, 64
Hannay, James, 28
Harding, Arthur, 108, 120–21
Hardy, Thomas, 131, 137, 178
Harkness, Margaret (a.k.a. John Law), 23, 66, 87–9, 91, 95, 102–3, 109, 124–25; *A City Girl*, 87–9, 109; *Out of Work*, 102
Hazlitt, William, 27
hegemony, 19, 24, 45, 64, 73, 91, 94–95, 97–98, 116–17, 123, 125, 176, 180–81
Hertz, Neil, 134
heterosexuality, 46
Hill, Octavia, 50, 76, 93
Himmelfarb, Gertrude, 1, 18, 40, 164
Hitchcock, Alfred, 32; *Psycho*, 32
Hobson, J. A., 174; *The Psychology of Jingoism*, 174

Hoggart, Richard, 108; *The Uses of Literacy*, 108
Holmes, Sherlock, 140
home, 3, 36–62, 143
homosexuality, 46, 139
Hooligan, Patrick, 122
Housman, A. E., 130
Hughes, Winifred, 41–42
Huxley, T. H., 155
Huysmans, Joris Karl, 137, 139

identification, 55, 132, 161–62
ideology, 3, 14, 26, 29, 32, 66, 73, 100, 124, 128, 155, 162, 176
ideology and rhetoric, 29, 32, 66
The Illustrated London News, 28
The Illustrated Times, 28
imaginary and imagination, 1, 4–5, 22, 31, 33, 103, 121, 124, 132, 144. See also male imagination
imperialism, 69, 93, 146, 170
incest, 39, 59, 62–63
individuality, individual, individuation, and individualism, 22, 31, 44–45, 63, 70, 77, 89, 91, 93–94, 99, 102, 124, 126, 155, 165, 173–74
innocence, 51–54, 58, 65, 104, 129, 157
inscribed reader, 32
instinct, 45

Jack the Ripper, 41
James, Henry, 42, 89; "The Art of Fiction," 89
Jameson, Fredric, 80, 127, 132
Jefferies, Richard, 24, 140, 148–56; *After London; or, Wild England*, 149–55; *Bevis*, 15; *Hodge and His Masters*, 150; *Wood Magic*, 150
jingoism, 124
Jones, Gareth Steadman, 36, 56–57, 144–46
journalism, 23, 25, 32, 36, 105, 163, 169
Jowett, Benjamin, 91

Kaplan, Amy, 119
Keating, Peter, 90, 122–23
Kipling, Rudyard, 106–7, 110, 141, 178; "The Record of Badalia

Herodsfoot," 106–7, 110
Krafft-Ebing, Richard von, 46
Krebs, Paula, 124
Kristeva, Julia, 55–57

labyrinth, 9, 21, 23, 89
Lamarck, Jean-Baptiste, 148
Lambeth workhouse, 10
LeBon, Gustav, 173–74
Lester, John, 131
Levine, George, 138–39
liberalism and Liberals, 68, 82, 124, 146–47
Lombroso, Cesare, 145
London, Jack, 6, 10, 24, 140, 144, 149, 164–74, 180–81; *People of the Abyss*, 164–73
Lukács, Georg, 80, 89

Mafeking, 124, 174
male(s), 80, 93, 109, 137, 144, 156, 179–80; body, 133, 136; competitiveness, 11, 27; construction of poverty, 77; desire, 24; detachment, 3, 23, 25–28, 66, 141; gaze, 140; homoerotic relationships, 16; hysteria, 134; imagination, 110, 149; intellectuals, 137; subjectivity, 61, 110
Mallock, W. H., 130
Malthus, Thomas, 75, 146–47, 172
management, 171
Marshall, Alfred, 75–80, 146
Marx, Karl, 68
mass culture and the masses, 153, 166, 173, 176
Masterman, C. G., 6, 24, 140–41, 149, 173–78, 180–81; *The Condition of England*, 177; *From the Abyss*, 141, 173–78
Maugham, W. Somerset, 122–23; *Liza of Lambeth*, 122–23
Maxwell, Richard C., 7, 12–13
Mayhew, Henry, 6, 8–13, 16–22, 25, 28–9, 39, 109, 151, 164; classification, 16–18; costermongers, 11, 19–20; criminals, 11; fly-paper seller, 12–13; *London Labour and the London Poor*, 11, 13, 16–22, 39; street-people, 12, 18; street-sellers, 11, 18; working classes, 16–17, 22
Meacham, Standish, 92–93
Mearns, Rev. Andrew, 36–62, 65, 147, 164; *The Bitter Cry of Outcast London*, 36–62, 65, 143, 147
melodrama, 52, 64, 88, 102, 104, 132–35, 141–44, 148, 164. *See also* sentimental
miasma, 23, 26, 38, 89
middle class, bourgeoisie, and bourgeois, 1, 3–5, 8–9, 13, 20, 24, 25, 27, 42–43, 73–74, 77, 87, 89, 99, 101, 103–4, 108–9, 112, 117–18, 123, 137, 141, 144–45, 151–52, 163–64, 173–74, 177, 179; emotionality, 43; ethos, ethics, and ethical mission, 14, 24, 38, 43–44, 54, 58, 63, 67, 73, 75, 77–83, 85–86, 91, 93, 104, 116, 179; families and nuclear families, 72–73; hatred of, 28; ideology, 14; individual and individualism, 31, 63; male, 9, 13, 77, 80, 94, 141; mediating role of, 6, 27, 87, 92, 94, 179; morality and moralism, 28, 49–50, 54, 66, 112, 132, 137, 140, 142–43, 166; notions of bodily decency, 40, 62; observer, 30, 52, 54, 78, 127, 138, 153; professionalism, 27, 62, 67, 141, 144; reader, 26–27, 29–32, 36–37, 43, 52, 63–64, 90, 104, 137, 148, 165, 170; self-definition, 2–4, 14; sentimentality, 38; subjectivity and self-definition, 31, 36, 67, 87, 102, 107, 140, 144; urbanity, 35; values, 30, 37, 40, 52–3, 92, 98, 104–5, 118
middle class male, 1, 3–5, 8–9, 10, 13, 20, 24, 25, 27, 67, 89, 94; manliness and masculinity, 5, 8, 10, 20, 22, 83; masculine domesticity, 8, 21–22, 78; professionals, 62, 66–67, 142–44, 179; subjectivity, 59, 71
Mill, John Stuart, 14, 68
mimicry, 19
misogyny, 8, 55, 104, 106, 110
Moore, George, 109–10; *Esther Waters*,

109–10; *Morning Chronicle,* 164
Morris, William, 68
Morrison, Arthur, 24, 74, 90, 93–125, 129, 132, 137, 140, 149, 164; "Behind the Shade," 107–8; *Child of the Jago,* 107, 110–25; *The Hole in the Wall,* 110; "Lizerunt," 104–6, 123; "Mean Streets," 90, 112; "A Street in the East End," 104; *Tales of Mean Streets,* 104, 120–21, 123–24; *To London Town,* 110
murder, 43, 172

nationalism, 129, 170, 172
Naturalism, 24, 89, 116, 118, 127, 137
netherworld, 6–7, 22–23, 91, 110, 115, 125–26, 129, 140
Nevinson, Henry, 123
Newgate Calendar, 7
Newgate Novel, 7, 28
New Journalism, 48
The New Review, 119
news, 43–44
The Night Side of London (Ritchie), 7

Oastler, Richard, 68
Old Nichol, 110–11, 120
Olsen, Donald J., 62
Osborne Jay, Rev. A., 90, 111–12, 119; *A Story of Shoreditch,* 90
"outcast London," 3
overcrowding, 62

Palace of Delights or People's Palace, 99–102, 104, 140
Pall Mall Gazette, 25, 28, 35–36, 47–49, 65, 143; "The Maiden Tribute of Modern Babylon," 39, 65, 139–42, 143
Pater, Walter, 138–39; "Conclusion" to *The Renaissance: A Study,* 138
paternalism and patriarchy and patriarchal power and authority, 2, 64–65, 72, 93, 97, 110
Pearson, Karl, 138, 141–42, 146
penny dreadful, 29–30, 42
permeation, 24, 162, 180
perversion, the perverse, 46, 55

Pharmakon, 170, 172
philanthropy, 68, 83, 95, 128, 140, 153, 159, 176, 179
The Pictorial World, 50
political, 49–50, 97, 133–34, 150, 172, 179–80
poor, the and poverty, 11, 24, 37, 40, 44–63, 76–77, 91, 98, 110, 122, 145, 149; domestic lives of, 11, 40, 44–63; as a subculture, 12, 17
Poor Law, the, 68, 76
Poovey, Mary, 170
Porter, Roy, 163
Potter, Richard, 69, 81
private sphere, 44–50, 61–62, 66, 78, 156
privatization, 63, 108
professional class and middle class professionalism, 4, 23–24, 26–27, 35, 62, 67, 78, 138, 145, 150, 152, 158, 162, 176, 180
prostitution, 55, 65, 106, 108, 125, 139, 143–44
public sphere, 42, 44–50, 66, 78, 156
Pugh, Edwin, 123
Punch, 28
purity, 58, 60, 65, 128

Quarterly, 41
Quetelet, Adolphe, 168

"race suicide," 146
radical and radicalism, 49
Reade, Charles, 41
Reade, Winwood, 151
reading and ethics, 34
realist novel, 43, 89, 116, 118–19
Reeder, D. A., 56
reform and reformism, 4, 7, 68, 70, 74, 78, 80, 116, 126, 162
regulation, 69, 72, 77
reification and abstraction, 66, 80–81, 85, 87, 89, 92, 127, 164, 166, 173, 175–76
repression, 60–61, 63, 85, 125, 136
"residuum," 3, 103, 124, 144, 148, 153, 168
respectability, 19, 44, 107, 120, 164, 175
ressentiment or resentment, 132,

135–36, 155
Reynold's Newspaper, 36, 43
Ricardo, David, 75
Ricoeur, Paul, 54
Riley, Denise, 78
Ritchie, J. Ewing, 7, 10; *The Night Side of London*, 7
Roberts, Robert, 108; *The Classic Slum*, 108
Rook, Clarence, 121; *The Hooligan Nights*, 121
Rose, Jonathan, 91
Rugby School, 92
Ruskin, John, 47, 68–69, 73

St. Giles, 9
Sala, George Augustus, 28
Salvation Army, 86–87, 140–41
Samuel, Raphael, 120–21
Sanitary Ramblings (Gavin), 2
sanitary reform, 3
Sartre, Jean-Paul, 112
scandal, 41
Schopenhauer, Arthur, 131, 177
Schreiner, Olive, 141
Schultz, Raymond L., 48–49
science fiction, 80, 149
science of society, 70
self-consciousness, 22
sensation, sensationalism, sensational journalism, the Sensation Novel, and "newspaper novels," 23, 25, 28, 33, 35–37, 43–66, 68, 140, 143
sensibility, 32, 67, 89, 95
sentiment and sentimentality, 23, 30, 38, 50–52, 55–59, 68, 77, 105, 109, 124, 141, 172, 180
settlement movement or Toynbee Hall, 91–94, 97–98, 101, 116, 126, 140–41, 162, 176, 180
sexuality, 45, 59, 61, 89, 134–35, 138–41, 144, 156
Shaftesbury, Anthony Ashley Cooper, Seventh Earl of, 39, 68
Sharpe, Maria, 141
Simon, John, 39
Sims, George R., 50–51, 54–56, 58, 64, 89, 164; *How the Poor Live*, 50–51,
54–56, 58, 64, 89
Sinfield, Alan, 139
slum(s), 1, 3–4, 6, 10, 16, 22, 25, 28–29, 36–40, 75–77, 83, 86, 91, 104, 106, 108–9, 112–13, 115, 122, 125–26, 129, 136, 144, 166
slumming, 170
Smiles, Samuel, 13; *Self-Help*, 13
Smith, Adam, 75, 154; *On the Wealth of Nations*, 154
Smith, Llewelyn, 146
"social, the," 23, 67–76, 98, 168
Social Darwinism, 156–57, 165, 170, 172
"social purity," 142
social services and social work, 77–78, 81, 83, 87, 107
socialism, 36–37, 70, 88, 158, 170–72
Society for Authors, 89, 154
Soffer, Reba, 75–76
Soloway, Richard, 146–47
South London, 121–22
space, spatialization, 39, 56, 89, 102, 118, 144
spectacle, 6, 49, 113, 140
Spencer, Herbert, 71; *First Principles*, 71
Spitalsfield, 11
Stallybrass, Peter, 11
Stanley, Henry Morton, 86, 151
state intervention, 72, 77–78
statistics, 168
Stead, W. T., 36, 39, 47–49, 65–66, 87, 141–42
stench, 2
Stevenson, Robert Louis, 141, 145
subculture(s), 18–19, 90
subjectivity, 91, 107, 110, 159
Suez Canal, 70
surveillance, 68, 73, 77, 92, 95
suture, 32–33
symbolic, 24, 56, 88–89, 101–2, 115–16, 118–19, 169
Symon, J. D., 49
sympathy and pity, 40, 66, 81, 83, 132–3, 159, 173

Taylor, Charles, 5

Tennyson, Alfred Lord, 39, 50; *In Memoriam A.H.H.*, 50; "Locksley Hall Sixty Years After," 40
Thackeray, William Makepeace, 15, 28; *Vanity Fair*, 15
Thompson, E. P., 11, 18
Tosh, John, 8–9, 109
Toynbee, Arnold, 91
Traill, H. D., 117–19
Turpin, Dick, 7–8

underclass, 24, 40, 91, 104, 132, 136, 158. *See also* class, lower
underworld, 18, 94, 110
urban poor, 1, 6, 18–20, 23, 25, 28–30, 32, 44, 50, 52, 54, 56, 58, 62, 65–72, 74–75, 80–81, 85, 88–89, 93–94, 102, 108, 118, 123, 132, 144, 147, 149–50, 153, 163, 169, 172–73, 179–80
utilitarianism and Utilitarianism, 14, 34

Veblen, Thorstein, 177
victim, victimization, victimology, 25, 40, 58, 64–66, 88, 107, 109, 129, 132, 170
violence, 90, 103–4, 106–7, 124, 156
voyeurism, 15, 32

Walkowitz, Judith, 49, 65, 141
waste, 12–13

Webb, Beatrice, 23, 40, 50, 66–89, 92, 103, 125, 141; *My Apprenticeship*, 23, 67–89; *The Diary of Beatrice Webb*, 67–89; "a sense of sin," 68; "consciousness of sin," 167
Webb, Sidney, 87
Weeks, Jeffrey, 46, 62
Wells, H. G., 24, 139–40, 144, 148–50, 155–65, 171, 180; *The Island of Dr. Moreau*, 139, 159; *The Time Machine*, 149–50, 155–63
West End, 20, 88, 97, 159
Westminster Gazette, 36
White, Allon, 11
White, Arnold, 146–48, 156, 170; "The Cult of Infirmity," 146; *The Problems of a Great City*, 147–48
"Whitechapel Horrors," 144
Wilde, Oscar, 73, 137–44; *The Picture of Dorian Gray*, 138
Wohl, Anthony, 39, 118
Wood, Mrs. Henry, 41
Wright, Patrick, 53
Wyss, Johan, 151; *Swiss Family Robinson*, 151

Yeo, Eileen, 11

Zola, Emile, 109, 116–17, 123; *L'Assomoir*, 109; "The Experimental Novel," 116–17